ANGEL OF THE MOUNTAINS

ANGEL OF THE MOUNTAINS

THE STRANGE TALE OF CHARLY GAUL

PAUL MAUNDER

QUERCUS

First published in Great Britain in 2024 by

QUERCUS

Quercus Editions Ltd
Carmelite House
50 Victoria Embankment
London EC4Y 0DZ

An Hachette UK company

A CIP catalogue record for this book is available
from the British Library

HB ISBN 978 1 52942 958 9
TPB ISBN 978 1 52943 058 5
Ebook ISBN 978 1 52943 059 2

Picture credits (in order of appearance):
1, 2, 5, 6, 7, 8, 13, 14, 15 – Ministry of Sport/The Luxembourg Government;
3, 4, 9, 10, 11 – Offside Sports Photography; 12 – Shutterstock/Kristof Bellens.

1

Designed and typeset by CC Book Production

Printed and bound in Great Britain by Clays Ltd, Elcograf S.p.A.

Papers used by Quercus Editions Ltd are from well-managed forests
and other responsible sources.

New archangel of the mountain. Carefree ephebe, slender cherub, beardless boy, delicate and insolent, inspired youth, he is the Rimbaud of the Tour.

Mythologies, Roland Barthes

CONTENTS

Part Three

GLOSSARY OF TERMS

Bidon: bottle (in French, like most of these terms)

Broom wagon: the last vehicle in the race convoy, carrying riders who have abandoned – metaphorically sweeps up after the race

Domestique: team-worker, a rider whose job is to work for a team leader

Flamme rouge: a red triangle hung above the road to denote the final kilometre of a race

Grimpeur: climber

La Grande Boucle: a nickname for the Tour de France, meaning 'the big loop'

Maillot jaune: yellow jersey, awarded to the leading overall rider of the Tour de France and other stage races

Maglia rosa: pink jersey (in Italian), awarded to the leading overall rider of the Giro d'Italia

Musette: small cloth bag with a single strap, containing food and drink, handed to riders from the roadside during races

Palmares: a racer's record of results

Peloton: the main group of riders in a race

Rouleur: a rider whose strength is rolling along flatter roads

Soigneur: an assistant responsible for feeding, massaging and caring for cyclists

Souplesse: a supple pedalling style – literally translates as 'flexibility'

Tifosi: passionate Italian cycling fans (in Italian)

PROLOGUE

Up there, away from the road, beyond the crowds, this is a wild place. Desolate, even. The mountain is immense. Its rock faces are stern, its meadows are vertiginous. Clouds swirl around its summit. The road scissors upwards, horribly steep. Today, for one day only, it is lined with a ribbon of colour. Thousands of fans are waiting for the Tour de France. On the long trudge up from the valley, the grass sparkles with morning dew. Now it is early afternoon and many are drunk, some asleep in deckchairs, but most are standing on the tarmac, hopping from one foot to another, looking down the hill.

The caravan chugged past twenty minutes ago, a seemingly never-ending procession of ridiculous vehicles and promotion girls tossing plastic tat out like goddesses bestowing jewels. The fans – and not just the children – desperately scrabbled for anything they could grab – a key ring, a bidon, some sweets. The Tour does that to people. It is a story in itself with its own logic, its own rules. Standing here in the high Alps, one's sense of perspective is altered.

A transistor radio is babbling. There have been attacks further down the mountain. This is the last climb of the day. After this the riders hurtle down into the next valley to the finish town. If anyone is clear at the summit they stand a good chance of taking the stage, unless they misjudge a hairpin on the descent and fly into a ravine. A police motorbike crawls up the slope, flashing lights, fumes spewing, its pilot nonchalant. The fans who were sitting down now get to their feet. The sleepers are roused by their friends. Gaul. Charly Gaul. The man with the transistor radio nods authoritatively. An attack by Gaul. The name stirs the crowd. There are raised eyebrows, smiles.

More motorbikes. The organisers' cars push everyone to the side of the road and then are swallowed by the crowds further up, like a python digesting its prey whole. The cheers of the crowd further down float up on the clear Alpine air. Clear, that is, apart from the diesel fumes, cigarette smoke and the smell of red wine.

Everyone strains to peer down the road. No more chatter now. Even those sleeping off their lunch have staggered to their feet and are gazing blearily downwards. And then, all in a rush, a host of motorbikes, weaving around to clear a path. Hysteria. Fists pumping, beer spraying across the tarmac, a thousand voices calling 'Allez! Allez!'

There he is. Unmistakable in his red, white and blue tricolour jersey, which marks him out as the champion of his tiny country. Riding alone, free of all earthly troubles. His sinewy legs turn with clockwork efficiency. His silver-blue bike glistens underneath his slender frame. But it is his eyes that are so captivating – icy blue, staring ahead with such zeal, such focus. In the newspapers he is portrayed as a cherub, beautiful even. Yet this man is tanned, covered in the dust of the road, pained. Below that famous Brylcreemed quiff his face is old. For a moment he seems to gaze straight at you. The Angel of the Mountains, looking into your eyes, just for a moment, and then he is gone again.

I never met Charly Gaul. He passed away before I learnt of, then grew fascinated by, his story. Yet while researching this story I came across people who experienced a scene such as the imagined one above, for whom witnessing Gaul on the road was so intense, so transformative that it left a lasting impression on them, a legacy. He became their hero. In cycling such moments are fleeting, but unforgettable. Gaul was an enigma. Difficult to know, difficult to predict. In races he was sometimes brilliant, sometimes appalling. The newspapers eulogised him for his climbing and criticised him for the bitter insults he slung at his rivals (though, of course, the conflicts made for spicy headlines). He looked like James Dean, but his moods could be famously ugly. The fans loved him, at least until his mercurial powers faded. Then their rancour left an emotional scar that affected the rest of his life.

This is a book about the problems that sporting success can bring. When a young athlete strives to win an event as difficult as the Tour de France, the effort is all-consuming, verging on maniacal. And, for some – the charismatic, the enigmatic, the ferocious – that ascent to success becomes wrapped in a mythology over which the athlete has little control. Sometimes the athlete might actively create or encourage this mythology (today we rationalise it as branding), sometimes the athlete might merely watch in bemusement as a narrative forms around them, alien and confusingly unlike their own perception of themselves. Never, though, can the man or woman control this mythology about themselves. It spins further away from their grasp, enriched by storytellers, and a gap opens between truth and mythology. As sports fans we want to believe the myths, the grand stories. This sense of the otherworldly is part of the reason we watch sport. We embrace the idea of athletes as supernatural beings, existing on a plain somewhere above us mortals. But at the centre of all this mythology, and sometimes submerged under it, is a human being. And human beings, as we know, are fragile things.

Equally fragile, despite the image of the invincible athlete, is sporting success. It is always governed by time. At the summit of an athlete's career he or she can only look down, even if that view is murky. What does the descent look like? What happens when the athlete no longer has a mission ahead of them and instead becomes 'merely' a normal person?

When Charly Gaul won the Tour de France in 1958 he secured a place in cycling's history books. Yet there are many other riders who have accomplished the same feat and still receded into the past, only remembered by the sport's historians. Gaul is different. He is, and will always be, the original Angel of the Mountains, a figure whose story is told over and over by the cycling media.

To fit the ways in which we consume stories now, with online brevity, Gaul's story is often reduced to a neat 300 words, roughly summarised thus: a former butcher's apprentice from Luxembourg, Charly Gaul was one of the most gifted climbers the sport has ever seen. He won the 1956 Giro d'Italia after a memorably freezing stage to Monte Bondone, had bad-tempered disputes with his rivals, then won the 1958 Tour de France. After another Giro d'Italia victory in 1959, he underwent a slow and painful slide towards retirement. After a failed attempt to run a café, he disappeared for more than a decade, living as a hermit in a forest hut and shunning society. He put on weight (every story seems to mention this, as if the writers cannot quite believe a cyclist could let themselves go) and gave exceedingly grumpy responses to anyone who tried to coax him out of the forest. Eventually, in late middle age, he resurfaced and reconnected with the world of cycling. Charly Gaul died in 2005, two days before his seventy-third birthday.

As a journalist I have been guilty of such reductive summaries of cyclists' lives, so let me attempt, in this book, to do justice to Charly Gaul's life. He has been submerged and obscured by mythology. This is not the first biography of Gaul (it is, though, the first in English), and it certainly does not represent the last word on his life, but I hope it will clear away the tangle of fable and riddle to let the man underneath it all emerge.

Sport is littered with tales of disastrous retirements. We know it is hard for elite athletes to adjust to the 'normal' world. Charly Gaul's story is often held up as an extreme example of that, but is this fair? Is there another, more complex, more human story? And might we all actually learn something from this unlikely hero, this vanished Angel of the Mountains?

PART ONE

Tour of Austria, 1951

Stage 1

'WHAT DO YOU WANT ME TO NEED?'

In mid-December 1944 the densely forested valleys of the Ardennes were frozen and still. Snow weighed on the trees lining the fast-flowing rivers. The Nazis, having occupied Luxembourg since May 1940, had retreated across the border into Germany. After a swifter than expected advance across Belgium, the US army was exhausted, its supply lines stretched to breaking. The Allied advance paused on the ridges of the snowbound hills. Blizzards and thick clouds kept Allied reconnaissance planes on the ground. Briefly, everything was quiet. Then Adolf Hitler threw his final desperate offensive.

Before dawn on 16 December, the Germans launched a massive shell bombardment of the American line. The Fifth Panzer Division pushed west towards Bastogne, while the 7th Army headed south towards Luxembourg City. Taken by surprise, US forces suffered heavy casualties but quickly began to retaliate. Until then, the small valley towns of the Oesling region, many with ancient castles watching over picturesque river scenes, had gone unscathed. Now, they were the scene of bitter street-to-street combat and heavy shelling from both sides. The Battle of the Bulge had begun.

A week earlier, a schoolboy in the small village of Tüntingen, less than 20 kilometres away from the advancing German troops, had celebrated his twelfth birthday. Charly Gaul lived with his parents, his brother, Jean-Pierre and his sister, Suzette in the village inn, which his parents ran. As in most villages across Luxembourg at that time, the work was primarily agricultural; of the fourteen boys in Gaul's class, eight were listed as having fathers who were farm workers. The small village world that Gaul grew up in may have been quiet, bucolic even, but he and his family were living through an extraordinary era.

Charly was small for his age and slight. He was a bright boy, well-behaved and liked by his teachers. His school report for the academic year 1939–1940 shows consistently strong academic scores ('très bien' – the highest result) across religion, German, arithmetic and writing. His marks for conduct, application and order were equally impressive.[1] There were no signs, however, that Charly would one day become one of the greatest racing cyclists of all time and a hero of his small, beleaguered nation. Indeed, at that time, as families across Luxembourg watched those final fierce battles of the war play out in their countryside, Charly did not even own a bicycle.

Four years earlier, on 10 May 1940, German forces had invaded Luxembourg and swept aside what resistance the tiny country's army could muster. Tipped off before the invasion, Grand Duchess Charlotte fled to France, then to Portugal, before eventually settling in exile in London with members of her government around her. A German civil administration was created, a Gauleiter (a political official within the Nazi apparatus) appointed to rule, and the illegal annexation of Luxembourg was complete. Luxembourg's political and judicial systems were abolished, replaced by German law. Faced with the obliteration of her homeland, Charlotte and her politicians voted unanimously to relinquish Luxembourg's neutrality and join the Allies. Hitler, and his Gauleiter, hoped that the population of Luxembourg would embrace German language and culture. In 1941 they drew up plans to run a census, asking people to choose the national language. When it transpired, through a smaller preliminary poll, that 90% of the people favoured Luxembourgish, a strong symbol of their national identity, the Gauleiter abandoned the census plan. Instead, the Gestapo increased their presence and their brutality.[2]

The German occupation may not have had a direct impact on Tüntingen, but by 1944 the danger of the Gauleiter's regime was well-known. Those who engaged in acts of resistance ran the risk of execution or deportation. Gestapo units would not hesitate to put someone against a wall and shoot them if they deemed that person to have committed a crime, such as flying the national flag. Luxembourg's Jewish population, many of whom had fled Germany before the war, were systematically rounded up and sent to con-centration camps. Few survived. And in 1942 the Germans made it compulsory for young Luxembourgish men to serve in the German military. To avoid wearing the hated German uniform, to avoid becoming an enemy in one's own town or village, many young men went into hiding in the forests of the Ardennes. Groups of boys hid in a series of caves, deep in the hills, and those who brought them food risked their lives.

Another Luxembourg teenager, Marguerite Thill, having married an American officer and moved to the United States, later wrote about her wartime experiences. She remembered visiting a cousin in the north of the country, close to where Charly Gaul was growing up. Her cousin took her out into a field of wheat so tall they disappeared into it and then, without explanation, asked Marguerite to start singing the national anthem. She recalled, 'The singing was a sign to some Luxembourg boys in hiding that it was safe to let us in. We came to a place of thick underbrush where the boys had dug a cave right into the mountain . . . After the war we found out that hundreds and hundreds of boys had been hidden this way. Our farmers are a very close-knit people and saved a lot of lives.'[3]

Charly's uncle, also called Jean-Pierre Gaul, ran a successful

butcher's shop in the town of Diekirch, which was situated just
north enough for it to fall into the band of territory being fought over
during that snowbound winter. In November 1944 the town was a
rest and recreation centre for American troops. The local population,
finally liberated after four years of German occupation, received the
American soldiers warmly. In return the Americans shared delica-
cies that had never before been seen in the town – peanut butter,
spam and corned beef. That Thanksgiving the American troops even
shared their turkey dinners with the people of Diekirch.[4]

However, everything changed when the Nazis launched their
offensive in mid-December. A mile north of town the Americans
fought courageously to withstand the German advance, but eventually were forced to succumb to the enemy's greater numbers. By
19 December they pulled back through the town, booby-trapping
roads and bridges as they went. The terrified people of Diekirch hid
in their cellars while the German 7th Army exchanged fire with the
US 26th and 35th Infantry Divisions. The American troops evacuated the town. Most of the civilians were also evacuated. When the
people were able to return to their homes in January, they found
their town devastated.[5]

The winter of 1932 was not an auspicious time to be born. In Germany
Adolf Hitler was negotiating with President von Hindenburg about
forming a new government, and in Geneva the World Disarmament
Conference was about to allow Germany to rearm beyond the
constraints of the Treaty of Versailles. In November, Franklin D.
Roosevelt was elected as US president, defeating Herbert Hoover
with a promise to tackle the horrors of the Great Depression. Within
days of taking office, in January 1933 Roosevelt set about imple-
menting his now-famous New Deal legislation. Luxembourg was
not immune to the economic slump. A drop in prices forced a
contraction in the country's steel industry, though the impact on

Luxembourgers was mitigated by the high proportion of immigrants working in the steel plants. The immigrants were laid off to protect the jobs of the locals.

Charly Gaul was born on 8 December 1932 in Pfaffenthal, a working-class district of Luxembourg City. Rue Vauban, site of the now-vanished maternity hospital, runs alongside the Alzette river, whose steep-sided valley dominates the landscape of Luxembourg City. On the west bank the Ville Haute, the historic centre with all the country's grand apparatus of state packed into a picturesque square mile, sits on top of rock cliffs. On the Pfaffenthal side of the river the hillside is less dramatic, though still challenging on a bicycle. Twenty-six years later Gaul would race up and down these roads in the Grand Prix de la Forteresse, cheered on by thousands of his compatriots.

Though his birth certificate states his name as Karl Gaul, the family soon began addressing their new addition by the French 'Charly'. His father, Jean Gaul, came from Erpeldange, a neighbouring town to Diekirch. His mother, Catherine Moser, had family roots in the beer business; a Moser ancestor, originally from the Tyrol region of Germany, moved to Diekirch to establish a brewery. Alcohol, one could say, ran in the blood. Gaul and Moser married in 1925.

At the time of his birth Charly's parents, both from agricultural families, were farming an estate in Gonderingen, north-east of the capital. Here, in the farmyard, Charly began to totter around and fostered a lifelong love of nature and animals. In 1935 the family moved to Tüntingen, leaving agriculture behind to start a new life as innkeepers. Their career change reflected broader shifts in Luxembourg society in the 1930s; young people began to reject the grinding poverty of life in the fields, instead favouring the rapidly growing service industries or the steelworks for which Luxembourg was to become famous after the war.

Tüntingen is another small village set amid rolling fields, though being a little further north-east, it neighbours densely forested hills that speak of the Ardennes valleys not far north. With his friends Charly explored these fields and forests, careering about the village on scooters and any bikes that could be borrowed from older siblings.

After the war Charly's brother, Jean-Pierre decided on a career as a baker and the family moved to Eich, a northern suburb of Luxembourg City set in a forested valley. There Jean-Pierre started work as an apprentice at the Maas Bakery; Charly's parents subsequently took over the Café Feller in the Place François-Joseph Dargent; and Charly himself went to secondary school.

In Eich, Charly got his first taste of cycling. With his friend Roby Maas, son of the Maas Bakery's owner, he would visit a bicycle shop owned by Kurt Warnier, an accomplished professional rider, who was unfortunate in that the Second World War had coincided with the best years of his career. In Warnier's workshop Charly and Roby inhaled the scent of grease and liniment, listened to Warnier's stories of riding the great races, and admired the glittering rows of bikes and wheels. Charly became intoxicated by the sport that would come to define his life. Charly and Roby raced their bicycles around the suburban streets of Eich, no doubt each playing the role of their favourite professional rider, but before the games could develop into a more serious tilt at racing, the Gaul family moved again. While Charly was very happy in the suburban milieu of Eich, his mother found the busy streets played on her nerves.[6] This time they moved to the south of the city, to Bettembourg, where Charly's parents took on a project to rebuild an inn.

Instead of following his brother into the bakery profession, Charly chose butchery. With encouragement from his father, he learnt the basics of the craft from Uncle Jean-Pierre and, on finishing school at fifteen, Charly went to work as a butcher's apprentice with Jean Kirsch in Düdelingen. By now, however, Charly's ambitions lay in cycling. He was training regularly with the local club, Velo Club Hüncheringen, and his riding style caught the eye of Pierre Clemens, a former professional who finished fourth in the 1936 Tour de France. Clemens was impressed with the lightness of Charly's pedalling and arranged for his first racing licence.

In March 1949, only three months after his sixteenth birthday, the youngster lined up for his first race, the traditional Luxembourg season-opener for juniors, the Critérium des Jeunes. Charly finished seventeenth. In July he took part in the Grand Prix de Schuttrange, one of the most important races for aspiring Luxembourgish riders and, with its repeated climbs, one of the toughest. The hills seemed to suit Charly. Dancing on the pedals and moving with a grace and fluidity that impressed the race officials, his quality was obvious. The Grand Prix de Schuttrange was his first victory. Later that summer he won two more races and, together with a string of top ten results, the butcher's apprentice with the cherubic face was officially the best of the year's debutants.

Coached by Clemens and supported by his parents, Gaul took the bold step of moving up to the amateur ranks a year early, for the 1950 season. Only just past his seventeenth birthday, he would now be competing against much older and more experienced riders. He also changed teams, joining Velo Club Bettembourg, one of the oldest clubs in Luxembourg. This was to become a theme throughout his cycling career; when it came to teams, Gaul was a restless soul.

The year started successfully with fourth place in the National Elite Cyclo-cross Championships. It was a particularly satisfying result because the race finished with a sprint between the leading four riders, and Gaul'smuch older and more experienced rivals had been unable to drop him. Raced on short off-road circuits, cyclo-cross involves tackling mud, grass, sand and sometimes snow, in short but very intense races. Originating in France in the early twentieth century, its popularity centred on northern Europereplace with colon : the Netherlands, Belgium, Luxembourg and Switzerland. By the early 1950s, following official recognition by the sport's governing body, the Union Cycliste Internationale (UCI), cyclo-cross was becoming more professional and more visible.

On the road Charly started to show a talent for short-stage races, winning the Grand Prix Général Patton, a two-day race in the Ardennes hills named after the American general who led the liberation of Luxembourg. Already his talent for climbing was becoming apparent, as well as its more negative corollary – his inability to win races in a sprint. Those watching the young man's progress knew that, while technique can to some extent be learnt, a racer's niche was predetermined by their physiology. At around 65 kilograms, the slender Gaul was built for the hills.

Gaul really showed his true potential in the 1951 season. Early in the year he won two prestigious stage races on his home roads – the Flèche du Sud and the Circuit des Douze Cantons, beating quality competition. Observers in the tightly knit Luxembourg cycling community noted the speed of his recovery after each stage. The victories earned him a growing reputation and a place on the Luxembourg team for the Tour of Austria, a major event on the European amateur calendar. It would be Gaul's first race outside Luxembourg. Until now he had excelled on the steep hills of the Ardennes, the landscape he had grown up with. Now he faced a much bigger challenge: the high mountain passes of the Austrian Alps.

At 3,798 metres the Grossglockner is the highest mountain in Austria. Carving a spectacular path up the mountain's northern flank, the High Alpine Road climbs to 2,502 metres. In summer the road is a destination for drivers who want to test themselves against 30 kilometres of sinuous asphalt. With every hairpin bend the view sparkles a little more – crystalline lakes, edelweiss, the jagged peaks of the High Tauern National Park and, at the top, the Pasterze glacier. In the winter the road is closed, buried under several metres of snow.

The 1951 Tour of Austria tackled the Grossglockner on stage 4. Gaul had started the race strongly, winning the opening stage in a sprint – a rare occurrence for him – from a small group, only to lose the leader's jersey two days later, but as the race began climbing he discovered his true calling. Years later, he said, 'I'd never seen a road higher than 800 metres before I rode the Grossglockner, but I found I was good on climbs like that. I found a rhythm and it felt natural, and also on that climb the higher we went the colder it got and that suited me too.'[7]

What Gaul didn't mention was the storm gathering strength over the riders, who, for the most part, must have been cursing their choice of sport. Gaul was eighteen years old and climbing one of the highest mountain passes in Europe on a wet day, with temperatures in single digits near the top. Perversely, this cheered him. The editor of an Austrian newspaper reported on Gaul's 'captivating manner' as the Luxembourger caught and passed the leading rider two-thirds of the way up the climb. Alone, Gaul pressed on, despite his team manager's calls to ride with caution. The British writer Charlie Woods was later to write,

This show of force was greeted by another, a thunderstorm and the first squalls of rain probably cooled the fever of his labours and brought with it a lighter, freer atmosphere. He had always been at ease in rainfall and beginning to pedal now with an edge of fierce affirmation, he perhaps completely forgot himself for a long series of ramps and bends . . .[8]

The Austrian newspaper editor wrote: '"Need something?" we ask him as we drive past him in the cold, wet rain, thanking God that we're in the car and not on a bike. "What do you want me to need?" he smiles.'[9]

At the cloud-laden summit the timekeepers recorded one hour

and twelve minutes for the full climb – a new record. Charly had a lead of five minutes on a chasing group, which he squandered on the ensuing long descent. This was to be a valuable lesson; if he had taken the descent faster he would have taken not only the stage win but the leader's jersey too. As it was, local rider Franz Deutsch (a rider who later became famous for undertaking a solo escape of 195 kilometres in a race, during which he drank six beers) ran out the eventual winner of the overall classification. Charly was third and his flight up the Grossglockner was the story of the race.

'What do you want me to need?' Charly had responded to the newspaper editor's offer of help on that long climb. Even allowing for the imprecision of translation, it is a strange thing for an eighteen-year-old racing cyclist to say to a – presumably much older – member of the press on a wet mountain pass in the Alps. The sports editor was dry and warm in a car alongside Charly. He was part of the race entourage, part of the cycling establishment. The teenager's comment is almost provocative; hardly deferential to the authority of the journalist. Perhaps the journalist happened to catch Charly at the exact moment in his fledgling career when he was beginning to understand not only his talent but also his calling as a climber. Before the Grossglockner he had been a very good rider, capable of winning races with apparent ease, but on that climb he must have started to see where he could truly excel, the landscape on which he could beat the world's best professionals. More than that, perhaps Charly was feeling elated that his gift could let him escape – from the other riders with their chatter and insults, from the mundanity of the flatlands and from his destiny as a butcher.

'What do you want me to need?' The question also foreshadows the prickly relationship between Charly and the press that would come to play such an important role in his life. In that cheeky one-liner he seems to have intuitively understood that newspapers wanted to construct narratives around riders, wanted to show how vulnerable they were. Five years later, in the middle of a snowstorm on the Monte Bondone in Italy, Charly's most mythologised victory would be told in terms of how his team manager coaxed him out of a café halfway up the climb, how blue his lips were, how afterwards he needed to be lowered into a warm bath, still in his cycling kit. At eighteen, Charly understood what the writers wanted. He was no fool.

November, 1951

Stage 2

THE KILLER

Depending on your age, you may have different preconceptions of Luxembourg. If you're a baby boomer, you'll think of Radio Luxembourg, one of the first English-language commercial radio stations to play pop music, and a seminal moment in youth culture in the 1950s and 60s. If you're a bit younger you may associate Luxembourg with the European Union because since the Second World War this small country has been integral to it. But, of course, none of these preconceptions really describe a nation, however small it is (and for the record the population is around 650,000).

Luxembourg's history has always been bound up with its neighbours and wider European conflicts have played out on Luxembourg's soil. The same is true in neighbouring Belgium, and some observers have commented that this has resulted in something of a bunker mentality among Belgians.[10] Luxembourg, however, has always been an open country, its borders and culture porous. It needs to trade freely with its neighbours because it is too small to exist in isolation. In 1932, children in Luxembourg grew up trilingual. Luxembourgish was the language they spoke at home, while at school they learnt German and French. Today, many Luxembourgers are also fluent in English. Walk through the streets of Luxembourg City and you are as likely to hear English being spoken as any other language, in part because of the many international corporations with offices in the city. This trilingualism meant that Luxembourg could co-exist with its three neighbours – Germany, France and Belgium. Landlocked between these three stronger powers, Luxembourg has encouraged trade to flow across its borders. That openness, together with the nimble language skills of its residents, has, in turn, encouraged immigration. In 2022 only just over half of its residents were native Luxembourgers. While Belgians, French, Germans and Italians are well-represented in Luxembourg society, it is the Portuguese who make up the largest immigrant group, accounting for 20% of the country's working population.[11]

After the First World War there was a long period of settled prosperity. Luxembourg society was happy in its wealthy neutrality. The two principal industries of agriculture and steel kept employment levels high, and a progressive social insurance policy caught anyone who might have slipped through the gaps. Luxembourg's royal family, known as the Grand Duchy, was, and continues to be today, well-loved. One legacy of the Germans' invasion of Luxembourg on 1 August 1914, when they trampled over the country's neutrality, was that Luxembourg turned away from Germany, politically and culturally, in favour of its other neighbour, France. Yet three languages continued to exist in this land of less than 1,000 square miles.

Luxembourg re-established its independence as a Grand Duchy after the war, and its politicians set about building a more international role for the country. Of its three neighbours, they chose Belgium as an economic partner and, with the Netherlands, formed the Benelux coalition, which was to become a model for the later birth of the European Economic Community. Having abandoned its neutral stance during the Second World War, Luxembourg now began to put itself at the heart of the European bloc. And as the threat from Stalin's Soviet Union grew in the east, the western European countries firmly allied themselves with NATO and American doctrine. According to international law, Luxembourg was still theoretically neutral; in practice it was anything but.

This alignment with America and Western Europe, supported by a stable social and political system, and Luxembourg's openness to immigration, facilitated a long period of economic growth. Steel mining, Luxembourg's primary industry since the nineteenth century, grew steadily throughout much of the twentieth century and when it faltered, hit by the industrial crises of the 1970s, the financial sector was lining up to take its place. Successive Luxembourg governments have courted foreign investment, banks in particular, and the result has been the establishment of Luxembourg as a major financial centre. Today the outer reaches of Luxembourg City are populated by shiny glass and steel offices, many of them housing international banks and trading firms.

The Second World War was as traumatic for Luxembourg as it was for every other European nation. Charly Gaul was eight when his country was occupied, twelve when it was liberated, and the proximity of his childhood home in Tüntingen to the southern front of the Battle of the Bulge suggests that the war must have had a profound effect on Gaul as a boy. In April 1939, as the country faced the spectre of Nazism just across its border, a festival was held to celebrate the centennial of Luxembourg's independence (arguably the treaty of 1867 was a more important moment of national independence, but the London Conference of 1839 was chosen as a pretext to create an opportunity to face down Hitler's aggression). There was a parade through Luxembourg City with demonstrations of Luxembourgish crafts and folklore. The much-loved Grand Duchess, a powerful symbol of her country, toured towns and villages throughout the land, provoking a surge in patriotism and national pride. It seems likely that the Gaul family would have witnessed this festival and, as innkeepers, been part of a party in their village.

However, it's difficult to gauge the true impact of the war on Charly and his family. In keeping with much of his generation, Gaul never spoke publicly about the war and there is scant documentary record. Whether or not he remembered the events in later life, these were the times that shaped Charly. During his childhood his tiny country endured a deep trauma. Despite Germany's overwhelming military superiority, which made the invasion a foregone conclusion, Luxembourg's swift capitulation was a source of shame and humiliation for Gaul's father's generation. Not only had David failed to strike down Goliath, he had not even fired his stone. Two decades later Charly Gaul was to become his country's David, a focal point for re-establishing its sense of national identity.

The Grand Duchy was very much integrated into the wider European sports arena, with Luxembourg's sportsmen and women finding that their exploits tended to be amplified because they demonstrated the strength of their tiny nation on a larger stage. Throughout the first half of the twentieth century, along with Spain and Italy, France and Belgium were the dominant forces in cycling, and Luxembourgish cyclists inevitably looked to their neighbours for opportunities to showcase their abilities. Cycle racing was as popular in Luxembourg as it was in France and Belgium, and the exploits of the country's professional riders were followed closely in newspapers and on the radio.

Aspiring riders from the Grand Duchy had a lot to live up to, though. Luxembourg already had two Tour de France winners: François Faber won in 1909, Nicolas Frantz in 1927 and 1928. Faber had Luxembourg nationality but lived in Paris and considered himself French (his mother was French, his father Luxembourgish). His Tour de France victory was accomplished amid some of the worst weather the race has ever seen – rain, snow, mud and freezing temperatures – and, along with the long distances of the era, this made the race an awful experience for the racers. However, Faber seemed to revel in the bad weather and dominated the race, winning five stages in a row, a record that still stands today. When the First World War broke out he joined the French Foreign Legion and was posted to Arras. On 9 May 1915 he received a telegram to inform him that his wife had given birth to their daughter. Later that day he was shot dead while carrying an injured comrade back from no man's land.

If Faber was heroic in the truest sense of the word, his divided loyalties meant that he was never quite adopted as a sporting hero of Luxembourg. Frantz, however, was very much a son of the nation and of the land. Born in 1899 into a wealthy farming family in the south-west of Luxembourg, Frantz had no interest in taking over the family business. From his early teenage years, competing in local races before the outbreak of the First World War, he was unbeatable. One of his first victories as a professional was the Grand Prix François Faber, a Luxembourg race to commemorate his predecessor. Frantz wore the red, white and blue tricolour jersey of National Road Race Champion for twelve years and twice finished on the podium of the Road Race World Championship, but it was his pair of Tour de France wins that set his place in cycling history. He so dominated the race in 1928 that the following year his rivals referred to the race as the Tour de Frantz.

On retirement Frantz managed the Luxembourg and Luxembourg Mixed teams at the Tour de France. It was in this capacity that the young Charly Gaul came into his orbit; the two were to have a respectful but difficult relationship.

In the autumn of 1951 Gaul was facing an awkward obstacle in his career progression – compulsory military service. With the support of another new team, the Union Cycliste (UC) Dippach, an amateur squad that was building a reputation for fostering many national champions, Charly was able to negotiate a post at the Heilig-Geist barracks in Luxembourg, where his butchery skills were put to use in the kitchens. He was permitted to go on training rides but was often followed around the countryside by colleagues in a military jeep. Quite where his superiors thought he might escape to, or why, is not clear, but the change of routine meant his preparations for the 1952 season were less than ideal.

Gaul's 1952 Tour of Austria was a carbon copy of the previous year. For the opening stages he coasted along in the peloton, biding his time, then made his move on the stage going over the Grossglockner. The weather, however, couldn't have been more different. In intense heat Gaul led alone over the summit, but, like the year before, he was caught on the descent by Franz Deutsch and beaten in the sprint into Saalbach. After the final stage in Vienna, Gaul finished second overall to Deutsch.

One thing was markedly different – Charly's look. Photographs of him in 1951 and before look like throwbacks to an even earlier age of cycling, with Charly wearing dust goggles and a leather helmet, a spare tubular tyre wrapped across his chest. In 1952 he seems to have become more styled, more self-conscious. The goggles and helmet are gone, and he has a neat dark quiff, which, along with his disaffected attitude, led to comparisons with James Dean. In fact, it seems unlikely that the American actor was a direct influence on the young Luxembourger (by the summer of 1952 Dean was not yet a fully fledged star), although, of course, it is entirely possible that Gaul's hairdresser was a fan. Already the media was beginning to see the appeal of this young man with the handsome face and killer climbing ability. The Viennese newspaper, *Sport-Schau*, put him on their front cover, a photo of Gaul grinning and joking with other riders in the Tour of Austria, and the manufacturer of his bicycles, also Austrian, featured Gaul in their advertisements.

So far, so normal. Charly's rise through the junior and amateur ranks – by the time he turned professional in 1953 he had more than

60 wins to his name – was impressive, but essentially no different from that of any other talented young rider destined to become a professional. Charly knew that a contract would bring money, fame and a chance to ride his bike for a living. An introverted young man, he loved nothing more than disappearing into the countryside on long solo training rides. Being paid to do so, rather than work in a butcher's shop, was an attractive proposition, but in the summer of 1952 there was nothing to indicate just how spectacular Gaul's rise and fall would be, nor the mythical status that would later be attached to him. Sporting myths, however, can be ignited by apparently incidental details.

Later that year Gaul switched from the butcher's shop to working at an abattoir in Bettembourg. The reason isn't clear. Perhaps the new job would offer more time for training, maybe the money was better. It certainly wasn't an easy way to make a living. In the middle of the twentieth century, slaughterhouses were rapidly becoming mechanised and industrial in scale, but the work was still brutally hard.

Gaul's job was to kill cattle as they arrived, and he would have been under pressure to do so quickly and cleanly. Despite being slight in build and less than average height, Charly – according to his own account[12] – became very good at killing cows with a single blow. The animal's head was pulled down to the floor and Gaul would swing a heavy, long-handled hammer to strike it between the eyes. A strong clean hit would kill the cow instantly. Not only was Gaul good at his job, he later claimed to have enjoyed it.

Maintaining a high-paced production line was the priority in the slaughterhouse. The work was repetitive and intensely physical, with conditions that were cold and dirty. The stench of death was everywhere. Modern studies have shown that slaughterhouse workers can suffer from post-traumatic stress disorder, as well as being prone to accidents and many forms of work-induced injuries. Few workers continue in the trade to full retirement age, and health problems stop most by middle age. In the face of such conditions, workers develop a strong sense of solidarity. A dark sense of humour masks more troubling emotions, which are rarely discussed. A good knife makes the work easier. Abattoir workers become very attached to their knives, which become extensions of their hands.

Gaul only worked at the Bettembourg abattoir for a few months and doubtless was already eyeing up opportunities to turn professional. The job, though, has become a central part of his story. In every written narrative of his life, he is referred to as 'the former abattoir worker' or something similar. In part this is because he, too, referred to it when speaking to journalists. He liked to throw it into interviews, perhaps to shock, perhaps to create an identity for himself. Gaul was not a popular character in the professional peloton, nor was he a physically intimidating presence. To those who angered him, he could offer one of two threats: I will leave you for dead on a mountain or I will cut you open with my knife. 'Do not forget I am a killer,' he would say.

The director of Gaul's club, UC Dippach, had a good relationship with Pierre Dion, the sports director of Dijon-based professional team, Terrot-Hutchinson, and he negotiated a professional contract for his young talent. The team was a comfortable place for Gaul to take the plunge into the considerably more cynical and ruthless world of professional cycling; it also contained two experienced Luxembourgish riders in Jean Goldschmidt and Marcel Ernzer. Both men were to play critical roles in Gaul's career, Goldschmidt as a team manager, Ernzer as Gaul's most faithful domestique. Both men also became lifelong friends.

On 3 May 1953 Gaul travelled to his first professional race, the semi-classic Polymultipliée in northern France. Wearing his new green and white jersey, aboard his Terrot bike, Gaul was active throughout the hilly 154 kilometres and came to the finish in the leading group, only losing out to quicker riders in the final sprint. Just ahead of Gaul were the well-known Frenchmen Jean Robic, winner of the 1947 Tour de France, and Raphaël Géminiani, winner of the mountains classification in both the Tour de France and the Giro d'Italia. Gaul's new boss was impressed.

In early June Gaul finished third in the Tour de Luxembourg, before lining up for the week-long Dauphiné Libéré, a traditional warm-up race for the Tour de France, where the contenders for La Grande Boucle are always closely watched for signs of strength and weakness. The French newspapers noted that Charly was able to stay with the leading riders on the high Alpine passes, many of which were lined with solid white walls of snow. He finished second in two stages, eventually finishing second overall to his team-mate Lucien Teisseire.

In 1953 the Tour de France was contested by national teams, although because of the strength of French cycling and Europe as the geographical locus of cycling, the start sheet shows six French teams: a national team led by Louison Bobet and five regional teams. Posed against this half-peloton of Frenchmen were teams from Switzerland, Belgium, Spain, Italy, the Netherlands and Luxembourg, which was able to field a full team of ten after the ignominy of having to bolster its ranks with two Australian riders the previous year.

With defending champion Fausto Coppi not taking the start in Strasbourg, the favourites were Bobet and the Swiss rider Hugo Koblet. There was, however, a heavy question mark hanging over the Frenchman. He had already ridden five Tours with little to show for his efforts. The French newspapers, and some of the French team, doubted he would ever find the strength to seriously challenge for the yellow jersey.

Gaul was selected for his Tour debut, not surprisingly given his performance at the Dauphiné Libéré, though some newspapers questioned whether, at twenty, he was too young for such a challenge of endurance. At the traditional – and entirely cursory – medical check on the eve of the race, the Tour's official doctor, Dr Berty, declared that Gaul was fit to race. His pulse was a little high, he noted, but his blood pressure was excellent, and there was nothing to indicate he had suffered damage from over-exertion.

Gaul may have been physically fit, but mentally he wasn't up to the pressure of the Tour. His team, other riders and even journalists warned him to stay attentive in the fast-moving peloton, to stay protected from the wind on the long flat stages through northern France, but repeatedly Gaul was to be seen drifting along at the back of the race and when the wind was strong he got spat out. Losing contact with the peloton always means losing time. A lone rider can never hope to ride as fast as the tightly packed group. On stage 6, from Caen to Le Mans, across the exposed plains of northern France, Gaul again slipped out of the back of the peloton. Disheartened, he pulled out of the race.

His behaviour, a mix of arrogance and naïveté, perplexed those who were trying to help him. 'Charly is a peculiar lad,' Nicolas Frantz told journalist René de Latour. 'Most novices are only too anxious to listen to the advice given them by old-timers. But not Charly – and that's too bad because in going his own way he makes bad mistakes and loses precious time.'[13]

There were the inevitable comments in the press about his age and lack of experience. Gaul himself was tight-lipped about the reasons for his exit. His friend François Mersch, who formed part of the small trusted entourage around Gaul and later wrote a biography, *Bergauf, Bergab mit Charly Gaul* (*Uphill, Downhill with Charly Gaul*), hints that the atmosphere in the Luxembourg team was not to Gaul's liking. Even if this was true, it was hardly a credible excuse. Charly had a lot to learn about professionalism.

After his second place in the Dauphiné Libéré, Gaul's mysterious exit from the 1953 Tour de France was a disappointment for his growing contingent of fans and the newspaper writers who wanted to see him confirm the promise he'd shown a few weeks earlier. There was no obvious physical problem – he couldn't have lost his Dauphiné form so quickly and there was no mention of illness in the Luxembourg camp. In later years Gaul also lost time on the flat, windy stages of the Tour and accepted it calmly because he knew the mountains were coming. Perhaps in 1953 he withdrew because he was just too self-conscious to accept the humiliation and criticism. The peloton gives anonymity. Being alone behind the race singles you out and puts you in the full glare of the photographers' lenses. Doing that takes some mental toughness.

In later interviews,[14] Gaul dismissed any hint of mystery around his withdrawal from the Tour, saying only that he wasn't ready. One benefit of his early exit was that he retained good form throughout August and, at the Road Race World Championship in Lugano, Italy, finished a creditable sixth in a race dominated by a long solo attack from Fausto Coppi. At thirty-three, Coppi was riding out the last days of summer of his career. His fame was intense, his charisma on and off the bike magnetic. In Lugano his performance was imperious. The World Championship was the only major race missing from his palmares, and he had prepared carefully for the hilly, 270-kilometre race. He had even skipped the Tour de France to ensure he was fully trained and rested. With 90 kilometres to go he rode away on the Crespera climb and only the Belgian Germain Derycke could hold his wheel. The pair rode together until Coppi attacked again, at the same spot, with 22 kilometres to go. In those last 22 kilometres the exhausted Derycke lost over six minutes, but hung on for a deserved silver medal. Gaul finished with the Italian Nino Defilippis, over nine minutes behind *Il Campionissimo* – the Champion of Champions – as Coppi was known.

In those post-war years, even being a celebrated professional cyclist did not excuse you from the requirements of military service.

Gaul had completed his in 1951, but he was still obliged to participate in military manoeuvres, so his season ended not with the planned Polymultipliée race in France, but with another form of simulated battle – a military exercise in the Luxembourg countryside.

Stage 3

THE ANGEL

Since the start of his career, Gaul had raced cyclo-cross during the winter months as part of his pre-season training. Faced with the prospect of a steady, six-hour road ride in single-digit temperatures, it was much better to race so intensely for one hour that the body barely had a chance to feel the cold. The racers may not have felt it during the race, but they certainly did before the start. The art of undressing on the starting grid was critically important. Racers would keep their woolly tracksuit tops on for as long as possible, then, when the officials called out one minute to go, they would unzip the tops and toss them to helpers.

Gaul's first race of 1954 was an international cyclo-cross race in Zug, Switzerland, in early January and, although Charly probably didn't find it very funny, it was marked by a note of comedy. Not only was it bitterly cold, but the track was also covered in ice and compacted snow. Gaul and a French rider were therefore overjoyed to find a building near the start with a roaring furnace, but they were so happy warming themselves by the fire that they missed the start and had to dash to the line, several minutes after their competitors had departed. Both men chased hard, principally motivated by embarrassment. Gaul eventually finished in twelfth spot, exhausted and abashed.

For climbers like Gaul, although they raced on the road from February, the season only really started in May. By this time the tough one-day classics in France, Italy and Belgium were out of the way, and the cycling world shifted its attention to stage races of varying lengths. There was a practical reason, too – stage races needed the high mountain passes of the Alps, Dolomites, Pyrénées and a host of other European mountain ranges, and these were often impassable well into the spring. Even in May the snow-ploughs sometimes had to be employed to cut a path for a race.

Between cyclo-cross races, Gaul prepared for the season ahead with long chilly rides through the Ardennes forests, often alone. The orthodoxy of the time was that elite riders had to commit to putting in thousands of kilometres of steady riding through the winter, whatever the weather. Lifting weights, running and even cross-country skiing, if you lived close to the mountains, were all seen as complementary activities, but there was no substitute for time on the bike. This is where cycling became an almost monastic activity. Every sport requires training and dedication, but cycling fans have always revelled in the idea that its elite riders have to repeatedly put in six-hour rides in temperatures barely above zero. The workload and prolonged exposure to the elements is what sets professional riders apart from mere club cyclists. They are not only fitter and stronger but also harder and more weather-beaten. This is part of the reason why road riders become legends and track riders disappear into anonymity. When asked how to train to be a champion, Fausto Coppi famously said, 'Ride a bike, ride a bike, ride a bike.'

For the most part, however, Gaul enjoyed training. As an introverted person, the time spent alone was good for recharging his mental batteries and, put simply, he did love riding his bike. Talking to the media did not come so naturally, but he was not yet suspicious of journalists. He also understood that giving an upbeat interview was all part of the path towards a professional contract. An article in

Lëtzebuerger Sport in January 1954 described his cheerful disposition, how much he loved children and his sense of national loyalty. Asked about his ambitions for the Tour de Luxembourg, he said, 'I frankly admit that I am keen to win in front of my compatriots.'[15]

Before his home race, however, came the Circuit des Six Provinces. This week-long stage race for riders under twenty-five was an important opportunity for young professionals to demonstrate their abilities. Organised by the same people who ran the Tour de France, the Circuit des Six Provinces was watched carefully by the professional cycling community. Its route, starting and finishing in the city of Lyon, took the riders through the mountain ranges of the Haute-Loire, which was challenging enough to sort the grimpeurs from the rouleurs.

In the first stage, from Lyon to Beaune,[16] Gaul was attentive, but held back from attacking, the terrain not tough enough to present him with an opportunity. The principal challenge of that first day were the hail storms that lashed down on the peloton. The next day, too, a 215-kilometre stage from Beaune to Roane, Gaul followed the moves of others, biding his time, learning about his rivals. Run off under cloudy skies, the race was constantly under pressure, splitting and re-forming as the strongest riders tried to force the decisive breakaway. *L'Équipe*, the official newspaper of the race and of the Tour de France, had predicted Jean Forestier as a favourite for the stage, but Forestier's luck ran out in the final kilometres; taking a drink while rolling down a hill he hit a parked car and crashed heavily. Though he remounted to finish the stage, the time lost put him out of contention. That evening in Roane, Gaul lay in thirteenth place overall, two minutes and sixteen seconds down on the leader, Belgian Fred De Bruyne. This was the only piece of good news for Terrot team manager, Pierre Dion. By the end of the second day, four of his riders had pulled out of the race, leaving only Gaul, Marcel Guitard and Raymond Elena.

The third day was predicted to be much more selective. The two principal climbs – the Col des Sauvages (725 metres) and the Croix de Chaubouret (1315 metres) – bookended the 215-kilometre route, the latter coming just 18 kilometres before the finish line in Saint-Étienne. Between them were many smaller uncategorised climbs. The weather continued to be unseasonably grey; showers were forecast in the afternoon.

A group of four jumped clear soon after the start. On the Col des Sauvages Gaul gave chase alone, but he was unable to make the contact before the summit and was absorbed back into the peloton. Further back race leader De Bruyne was struggling after an early puncture. On the climb of Saint-Symphorien-sur-Coise the promising Peugeot rider, René Privat, launched a strong attack and, by the small town of Saint-Chamond, at the foot of the final climb, with the rain now falling heavily, Privat was more than two minutes clear of a chasing group. The peloton, including Gaul, began the climb three minutes back.

For those spectators standing huddled under umbrellas and in shop doorways in Saint-Chamond, that three-minute gap between Privat and the bedraggled, tyre-hissing peloton must have seemed like an eternity. Surely his victory in Saint-Étienne, just a few kilometres away down the valley road, was assured? Yet the race wasn't going down the valley. It was going to hit a 15-kilometre climb with an average gradient of 5.4% and maximum gradient of 10%. If the Croix de Chaubouret is not as high or spectacular as the fabled passes of the Alps or the Pyrénées, it was certainly difficult enough to blow apart a peloton of tired and soaked young riders.

As soon as the road began to tilt uphill, still in the streets of Saint-Chamond, Gaul attacked. He quickly caught and passed the chasing group, then Privat. Now he was alone. No one even attempted to follow his pace and the journalists on the race watched with wonder as the twenty-two-year-old danced away from his rivals.

Pierre About wrote in *L'Équipe*, 'When Charly Gaul met with the terrible ascent of the Chaubouret, one forgot that he had been looking like a man who fought and suffered. An irresistible lightness suddenly took hold of this young boy with the doll's eyes, and he gave the impression of an angel for whom nothing is difficult. Light, harmonious, he rode away from the field.'[17]

With its dark banks of pine trees, patches of exposed moor and low cloud cover, did the Chaubouret climb remind Charly of the Ardennes? Did he have any idea of how his escape might be perceived and described by writers? Probably not. A professional cyclist is paid to pedal, not to ruminate on his own mythology. This day was, however, the start of the mythology that attached itself to Charly Gaul. Whether or not Gaul took delight in his exploit, whether or not his race-winning attack really did feel effortless and harmonious, does not really matter. About's report in *L'Équipe* (which included several more paragraphs of purple prose devoted to bringing the scene to life for readers) created the idea of Charly Gaul as the Angel of the Mountains. It was an attractive proposition.

In 1954, Fausto Coppi's presence – and the somewhat scandalous mythology that swirled around him – still dominated professional cycling. Coppi, and his Italian rivals Gino Bartali and Fiorenzo Magni, were loved deeply, but they were certainly no longer innocent and fresh. Among the wider populations of Europe, memories of the Second World War were still vivid. Economic hardship, and the emotional aftermath of war, made life tough. Cycling, while it was diverting entertainment, had yet to acquire the glamour that came with Jacques Anquetil in the 1960s. Louison Bobet was talented and charming, but he was considered rather snooty by a peloton made up of working-class men. A baby-faced innocent, naïve, gifted and aloof, was an exciting proposition for the cycling press. Like all natural climbers, his ability seemed almost otherworldly and the fact that he'd appeared suddenly, apparently fully equipped to beat the world's best riders, and that he came from Luxembourg, of all places, only added to the mystique.

The nickname Angel of the Mountains stuck. Other writers adopted it, in part because it could be used in headlines in different ways. Pierre About surely knew the connotations of the name he bestowed upon Charly. Since the fifteenth century the term 'angel' has been used to describe someone with divine qualities, and angels are important in Judaism, Catholicism and Eastern Orthodox religion. The word has its origins in Hebrew, in which it means 'messenger'. However, the position of messenger is relatively low in the divine hierarchy, and angels have traditionally bridged the gap between the human realm and the divine. If About had named Charly Gaul a god or a saint, it would not have captured the imagination in quite the same way. An angel, though, is a distinctly imperfect distillation of something higher. Just think of the angel Clarence Odbody, who rescues George Bailey in Frank Capra's 1946 film, *It's a Wonderful Life*.

The nickname soon became double-edged for Gaul; as his career progressed and his behaviour towards fellow riders and the press became erratic, the moniker took an ironic slant. On the ascent of his career, his was a divine calling; on the descent, he was a fallen angel. An angel with a dirty face.

In 1954, however, Gaul paid scant attention to About's mythologising. He was focused on less abstract matters – training and racing. Plus he had a girlfriend. In an interview with a French newspaper in May 1954, he told the journalist Robert Silva of his relationship with Georgette Schmit, daughter of the president of his amateur cycling club UC Dippach. Georgette, wrote Silva, worked in the office at the slaughterhouse and had been immediately attracted to this handsome young man. There is no evidence to corroborate this last claim, which presumably came from Gaul himself. Gaul also said how fortunate he was that Georgette was not jealous of his bicycle.

In these comments we can hear a wry sense of humour undercutting what could be perceived as arrogance and vanity.

In this early stage of his career, Gaul was remarkably open with journalists that he trusted. In February 1956 Pierre Chany, one of the most respected cycling writers of the era, wrote in *L'Équipe* that Gaul had picked a fight with the Luxembourg taxman. 'Since my successes in the Tour, I have been harassed by . . . the tax department. Consider that the tax collector currently takes 50% of my earnings. It cannot last. Now I categorically refuse to pay, which obviously gets me into a bit of trouble. So, I have an appointment this week with the Minister of Finance! If we do not find common ground, I will simply give up pursuing my career! I am willing to make sacrifices to remain a champion, I am ready to accept all the risks of the job, but I also want to reap the benefits,'[18] Gaul reportedly told Chany.[19] The article went on to say that a socialist newspaper was advising Gaul to marry – doing so would reduce his tax burden and therefore keep him in the sport. Just a month after the *L'Équipe* article was published, Charly and Georgette did indeed get married in the Cathédrale Notre-Dame, Luxembourg City.

Whether his tax bill played any part in Gaul's motivation for marrying Georgette is impossible to say. It is more likely that his comments to Chany were ironic. Here we begin to see the opening of a gap between Gaul's life and the way it was presented in the cycling press, who were as guilty of succumbing to tabloid sensationalism as they were of mythologising racing exploits. In an era when professional cyclists were household names across mainland Europe, it wasn't only avid cyclists who read newspaper stories. The audience was broad, and journalists knew that professional riders were becoming household names.

In this early part of his career Gaul was probably more amused than anything else. Close friends in the peloton portrayed him as a bit of a joker and, in his naïveté, he perhaps thought that joking with the press would keep them at a certain distance. Within a few short years, however, any humour in this relationship had evaporated.

In 1954, as Charly Gaul got to grips with his new-found celebrity, Louison Bobet was at the peak of his fame. The Frenchman was in the middle year of his hat-trick of Tour de France victories and enjoying adulatory reviews in the French newspapers. More than any other rider, Bobet was to play an important role in Gaul's story. The antipathy between the two men shaped the outcome of races and influenced Gaul's position within the peloton, and long after both riders retired, their relationship tainted the way Gaul was portrayed. Bobet's own story also provides a useful counterpoint to Gaul's. There were similarities between them as well as some deeply entrenched differences.

Born in Brittany in 1925, in the village of Saint-Méen-le-Grand just west of Rennes, Louis Bobet was one of three children. His father was a baker and also called Louis, so the family adopted the diminutive Louison for the boy. The French philosopher Roland Barthes, writing on the Tour de France in his seminal book *Mythologies*, associated this use of the diminutive with the role of the hero: 'Diminished, the name becomes truly public; it permits placing the racer's intimacy on the heroes' proscenium.'[20] In other words, by giving a favourite rider a nickname, the public makes a possession of him and expects to understand him intimately.

The Bobet children were talented at sport. Louison's sister played table tennis, and his brother played football and later took up cycling. Despite being Brittany champion at table tennis, Louison chose to focus on cycling after his Uncle Raymond, president of a cycling club in Paris, had a quiet word with him. Bobet's results as a young rider were solid, though not exceptional, but he was dedicated to his sport and eventually his hard work paid off.

After being demobilised from the French Army in 1945, an

administrative error gave Bobet the chance to prove himself on a bigger stage. He'd applied for an amateur racing licence, but instead was sent an independent one, which allowed him to compete against both amateurs and professionals. He came second in the Brittany championship, then travelled to Paris for the French amateur National Road Race Championship. In the closing kilometres two riders were clear. Bobet attacked the field, bridged to the leading duo, dropped one, then outsprinted the other on the Piste Municipale velodrome. No one had heard of him, and he had to explain his background to intrigued journalists.

'I am a baker,' he told them. 'I work for my father and we are so busy that I have to do all my training at night.' Bobet was not a baker for much longer. He signed as a professional for Stella, a small team based in Nantes, and rewarded their faith in May 1947 when he won the Boucles de la Seine, a French classic, with a 60-kilometre solo breakaway. That victory earned Bobet an invitation to ride the 1947 Tour de France on the French national team, but he wasn't prepared for the higher level of racing. His first experience of the Tour was a baptism of fire. When the race entered the Alps, Bobet was dropped and began to cry. Other riders in the peloton called him a crybaby and, on stage 9, a traumatised Bobet left the race.

The following year, however, Bobet was back at the Tour with a new-found toughness. He won two stages and wore the yellow jersey twice. Coming into the Alps he had a twenty-minute lead over Gino Bartali, but Bartali and his fellow Italians combined to demolish the gap. By Paris, Bobet was more than thirty-two minutes behind Bartali, but he had finished fourth and shown his true potential.

Despite a cycling career in the ascendancy, Bobet never lost touch with his roots. With the proceeds from his successful 1948 Tour, he bought a grocery shop in Rennes, and every morning before dawn he got up to deliver milk to houses in the neighbourhood. Admirable, but unwise. His exhausting routine contributed to his disastrous

1949 Tour, and he quit the race and was on the verge of quitting the sport altogether. Ultimately, though, he wanted fame and money too much; Bobet just could not see himself as a humble grocer and milk delivery man. In the autumn of 1949, he won the Critérium de l'Ouest and decided to persevere.

In 1950, he finished third in the Tour, but dropped to twentieth the following year and was again heavily criticised in the French newspapers. He didn't ride in the 1952 Tour, which was dominated by Fausto Coppi, and after his poor performance at the 1953 Giro, few expected him to perform well at the 1953 Tour. Bobet, though, had other ideas.

Near the top of the Col d'Izoard a pine forest gives way to a landscape of bizarre, tawny needles of dolomite rock amid searing grey scree. This is the Casse Déserte, the 'broken desert'. At its summit the brave cyclist will have climbed for more than 31 kilometres to an elevation of 2,361 metres. In 1953 the Tour de France ascended the Col d'Izoard and Bobet rode clear of his rivals. Ahead of him a convertible car laboured upwards, a cameraman standing precariously in the passenger seat. Around Bobet a horde of motorbikes and a jeep bounced over the road's rutted surface. There were few spectators up there in the baking mountain amphitheatre.

Bobet, who had attacked going over the top of the preceding Col de Vars and was paced along the valley between the two passes by his team-mate, Adolphe Deledda, was slightly over-geared for the final climb and had to wrestle his bike to keep it moving. As he came around a bend, Bobet saw an unusually large group of fans. At its centre, grinning broadly and pointing a camera, was a tall man in a stylish black sweater – it was Fausto Coppi. Beside him stood his famous mistress Giulia Locatelli. Coppi shouted his encouragement; Bobet called out 'Merci!' and pushed on towards the summit.

For all his later accomplishments, Bobet would always be associated with that ascent of the Col d'Izoard. Above all, to ride with such fury and panache, after so many setbacks, showed the world how hungry he was to be a champion. He won the 1953 Tour de France by fourteen minutes from compatriot Jean Malléjac.

Twelve months later Bobet arrived in Amsterdam for the start of the Tour de France with the support of a strong French team and with the weighty tag of race favourite. Gaul, with his Luxembourg Mixed team, was more a curiosity than an outright favourite. After his success at the Circuit de Six Provinces and a subsequent second place at the Dauphiné Libéré, the press were intrigued to see what he was capable of, but everyone knew that the Tour de France was a very different proposition to its warm-up races.

In the days after the Dauphiné there had been a disagreement about whether Gaul should ride the Tour. Representing Terrot, Dion had sent a telegram to Gaul and the Tour organisers, saying that the team objected to Gaul riding. Terrot wanted to protect its asset; at twenty-one he was still too young for the brutal physical test that the Tour de France entailed. Gaul's response to Dion was unequivocal – he had certain obligations to Luxembourgers and therefore was going to ride – but privately Gaul shared his director's concerns. The Tour was a daunting enough prospect with a solid team around you, but being part of a Luxembourg Mixed team, bolstered by three Austrians and a rider from Liechtenstein, was bordering on foolish.

Dion was proven right. During the first week Gaul was active whenever the road went uphill; clearly he had carried his great form from the Dauphiné. In the first major mountain stage, 241 kilometres from Bayonne to Pau, crossing the Col d'Aubisque, Gaul followed Bobet, Jean Malléjac, Ferdi Kübler of Switzerland and all the other yellow jersey contenders, finishing tenth on the stage. The next day, however, Gaul was suffering with a stomach upset that the Tour's doctors couldn't bring under control, and 70 kilometres into the stage he was forced to retire. His friends blamed the Luxembourg team management for letting Gaul descend the Aubisque on a chilly day in just a short-sleeve jersey, with no arm-warmers or jacket. As Gaul's friend François Mersch has pointed out, riders in great form are also very vulnerable to colds and viruses. Gaul was frustrated with his enforced exit, sensing that in the high mountains he had the ability to make his mark, but that would have to wait.

After France's Jean Robic and Switzerland's Hugo Koblet, both previous winners, crashed out of contention, Bobet's waiting game for the first two weeks of the Tour paid off. The Swiss team valiantly tried to put him under pressure for their other star rider, Ferdi Kübler, but Bobet was dogged. In 1953 he had used the stage to Briançon, crossing the Col d'Izoard, to win the race. In 1954, with the competition demoralised, he would employ the same tactic. Having crossed the summit of the Izoard alone, Bobet won in Briançon by nearly two minutes from Kübler. And if any doubt remained, three days later he won the 72-kilometre time trial at Nancy by more than two minutes.

While Gaul recuperated at home in Luxembourg, Bobet was obliged to undertake the customary circus of post-Tour de France criteriums – races in towns across France and Belgium where the crowd paid a small fee to see the star riders they'd been reading about in their newspapers. This was sport as entertainment. Those who had performed well in the Tour were given prominence and, after a local rider or two was allowed to go off the front, a big name like Bobet took the win (agreed in advance). For the paying spectators it gave them a chance to see the fabled yellow jersey. For the riders it was a lucrative, if exhausting, circuit. They received personal fees for riding, but the races were packed together in a schedule that meant driving huge distances back and forth across northern Europe, fuelled by amphetamines to keep them awake.

On 15 August, Bobet travelled to the Critérium de Bellegarde. Before the race it had already been agreed that he would cross the line in first place, resplendent in the yellow jersey he'd secured in Paris two weeks earlier. But Bobet had a more devious plan. His next major objective, the Road Race World Championship in Germany, was in two weeks. He needed to test his form and, specifically, he needed to work out where he was in comparison to Fausto Coppi, his biggest rival for the coveted rainbow jersey that only the World Champion can wear. So in Bellegarde, Bobet attacked hard early in the race. The peloton split in two, with Coppi caught in the second group. One imagines many of the riders were muttering darkly about Bobet's tactics – criteriums were a show race, they weren't supposed to be *this* fast. Coppi, either out of pride or because he too wanted to test his form, went to the front of his group and gave chase. For lap after lap neither man relented, dragging their group around the town. It was great viewing for the crowd. Finding he couldn't reduce the gap, Coppi retired from the race, telling the press that his derailleur had failed. Bobet's helpers weren't convinced and sneaked over to find the Italian's bike. When they returned to tell Bobet that Coppi's derailleur was perfectly fine, the Frenchman just smiled.

The World Championships were staged that year in Solingen, a German town famous for the manufacture of steel products – swords, knives, razors. Perhaps the connection to his homeland made Gaul feel comfortable. The racing conditions certainly suited him, too: the road race would tackle 15 laps of a 14.5-kilometre circuit, with every lap tackling the Herscheid climb to the south of the town. The climb promised to make the race one of the toughest in living memory. For two days before the race it had been raining heavily. On the morning of the race the rain did not abate. For Louison Bobet this was a critical career moment. He had won the Tour de France twice, but he had yet to win the rainbow jersey. The World Champion was permitted to wear the rainbow jersey – white with the rainbow colours in bands around the chest – in every road race until the following year's event. It was, and remains, cycling's ultimate status symbol and, until he had won it, Bobet could never emerge from the shadow of Fausto Coppi. Bobet's self-applied pressure ratcheted up even further when he realised that among the thousands of spectators around the sodden circuit were hundreds of French soldiers, stationed nearby as part of the occupying forces from the war.

If you do not win today, you will never be World Champion, he reportedly told himself at the start.[21] Seven hours later, with one lap to go, Bobet led the race. But he was not alone. The small and annoyingly tenacious Swiss rider Fritz Schär had attached himself to Bobet's back wheel and was refusing to let go. Bobet may have been riding like the champion-elect, dominating the race, but he did not want to take Schär to the finish. A two-man sprint at the end of a long race is always a risky proposition. A rider who on paper should easily win may find his legs are not of the same opinion. Behind this pair, Charly Gaul was in a small chasing group with Michele Gismondi, Fausto Coppi and Jean Forestier. It was the first time Gaul had been in such close proximity to the legendary Coppi, who, at thirty-four, was coming to the end of his career.

Bobet and Schär crossed the finish line to a bell ringing amid the cheers of the crowds packed into grandstands. They passed the feed zone, where team mechanics waited with bottles, bags of food and spare wheels. It was, of course, too late for food and drink. That part of the race was behind them. In a World Championship road race everything is designed to build to a crescendo in the last lap. If you are still there near the front, you go all out for the win or at least a medal. Then Bobet realised that he had a flat tyre. He turned to shout to his mechanic, who was now 100 metres behind him. The mechanic jumped on Bobet's spare bike and sprinted up to his stranded rider. Bobet leapt on to the new machine, but Schär, sensing the opportunity of a lifetime, had disappeared.

The crowds fell silent, hanging on every word coming over the tannoy from the speaker, but the organisers had pulled out most of the following cars, so scant information was coming back over the race radio. The two men were having their own private battle in the mist and rain of the Herscheid hills. Then word came – Bobet had caught Schär. There was a huge cheer of relief from the crowd. There could only be a few kilometres left. Cars and motorbikes began to emerge at the end of the finishing straight. There was a rider alone, his silhouette illuminated by the yellow headlights of the car behind him. Everyone knew that silhouette. It was Louison Bobet, World Champion.

While the French celebrated, Gaul's quartet was splintered across the circuit – and it was Charly who had done the damage. Apparently impervious to the rain, he had used his climbing ability to break free, taking the bronze medal, two minutes behind Bobet. Coppi, demoralised by Bobet's dominance, finished in sixth.

It was a stunning result for Gaul and, even if it was overshadowed by the drama of Bobet's victory, his bronze medal did not go unnoticed by the peloton or the press. The World Championship was one of the most important one-day races of the year, always fiercely contested and a stressful race to ride. To get on the podium required not only good legs but also a cool head.

The years 1953 and 1954 were Charly Gaul's apprenticeship in the professional ranks. For such a young rider his results were impressive, and the manner of his victories promised a great deal more to come. As the winter of 1954 set in, Gaul had shown what he was capable of. His flashes of brilliance were counterbalanced by lapses of concentration and tactical naïveté, but surely this would come with maturity. He had married a woman who loved and supported him and came from a cycling background. His sense of quiet self-assurance was impressing those around him and in terms of attracting public attention he had that most important thing – a nickname. The Angel of the Mountains finished 1954 strongly. In 1955 he was to climb to an even higher level.

Tour de France, 1961

THE CHERUB AND THE CRYBABY

On Bastille Day 1955, the peloton of the Tour de France gathered in the small town of Thonon-les-Bains, on the southern shore of Lac Léman (Lake Geneva). There was an air of trepidation among the riders as they made their final preparations for the day's stage; they were about to enter the mountains, the arena where the Tour would be won and lost. During its opening week the race had followed a familiar pattern: 130 riders took the start in Le Havre and, after pilgrimages to the cobbles of Roubaix and the Belgian Ardennes, the race turned south to Metz and Colmar, then crossed the Swiss border to Zurich. The day before, 13 July, an opportunist breakaway group finished some seventeen minutes ahead of the peloton, handing the yellow jersey to Dutchman Wim van Est. But no one was very interested in that. All eyes – those of the riders, fans, journalists and team managers – were on the Alps. Ahead of the riders lay 253 kilometres across three major climbs – the Col des Aravis, the Col du Télégraphe and the Col du Galibier – before a fast descent into the town of Briançon. This was the moment when the favourites would have to show themselves. There would be nowhere to hide.

Tucked into the middle of the peloton as it spun out of Thonon-les-Bains that July morning was Charly Gaul. At twenty-two, this was his third participation in the Tour. He was yet to prove himself on this stage, but his performances in other races, notably the Dauphiné Libéré and the 1954 Solingen World Championships, prompted the newspapers in Luxembourg and beyond to frame him as a future Tour contender.

At the Tour the difference was not just in the intensity of the racing; here every pedal stroke was watched and analysed by the press. The crowds were bigger and there were photographers everywhere. Film stars turned up in the start village wanting a photo with their heroes, and every night the stage town hosted raucous parties that went on into the small hours.

More than any other race, the Tour was where a rider could make his reputation. Even by the 1950s it was a sporting event that defined the idea of European sporting heroes. In their book on the symbolism of sport, Richard Holt and J.A. Mangan describe the Tour as an event requiring 'almost superhuman powers of endurance, . . . a kind of mythic journey through ancient provinces, littered with sacred ruins, the bones of saints, great mountain ranges, and the scenes of former battles.'[22]

Charly started the 1955 race in good form, though again hampered by a weak team. France was the dominant force. Again they lined up with a powerful national team that included defending champion Louison Bobet and five regional teams. Charly was the leader of the Luxembourg Mixed team – so called because there were only four Luxembourg riders in it. A 'ragtag collection', as one journalist called it, the team included Germans, Austrians and two Australians. Not only did it lack the unity of a shared nationality, its collective firepower was well below that of the French, Italians and Belgians. Effectively, Charly was on his own.

But Charly had a plan. And he'd let it slip, quite intentionally, the evening before. Shortly after the end of the stage into Thonon-les-Bains, the journalist Marcel Hansenne of *L'Équipe* found Gaul looking relaxed, leaning over his bike. Remarking on how fresh

Gaul looked after seven stages of intense racing, Hansenne asked if Gaul thought his Tour had gone well so far. Gaul looked at him in astonishment.

'Didn't I say I would save myself for the Alps?' he said in what Hansenne described as a 'soft, almost shy' voice. Hansenne pointed out that Gaul had lost a lot of time, perhaps too much, but Gaul shook his head. 'Everything went as planned. I arrived here with minimal effort.'

'Really, you haven't suffered at all?' replied Hansenne incredulously. In 1955 the idea of cruising through the opening week of the Tour de France was unheard of; even if it did happen, no journalists were interested in that narrative.

'Tomorrow they will see me,' said Gaul, and Hansenne wrote about how pained Gaul seemed that anyone would doubt his assertion that he had not suffered yet in the race.

At the start Gaul spoke to journalist Gaston Bénac of *France-Soir*, asking him whether the weather was usually cooler in the high mountains at this time of year. This was an odd question, for Gaul must have known the answer. He was, perhaps, trying to provoke Bénac into asking about his plans for the day. Normally, yes, came the reply. Then another journalist, Pierre Chany, asked Gaul if he was going to go on the offensive. 'Just wait another hour,' teased Charly. In fact, he had already picked out the place where he would attack, and had cut the stage profile out of the road book and taped it to his handlebars.

As the riders picked their way through the streets, the crowd looked for their hero, Louison Bobet. Resplendent in the rainbow jersey that he had won a year earlier on that wet day in Solingen, Bobet was the outright favourite to win the Tour. Today was particularly special for Bobet because in both previous years he had used a stage into Briançon to set up his overall victories.

Predictably, before the roads began to climb, four opportunists went on the attack. The race skirted Geneva and headed south towards the high mountains of the Haute Savoie, the playground of the Tour de France since its inception. The first climb, the Col des Aravis, is typically Alpine – some 19 kilometres long with a relatively steady gradient. On its higher slopes those with the energy to look up from the road are rewarded with spectacular views of Mont Blanc. The leading quartet splintered, Dutchman Jan Nolten proving to be the best climber and moving away from his companions. But Nolten was no more than bait. Behind, race radio reported an attack from the peloton by Charly Gaul.

As the first French Tour winner since fellow Breton Jean Robic in 1947, it is not surprising that Bobet was popular. He was a stylish rider, fastidious about his appearance and health. When he rode, he raced. Whichever group he was in, Bobet would sprint hard for the line. Not only was this good training, it also endeared him to the fans.

His dominance of the Tour de France, though relatively brief, came at a crucial time in the history of the event and its host nation. After the Tour's long break through the Second World War, the race set about re-establishing itself as cycling's flagship event. Like today's race director, Christian Prudhomme, post-war boss Jacques Goddet introduced innovative ideas, although without turning the race on its head. He understood that the appeal of the Tour lay in creating legends. Innovation, such as introducing the green jersey competition in 1953 and the Tour's first foreign start in 1954, helped to modernise the race, yet it was exploits like that of Bobet on the Izoard that made the Tour deeply loved.

Like the Tour, France was attempting to find its way in the post-war world. If, by the early 1950s, the physical scars in the landscape were beginning to heal, the psychological scars were still raw. Occupation, collaboration and resistance had divided the nation. Now a new political and economic reality was developing, and France had to keep pace. The loss of its colony of Indochina (today's Vietnam, Cambodia and Laos), whose war and bloodiest battles coincided with Bobet's reign at the Tour, was felt keenly by the French people. While no one could compare Tour de France victories to the loss of an empire, Bobet's redemption did at least provide a comforting distraction.

Louison Bobet may have been a champion, but he wasn't invincible. His fans saw him struggle, they experienced his pain with him and they rejoiced in his successes. He was not head and shoulders above his rivals; indeed, he was frequently defined by the press only in relation to his peers – Gino Bartali, Fausto Coppi, Hugo Koblet and Charly Gaul. In *Mythologies*, Roland Barthes described Bobet as a 'Promethean hero; he has a magnificent fighter's temperament, an acute sense of organisation, he is a calculator, he aims realistically at winning . . . In 1955, he had to face a heavy solitude. Without Koblet or Coppi, having to struggle with their ghosts, without declared rivals, powerful and solitary, everything was a threat to him, danger could appear from anywhere and everywhere.'[23]

On 14 July 1955 Charly Gaul did not yet count as a dangerous figure. By the end of the day Bobet and his team were revising that assessment. Charly's attack on the lower slopes of the Aravis was ferocious, but there was no sense of an imminent danger to Bobet's position. The peloton simply watched as the young Luxembourger danced away from them. They were probably as curious to see what he could do as the journalists.

Charly soon caught Nolten, who was able to latch on to Charly's back wheel and hang on over the top of the Aravis, where Nic Frantz shouted at Charly to slow down, not get over-excited. Charly was happy to have the Dutchman with him; they could work together on the valley road leading to the Col du Télégraphe. Once on the climb,

Nolten could no longer hold on. Charly was alone with two huge Alpine passes ahead of him. Flanked by photographers on motor-bikes, he pressed on, pedalling fluidly, apparently undaunted. At the top of the Col du Télégraphe, Charly led Nolten by five minutes, a chasing group of favourites including Bobet by thirteen minutes, and yellow jersey Wim van Est by seventeen minutes. Van Est knew by now that he would be back in his regular team jersey the next day.

After the brief respite of the descent from the Col du Télégraphe, Charly set about conquering the Col du Galibier. One of the highest roads in the Alps, at an altitude of 2,556 metres, the Col du Galibier is a giant of the Tour de France. When it was first used in the Tour de France in 1911, only three riders managed to cycle up; the rest got off and walked.

If anyone expected Charly to falter now, they were mistaken. The race was witnessing something special – the emergence of a unique talent. Charly fixed his eyes on the next bend in the road, still pedalling with *souplesse* on a tiny gear, his dark hair swept back immaculately, and the writers were already conjuring the superla-tives that would be hammered into typewriters later that evening in Briançon. In the oppressive heat, which softened the tarmac under his wheels, Gaul took on bottles from spectators, drinking some, pouring others down his neck. At the summit an observer holding a notebook shouted out 'Gaul!' to signify that he'd taken the mountain classification prize there. Charly took another drink, glanced across at the memorial to Tour de France founder Henri Desgrange and plunged into the steep descent towards Briançon.

Behind Charly the chasing group broke up, then reformed. Bobet was watchful. His team-mate, Antonin Rolland, had been riding strongly during the first stages, giving rise to whispers of a sim-mering rivalry within the French team. Swiss rider Ferdi Kübler, winner of the Tour in 1950, was also in the group. He looked to be suffering, but could never be totally discounted. If anyone had any energy left for an attack, they decided to leave it for another day. At the top of the Galibier there was 33 kilometres of descending towards Briançon. Having learnt the lesson of the Grossglockner – that you can't afford to descend slowly – Charly pushed himself to the limit on the descent of the Galibier. At the finish line, underneath the battlements of the citadel, he had a margin of nearly fourteen minutes on the chasers.

After the ceremonies, the bouquets of flowers, photographs with dignitaries and newspaper interviews, Gaul and his entourage drove down the valley to their hotel in Sainte-Catherine. There was, however, no one at reception to allocate their rooms. Hearing a radio report about the day's stage, they wandered into the bar where they found an old woman listening to an account of Gaul's victory. The old woman put a finger to her lips and said, 'Someone will come soon. Wait, gentlemen, with me and listen to the report of the finish.'

Frantz laughed and said, 'Here's the winner!'

'Allez! Allez!' said the old woman in disbelief. 'This child?'[24]

While Charly celebrated, with newspapers proclaiming that the Angel of the Mountains had finally delivered on his promise, within the French team the stage to Briançon seemed to exacerbate a sense of persecution. Louison Bobet's younger brother, Jean, was on the team that year, a loyal presence whose principal duty was shoring up his brother's fragile morale. Jean was a lesser rider than Louison, but the greater intellectual. After his racing career Jean became a writer and, for a time, head of sport at Radio Luxembourg. In his 2004 book about life on the road with Louison, *Tomorrow We Ride*, Jean recounted the atmosphere of the 1955 Tour: 'The race was wild and unbridled. Untameable … We thought we had effectively controlled the race when suddenly the situation deteriorated … The Luxembourg climber, Gaul, quickly baptised "Angel of the Mountains", took off up the Galibier and, in Briançon, made up ten minutes on Louison. The newspapers laid it on thick again. "Was Bobet as strong as they said? Were his team-mates not overstepping the mark? Was mutiny on its way?" I tried to conceal or play down the unkind words and the nasty questions put to me for transmission to my big brother, who was worried, frustrated, on edge.'[25]

In a somewhat petulant attempt to reassert his authority, big brother Bobet ordered his team to attack through the feeding station on the Monaco to Marseille stage, with the intention of 'boxing Charly Gaul's ears.' Accelerating through the feeding station ran against the peloton's unwritten code of conduct because it meant riders were unable to pick up fresh bottles and musettes of food, and it made the French team even more unpopular. Still, the tactic worked. On the exposed flat roads, in searing heat, Charly was unable to stay with Bobet's group and lost time. At the stage finish he declared himself 'weak at the knees', blaming the heat rather than his own questionable positioning in the group.

Nicolas Frantz disagreed. The two-time Tour winner was now technical director of the Luxembourg Mixed team and was attempting to manage his new star rider. Frantz had watched Charly emerge from the junior and amateur ranks and felt that Charly had the ability to win the Tour one day, but he was frustrated by his protégés tactical naïveté. Daily, the pair had heated arguments. Charly liked to sit at the back of the peloton, making him susceptible to crashes, splits and attacks. Throughout the first week Charly coasted along like this, losing time to Bobet, who was always near the front and always on the lookout for an opportunity to grab some time on his rivals, whatever the terrain. It was as if Charly had decided that the mountains were the only place he was prepared to take the race seriously. No one ever won the Tour like that, Frantz repeatedly told him.

'If you were my son, I'd spank you. I could write a book about your mistakes in bike racing,' he told Charly, who just shrugged in response.

Charly was not making any friends with his team-mates either. By 1955 the top riders had all adopted the custom of sharing their winnings with their team-mates, a practice initiated by Louison Bobet that continues today. This was less about altruism and more to do with motivation. Charly, however, saw no reason why he should share any rewards with his team.

'I know I can win the best climber's prize,' he told his team-mates. 'That's all I'm going for – at least this year. I know only too well that you can't be much use to me in the hills. You'll be too far behind. Why should I split my money with you? I'll manage my own race. You manage yours.'

Having 'boxed Charly Gaul's ears', Louison Bobet now focused on winning the Tour de France. Frustrated with the way he was being treated by the press and sensing that the French public were getting impatient with him, he began planning an attack that would secure his third victory.

By 1955 Bobet was thirty years old and used to winning. It was expected of him – by his family and friends, his team, indeed all of France. And he expected it of himself, though he was riddled with self-doubt. He enjoyed everything that came with victory, not just the money, but the fame too. No longer referred to as a crybaby, Bobet nonetheless was not popular in the peloton. Many riders thought him a self-important snob. After all, wasn't he just the son of a Breton baker? Professional cycling in the 1950s was a sport for working-class men, a way to make better money than being a baker or a butcher or a farmer. Anyone who forgot their roots risked the wrath of his peers.

Nevertheless, Bobet seemed to see himself as the hero of a grand narrative. In modern terms, he cultivated his own brand. Had he been racing in the twenty-first century, he would have had a big social media presence. Bobet understood that a bike racer's career is short and the best years even shorter. Retirement, when it comes at thirty-five, is a second career. Having a well-established brand will open doors. Bobet felt that he needed to *use* his victories to build the post-cycling life he desired.

Charly was never so calculating, either in his racing tactics or his career. He raced on instinct, and his dogged determination to ride at the back of the race on days that weren't suited to him was almost insolent. He seemed to be thumbing his nose at the conventions of racing and, consequently, at all those who followed them. Perhaps a perceived lack of respect was why Bobet disliked Charly so much. On climbs Charly could drop his rivals with apparent ease; on the flat he didn't seem to care about the race.

The 1955 Tour de France had ignited. On the fearful slopes of Mont Ventoux, Bobet was about to cement his place in history and Charly would be humbled, while others would come close to death.

THE BALD GIANT

'Wise is he who does not return there. But mad is he who does!' These were the words of an old man to Provençal poet, Frédéric Mistral, on discovering that Mistral and two friends had just climbed Mont Ventoux for no reason other than to appreciate the view from the top. Nine years after his ascent, in 1866, Mistral – himself named after the famous north-westerly wind that blows across the mountain and is said to drive people mad – published an epic poem about Ventoux:

> *From the North, the Ventoux is frightening:*
> *One would say like a wall*
> *It arises, grandly chiselled from foot to peak;*
> *A black crown of trees,*
> *A forest of larch, a hard line*
> *Serves as the entrance*
> *And the portal of the formidable rampart.*

Mistral valued the Mediterranean way of life over the cold north, hence his emphasis on Ventoux as a rampart, intimidating when approached from the north. Provençal folklore about the mountain says that one of the caves on the north face, the Baume de la Mene, is an entrance to hell. The mountain is strange, frightening, unique.

Mont Ventoux rises to 1912 metres. Geologically it is part of the Alps, yet it sits alone, dominating the landscape. The white scree at the top, often described as lunar, is limestone. Over the centuries the mountain was stripped of its forests for charcoal production, then timber for shipbuilding. Since the nineteenth century, conservation efforts have had some success in replanting trees. The flora and fauna on the mountain have long attracted collectors and medicine-makers.

It is also the windiest place on earth. In February 1967 a wind-speed of 320 kilometres per hour was recorded on the summit. The name Ventoux is often thought to originate from the French word for windy, *venteux*, but the correct etymology is the word *vinturi*, simply meaning mountain.[26]

The Tour de France has a special relationship with the landscape it passes through, but only Ventoux inspires fear, awe and joy on such an instinctual level. In 1955 the climb was a relative newcomer to the Tour, having only been included in the route twice before, and on both occasions the organisers had used the slightly easier approach from Malaucène. Now they switched to the Bédoin route.

The ascent is open, straightforward and brutal, 21 kilometres long, with an average gradient of 7.5%. On paper this sounds manageable, but within it is the long section from Saint-Estève to Chalet Reynard, through the forest, with an average gradient of 9% and some ramps up to 12%. Pass this test and you emerge into the infamous blasted cauldron of the upper slopes. The air is dry and scarce. Crosswinds can have you leaning your bike just to stay on two wheels, while the heat reflects off the merciless rocks. Here a cyclist should not fear the gradient, the heat or the wind. He should fear the combination of all three. By this point in a race, tactics are minimal. By the last few kilometres, towards the aptly named Col de Tempêtes, there is only road, white rock, wind and pain.

Not only is the Bédoin ascent harder, but on 18 July 1955 a heatwave was hanging over Provence. Everyone was nervous. The French team were particularly worried about Gaul. Would he attack them on Mont Ventoux? On such a slope a pure climber in good form could gain significant chunks of time. From the summit of Ventoux the race would plunge down a fast descent to finish in Avignon; barring accidents, the rider who led over the top would go on to win. Frenchman Antonin Rolland, one of Bobet's lieutenants, was in the yellow jersey. Behind him Bobet, the Italian Pasquale Fornara and Gaul were grouped closely together, a little more than eleven minutes back.

Bobet's French team went into the stage feeling that they were under attack by the newspapers. Questions were being asked about their leader's strength and about the loyalty of his lieutenants. The expectation that they would deliver a yellow jersey rankled. On the stage to Marseille, despite having put time into Gaul with the audacious feeding station attack, Bobet had been whistled at. The French public had grown used to his dominance. Signs of weakness were not acceptable.

Meanwhile, for the wider European audience, the arrival of Charly Gaul gave the race an exciting new dynamic. This good-looking young climber was clearly shaped from a different mould. His presence was both disruptive and unpredictable. The French dominance was becoming boring. Could the newly christened Angel of the Mountains be the one to unseat them?

That morning the atmosphere on the start line was tense. Everyone knew this was going to be an important day, perhaps *the* decisive day of the Tour. Though the Tour had not previously tackled the Ventoux from Bédoin, many of the riders knew the climb, either from training or rumour. For the leaders there would be nowhere to hide. For the rest it was simply a matter of survival.

The moment the flag dropped, the French team attacked. On a long, exposed stretch of main road the peloton strung out, those at the back breathlessly cursing their tormentors. Eventually the elastic snapped and a group of twenty went clear, including all the favourites and most of the French team. The group rode hard through Carpentras. Through the morning haze the bulk of Ventoux loomed. The ageing Swiss champion, Ferdi Kübler, attacked on the false flat towards Bédoin, taking French road captain Raphaël Géminiani with him. Jean Bobet, dragging the group along at what he thought was a high pace, was surprised that the pair could jump clear, but Kübler was not a serious contender for the maillot jaune. Jean was more concerned with his brother's legs. Louison rode up to Jean and asked him to drive the pace of the group all the way to the foot of the mountain. After that it would be every man for himself.

Approaching Bédoin, Louison again came up to his brother and whispered to him that his legs were not feeling good. Jean was relieved. He knew Louison well enough to know that meant his brother would have a good day. The small town was packed with spectators spilling out of bars and *en fête* – in the mood for partying. Jean Bobet and his French team-mates were close to implosion, and the start of the climb – marked by a steep, left-swinging bend – was only a kilometre away.

In front of them Kübler and Géminiani were talking. The Frenchman said, 'Be careful, Ventoux is a mountain not like any other.' Kübler replied, 'Yes, and Ferdi is a champion not like any other.'

On the early slopes of Ventoux, through the forest scented with pine, cicadas buzzing, fans spraying water on their heroes, Kübler tried to escape Géminiani, but the Frenchman would not give up. Behind, the main group of favourites was being whittled down. Bobet was prominent near the front, Gaul in close attendance but beginning to suffer.

Emerging into the searing heat at Chalet Reynard, Géminiani pushed on. The road there bends past a café where spectators and leisure cyclists can get a welcome drink, then it ramps up once more, now into the desolate white scree. There is no protection from the elements. For the riders of the 1955 Tour there were only two ways out. Kübler tried, but failed, to respond to his companion's pace. Close to the summit he slowed to walking pace, eyes in a trance. As his team manager jumped out of a following car to give him a push, Kübler yelled abuse at the crowd staring at him. He frothed at the mouth. Then he fell from his bike and lay on the tarmac, his legs still pedalling.

His manager cast around desperately for the race doctor, Dumas, but he was nowhere to be seen. As the race convoy crawled past, throwing out dust and exhaust fumes, and the intense heat saturated the lunar surface around them, Kübler summoned his senses and got to his feet. He wasn't going to let Ventoux defeat him. He clambered back on to his bike and – now at the back of the race – managed to pedal the last torturous section of the climb, then descended towards the finish in Avignon. During the final flat kilometres coming into town he stopped at a bar, drank whatever they gave him, then set off again – in the wrong direction. The bar's drinkers had to run up the road yelling at him to turn around. 'On the finish line they had to scoop him off the road with a teaspoon,' Géminiani later said.[27]

That evening, the chastened Swiss told the press, 'Ferdi killed himself on the Ventoux.' He then announced his retirement from his Tour de France career, effective immediately. One wonders what kind of madness went through his mind during that infernal experience.

Kübler's helpers had been unable to find Dr Dumas because he was already on his way to hospital in an ambulance with another rider. Ten kilometres from the summit the talented Breton rider, Jean Malléjac, also succumbed to the heat and exhaustion. Grey-faced, drenched in cold sweat and barely conscious, Malléjac wobbled across the road then collapsed beside it, one foot still strapped into the pedal. A rival team's manager moved him off the road, laid him on a blanket and flagged down the doctor. For fifteen terrifying minutes the doctor gave him mouth-to-mouth resuscitation, Malléjac staring skywards, empty-eyed, silent spectators encircling him. Pierre Chany described him as, 'completely unconscious, his face the colour of a corpse'. A freezing sweat ran on his forehead. Dumas forced open Malléjac's jaw to get a drink into him, then injected him with solucamphor, a nerve stimulant and painkiller. Once he had also been given oxygen, Malléjac regained consciousness. On the journey to hospital in Avignon the rider grew furious at being taken out of the race. He shouted at Dumas, demanding his bike so that he could continue the Tour. Dumas was forced to strap him down and the two men shouted violently at each other all the way. Malléjac claimed that he had been drugged and taken out of the race against his will.

After the drama had subsided and the riders lay on their hotel beds, the underlying reason for Kübler and Malléjac's problems became clear. Bottles of the same pills were found in both their bedrooms. Both denied wrongdoing and a soigneur was blamed, but rumours of widespread doping practices began to envelope the Tour. These incidents were a chilling foreshadowing of cycling's darkest Ventoux moment – the death of Tom Simpson in July 1967.

For Charly Gaul that ascent of Mont Ventoux underlined what he already knew, but others had not yet fully appreciated – that he did not ride well in extreme heat. On the upper slopes the leading group splintered. It was a game of survival. Bobet rode conservatively until he saw weakness in the others, then ratcheted up the pressure.

Gaul tried to follow, but his head was throbbing. His knees buckled, forcing him to come to a stop at the side of the road. He was moaning, rambling, on the verge of fainting. In an effort to stay hydrated, Gaul and his rivals had been accepting drinks from the crowd, and pouring iced water, red wine, fizzy soda and Pernod into

their empty stomachs had not helped their bodies manage the combination of intense heat and intense effort. Sensing that what Gaul
really needed was some solid carbohydrates, a spectator produced a
baguette, tore off a chunk and gave it to the rider to chew on. Brought
to his senses by this simple act, Gaul remounted and set off. Victory
was long gone, but he could at least limit his losses.

On the upper slopes of the climb Bobet was alone, looking for
his team-mate Géminiani, though when he was caught 'Big Gem'
could offer his leader no assistance. 'I'm cooked,' was all the conversation Gem could muster. Bobet pressed on. Crossing the summit
of Ventoux alone, in the rainbow jersey of World Champion, may
have looked like a symbolically powerful image, but Bobet only
had a minute on Belgian climber, Jean Brankaert. A small group
had formed around Géminiani a further three minutes back. Gaul,
suffering, was five and a half minutes behind Bobet.

There were still 60 kilometres of descent and flat roads to Avignon.
Bobet's team manager told him to go for it and, if the chasers got to
within forty-five seconds, he would tell Bobet to sit up and wait. So
Bobet hammered down the hot roads off the Ventoux, determined
to claim the yellow jersey that everyone expected him to be wearing.
A puncture on the outskirts of Avignon reduced his lead and by the
finish the had only forty-nine seconds on the chasing group.

That evening Antonin Rolland was still in the yellow jersey, with
his team leader Bobet now four minutes behind in second place.
Bobet had won the stage and taken back time on his rivals, but at
what cost? Bobet lay on his bed, still wearing his racing clothes,
exhausted, despairing, furious with himself and the agony he'd just
put himself through. His brother, Jean, tried to console him, telling
him about Malléjac and Kübler, about the destruction of so many of
Louison's rivals. It was very late in the evening by the time Louison
began to come round, and something in him changed that day. He
felt no glory in his achievement, only sacrifice. When asked to talk

about his famous escape on Ventoux he would only talk about the pain, never the joy of victory.[28]

For Gaul, that ascent of Mont Ventoux was physical purgatory – at the finish, when he climbed off his bike, he was violently sick and he vomited again in his hotel room that evening – but there is no evidence it had anything like the psychological effect on him that it did on Bobet. Perhaps this was the imperviousness of youth. Instead, Gaul was plagued by rumours of doping. Malléjac was quick to blame his body's failure on doping products given to him without his consent by his team's soigneur and there were mutterings about Gaul's near-collapse too. At the time, doping was not against the rules and a variety of dangerously amateurish practices were going on. The very public dramas of Mont Ventoux had suddenly brought doping into the spotlight and such rumours were to float around Gaul throughout his career.

After Ventoux the race settled down for a few days, although Gaul's physical condition was still delicate and he could only consume cold tea and plain biscuits. The race doctor, Dumas, checked on him and gave him medication for his stomach. Gaul suspected that Dumas was also checking for signs of doping. On the subsequent hot, flat days across the south of France the sprinters and opportunist breakaways had their chance. Rolland held on to the yellow jersey in the knowledge that he was just its temporary owner. In the Pyrénées everyone expected Bobet to claim it. The Frenchman, however, was not so confident. An old and painful injury, inflammation of the perineum, had recurred. 'I shared a room with him,' Géminiani told British writer, Isabel Best, when she interviewed him in 2020, 'He had a boil the size of a golf ball. I couldn't have ridden with that.'[29] Bobet was riding through agony and his team were doing their best to hide it from the rest of the peloton.

On the rest day at Ax-les-Thermes, Gaul felt his strength and appetite return, and he planned a revenge that would redress the shame of the Ventoux stage. Two days after the rest day, the race entered the Pyrénées with a 249-kilometre stage from Toulouse to Saint-Gaudens that included the Col d'Aspin and Col de Peyresourde. Gaul was fourteen minutes behind Rolland in the general classification; in today's closely fought racing an insurmountable gap, but in the 1955 Tour fourteen minutes meant Bobet had to be wary of Gaul. If he had not listed the Luxembourger among his rivals three weeks earlier, he did now. Moreover, the peloton had ridden itself clear of the Provençal heatwave, and the weather in the Pyrénées was cool and rainy, and much more to Gaul's liking. Bobet, indeed the whole race entourage, expected the Luxembourger to attack on the Col d'Aspin and he did not disappoint.

On the lower slopes, Gaul pulled in two early breakaways and pushed relentlessly onwards. Bobet let him go, nervous of over-extending himself by trying to follow. If he spent too much energy chasing down Gaul, he would leave himself vulnerable to attacks by others later in the stage. So Gaul reached the summit of the Col d'Aspin alone, over three minutes clear of a group containing Bobet and the other favourites.

On the Col de Peyresourde, Gaul was still in the lead, but now Bobet was chasing alone. His escape on Mont Ventoux had given him a famous victory, but precious little time in the fight for the yellow jersey. This stage was to be the opposite. Ever-calculating, the Frenchman had seen his opportunity: Gaul could help him ride into yellow. Bobet caught Gaul on the descent from the Col de Peyresourde and the pair formed a temporary alliance on the road towards Saint-Gaudens. Half a dozen motorbikes buzzed around them, pillion press photographers contorting themselves to get the perfect shot. This was one of the key moments in the race, arguably in all of Bobet's distinguished career. The great champion in his rainbow jersey, powerful, determined, riding alongside the young pretender who had lit up the Tour, though remained something of a mystery. A photographer captured Bobet and Gaul sharing a bottle. There was, for the moment at least, respect between the two men.

On the approach to Saint-Gaudens Bobet punctured and had to wait for a wheel change. Gaul pressed on to take a solo victory. Bobet came in second, just over a minute back, but more importantly he had taken big chunks of time over his other rivals. Team-mate Rolland, the maillot jaune, finished nine minutes down. While no one ever wants to lose the yellow jersey, Rolland was probably relieved that his leader took it off his shoulders. Such was the support for Bobet that the French public might have started booing Rolland had he taken it much further.

The next day, from Saint-Gaudens to Pau, was the final stage in the mountains and the last opportunity for anyone to challenge Bobet. The race crossed the Tourmalet and Aubisque, and the favourites watched each other, with the French team strangling the race. Gaul either couldn't attack or chose not to. He finished third on the stage in a small group with Bobet, Brankaert and Géminiani.

After two flat stages through Bordeaux and Poitiers, the final test was a 68-kilometre time trial to Tours. Bobet was in agony throughout, standing up on the pedals for prolonged periods to relieve his saddle sores, but incredibly he was able to still finish third on the stage, losing just over two minutes to the winner Brankaert. Gaul lost nearly six minutes to the Belgian, but maintained his third place overall.

For Gaul the 1955 Tour was a breakthrough moment. Third place in the general classification, the best climber's award and two stages was far beyond his expectations coming into the race. He returned to Luxembourg transformed from a promising young rider to a genuine Tour de France contender. A television documentary captured him at home with his family, smiling awkwardly for the camera, eating on the terrace and coming out on to the road to greet neighbourhood children on their bicycles.

As well as building his self-confidence, finishing the Tour made Gaul a stronger rider physically. He rode well for the remainder of the 1955 season, finishing third in his home Tour de Luxembourg and sixth in the Tour de Romandie. Bobet, by comparison, finished the Tour de France exhausted. He returned to Brittany and underwent surgery on his perineum, a delicate procedure that required a great deal of rest afterwards. Later he said that the 1955 Tour had damaged him permanently. Physically and mentally he had gone deep into his reserves of strength – he would never again be quite the same rider.

If Bobet restored French pride, by 1955 the wider cycling world was beginning to grow weary of his dominance. Here was a rider with panache and courage, yet there was something calculating and cerebral about his approach. Cycling has always been intensely tactical, but fans have rarely responded to riders who seem intellectual. Their passion has been inspired by riders who ride on instinct; those who attack on impulse and do not worry about the consequences.

There were two narratives of the 1955 Tour. Firstly, there was the intrigue within the French team. Was Bobet capable of controlling his ambitious team-mates? Was treason being plotted? Secondly, there was the coming of age of Charly Gaul, this singular prodigy from the tiny fairytale kingdom of Luxembourg. Here was a young man, good-looking and innocent, taking on the grizzled might of the traditional cycling nations. That he had no team support added to the story. Bobet, after the Tour had finished, half-joked that he was glad Gaul had not been born in Italy because then he'd really be worried.

And then there was the style of his riding. Gaul was erratic, unpredictable. On Ventoux, when everyone expected him to rip the French team apart, he sagged. On the flat stages he was caught out. Yet when he was inspired to attack, he did so with such a combination of force and style that the other riders were stunned.

Barthes portrayed the Tour de France as an epic contest, with the hero tested on such hellish sites as Ventoux. To take on these super-human challenges, the racers must channel spirit energies:

> The strength a racer possesses ... may assume two aspects: *form*, a state more than an impulse, a privileged equilibrium between quality of muscles, acuity of intelligence and force of character; and *leap*, a veritable electric influx which erratically possesses certain racers beloved of the gods and causes them to accomplish supernatural feats ... Charly Gaul, glamorous beneficiary of grace, is precisely a *leap* specialist; he receives his electricity from an intermittent commerce with the gods; sometimes the gods inhabit him and he works wonders; some-times the gods abandon him, his *leap* is exhausted. Charly can do nothing more of any use.[30]

Louison Bobet had no leap. His racing was based on form. Bobet – according to Barthes – used human qualities to triumph: will, intelligence, hard work. Bobet's celebrated solo ride over Ventoux demonstrated these qualities; he ground the victory out through sheer force of will. Gaul, by contrast, was complicit with the gods. When the spark came, he took off, pedalling fluidly, unruffled, eyes gazing up to the mountaintops. Gaul was an archangel.

Jean Bobet saw it:

> I have the Col du Tamie not far from Clusaz in the Alps ... in very clear memory. It was July 1955 and the climb to this pass looked really harmless. We were told that rider number 61 got away and had a lead of more than two minutes. After a short conversation we knew that the 61 was Charly Gaul and we wanted him to exhaust himself in front. That would teach him manners.

'The only annoying thing was that 60 kilometres further and 2,000 metres higher the number 61 had a fifteen-minute lead and kept fourteen minutes to the finish in Briançon. With a bang – but what a bang! – Charly had double fame. For his opponents he became a dangerous man, and that is an enviable reputation. For the big audience he became the 'Angel of the Mountains' and so the legend began . . . Since that July day in 1955, and I mean this sincerely, never again will a rider be so quick and so light in the mountains. And if you ask me to describe Charly Gaul in one word, then I still answer: 'Unreal.'[31]

Thonon-les-Bains to Briançon, Tour de France, 1955

Stage 6

ESCAPISM

The leap. The term may be obscure – Barthes's analysis of cycling has not made it into the popular lexicon – but the idea is familiar, even to casual sports fans. It is a moment of such brilliance that the athlete is transformed in our eyes. They become more than a mortal being. And it applies to any sport. It is Diego Maradona dribbling past half a dozen players, it is Roger Federer producing an impossible backhand, it is an Ayrton Senna overtaking manoeuvre that seems to defy the laws of physics. To the spectator the feat is conceivable, but only possible for this rare individual, and often the athlete himself is at a loss to explain it. It is a critical reason that we watch sport. Most of the time we know we will not see a leap, yet we always hope for it.

Due to technical challenges, live television coverage of the Tour de France did not reach households until the early 1960s. In the 1950s coverage was limited to short highlights films, recorded on 16mm and shown on a news programme the next day with a dry voiceover from the newsreader. By then, of course, the public had already bought and read the newspapers that reported the race in much more detail. In France the principal newspaper of cycle racing was *L'Auto*, (which became *L'Équipe* after the Second World War). In Italy it was *La Gazzetta dello Sport*, whose famously pink pages still stand out on news-stands across the country today.

The Tour de France and the Giro d'Italia were originally conceived to promote these two newspapers; their cultural identity was deeply connected to them. Writers for these newspapers looked for legends to build. They described in intimate detail the heroes of the road and the landscape – sometimes inhospitable, sometimes alluring – that these heroes were passing through on their three-week odyssey. The reporting of results was less important than building pictures in the collective imagination of the readership. This heightened the intensity of seeing the race in person. The peloton might sweep past in a few moments, but the anticipation and the electric connection to these embattled young men, forged in the newspaper pages, was essential.

When live television came along, cycling fans changed their habits. Newspaper reports remained popular, but now fans could judge for themselves how epic the race really was. The television commentator became responsible for heightening the tension, for reacting in astonished tones to an attack. In cycling the leap can be taken quite literally. A racer shelters in a group, chooses his moment, then attacks with as much venom as he can muster. It is a move designed to stun his rivals, and to quickly create a physical gap between attacker and group. Once a gap is established the attacker sets about widening it. This can only be achieved by a more steady, sustained effort.

Road racing can be a dull sport to watch live on television. The peloton rolls along, perhaps chasing an early and inconsequential breakaway of riders who are only trying to get their sponsors' logos on television – the sporting version of an advert break. The landscape is a salve for the bored television viewer, so too is the constant colourful swarm of the cyclists, but as a sporting experience it demands a fair amount of patience. Cycling fans invest their time because they know that there is a mountain looming and – if the gods inspire – one of their heroes might attack. For the riders, too, there is patience. Four or five hours of somnolent riding may pass before the right moment presents itself. Or it may not present itself at all. Legs turn out to be deader than expected. Tactical nuances stymie ambition. The wind is blowing in the wrong direction.

So what is a climber? Physiologically, the main difference between climbers and other riders is their strength-to-weight ratio. A climber's foe is gravity. If he can deliver the same amount of power into the pedals as his rival, but is five kilograms lighter, he will win the race. At a racing weight of 65 kilograms, Gaul fitted this mould. All professional cyclists are skinny compared with the general population, but climbers look even more emaciated than their peers. With such a lack of body fat, the immune system can be delicate, making the rider prone to picking up illnesses. This is why Gaul's love of riding in the cold and rain is even more noteworthy – most riders of his build feared such conditions. Indeed physically, Gaul seems to have been remarkably resilient, rarely picking up more than a cold during his career. After the Monte Bondone stage of the Giro, during which he wore hardly any protective clothing, many other riders would have succumbed to illness the following day.

The pure climber excels on the steepest climbs. Modern riders such as Greg LeMond, Miguel Indurain and Bradley Wiggins have been able to apply their power to the steadier climbs, grinding out a pace that keeps them in contention. Men like Gaul, or the Spanish rider Federico Bahamontes, however, relish the sort of climb that looks like a wall of tarmac. Pedalling a small gear, frequently jumping out of the saddle, they can attack the climb, rather than be beaten up by it.

A further, oft-quoted feature of a climber is the ability to vary pace. Non-climbers drag themselves up mountains by settling into a rhythm they know they can sustain. Climbers, when they are feeling good, can speed up, slow down, ride steady and repeat. While the non-climber plods along at the same unvarying pace, the climbers buzz around him, sometimes accelerating, sometimes dropping back. This is both tactical and physical. The climber wants to break free and uses his or her anaerobic capacity to make a sharp attack, then settles back into the same pace (or ideally slightly higher) as the group he's just left. If the attack fails, he is able to recover and try again.

The Italian Marco Pantani was famous for his searing attacks. Television audiences waited for his leap. If Charly Gaul was a throwback to a pre-modern time when races were won with feats of bravery and endurance, Marco Pantani was a throwback to Charly Gaul's time. He seemed to ride on instinct, with little support from a team, and his attacks in the high mountains won him legions of passionate fans. Pantani's career peaked in 1998 when he won the Giro/Tour double, a feat only achieved by seven riders. To this day he holds the record for the fastest ascent of Mont Ventoux, forty-six minutes, though comparing times across the years is imprecise, given the differences in weather, equipment and pharmaceutical influence.

Gaul, though he is celebrated as one of the sport's best climbers, did not quite conform to the image of a climber inflicting a horribly erratic pace on his rivals. He liked steep climbs and he was capable of devastating accelerations, but he did not like to vary his pace. His method was more cold-blooded. At the start of a climb he would shift down into a low gear, using a rear sprocket with twenty-seven teeth, and set about trying to break those around him. Accelerating gradually, Gaul's relentless pace deceived others into trying to stay with him. When he sensed their weakness, he accelerated again and left them behind. Raphaël Géminiani said, 'He was a murderous climber, always sustaining the same rhythm, a little machine with a lower gear than the rest of us, turning his legs at a speed that would break your heart; going tick tock, tick tock, tick tock.'[32]

Dr René Bürger, Gaul's personal physician and, along with Marcel Ernzer and Willy Kemp, part of Gaul's inner circle, told journalists that Gaul had a naturally low resting pulse and a naturally strong heart and lungs that processed oxygen efficiently. Progressively harder training over many years brought that system to a level of performance that could deliver devastating results in the biggest races. Of course, sports science was in its infancy in the 1950s and even if Dr Bürger was correct – and there's no reason to suggest otherwise – his analysis does not tell us much we couldn't already guess. Most professional cyclists have low resting pulse rates and very strong cardiovascular systems.

We know where climbers excel and how, but perhaps the more interesting question is why? And, relatedly, why do we fans love them so much? What is going on in the riders' minds and in ours?

Bike racing on the flat is fast and frenetic. The peloton may look serene from the outside, but it is anything but. Even on quiet days there are crashes, mechanicals, jostling for position and the kind of banter, eating and urination that we might expect from 150 young men engaged in physical competition. The group hurtles through towns and villages at 40 kilometres per hour, tossing bidons into front gardens, hopping on and off the pavement, ducking under spectators clapping hands. This is sport as travelling circus. A flat stage usually ends with a sprint; a shot of adrenaline in which a dozen or more men hurl themselves towards the line. These are the gladiators of the peloton, battle-scarred, rough, afraid of no one. The television camera looks down on the battlefield of the last 200 metres. Who will emerge from this melee?

A mountain climb is very different. The landscape is prehistoric, awe-inspiring, sublime in the Romantic sense of the word. Remote too; buildings are scarce. The road that snakes upwards is a reminder of man's ingenuity and fragility. The only sounds are mountain streams, sheep or goats, the wind. There is a sense of exploration and jeopardy, even on climbs that have been used many times before. Mountain weather is notoriously unpredictable. Storms can close in quickly. A warm sunny day in the valley bears no relation to the conditions 2,000 metres higher.

Most of the peloton drops back, resigned to dragging themselves up the climb at their own pace, a long way from the front. They know they will not see their climber team-mates again until the hotel that evening. The biggest challenge for the heavyset sprinters is to avoid elimination by finishing inside the time limit. In itself, this can mean a heroic effort. Meanwhile the television motorbikes are crawling along in front of the leading group, cameras trained on the group of skinny men who have endured a week of flat stages in order just to get here, to their terrain.

There is no hiding on a mountain. A poker face may mask pain for a time, but the legs always betray. Every rider is pitched against the hill. The winner is the one who beats it fastest. Compared with the flat stages the action unfolds in slow motion. It can be agonising to watch. There is time to think, time to witness someone's whole race, their whole season, falling apart, or coming together. Everything is exposed.

True climbers want to be alone. They want to be ahead of their rivals, with the freedom to take on the mountain, tiny David versus unmoving Goliath, the higher and more solitary the better. Many of the best images of Charly Gaul are those of him riding through the snow on a high Alpine pass, no other riders in sight, no crowds either, just a couple of motorbikes and his team car for company. When Charly, later in life, reflected on his career, these were surely the moments he treasured the most. For the climber to escape from earthly troubles, and from other men, is the goal. A victory is just a happy by-product.

We want to see a rider effortlessly conquering a mountain. If the effort is written on his face, we accept him as a martyr. He puts himself through purgatory so we can, vicariously, feel that freedom. Climbers are introverts, climbers are strange. It is a narrative that fits neatly into the mythology of the Tour de France; among this band of heroic figures, leaders, warriors and foot soldiers, here is a small group of men blessed by grace. Their gaze is set higher than those around them, for they only want to escape into the clouds, to free themselves of earthly troubles. Gaul is an angel. Bahamontes is an eagle. Writers like Antoine Blondin have embroidered this myth because they understand that cycling fans desire to witness that grace, that leap.

The mythology of ascension may have been lost behind the curtain of thousands of years of myths and religion, but it remains intrinsically built into our way of looking at the world. Charly Gaul would undoubtedly have laughed at the idea that he was, or represented, a shaman. Those who wrote about the Tour de France in the 1950s –Pierre Chany, Antoine Blondin, Pierre About – almost certainly understood the connection between cycling's climbers and Palaeolithic mythology, and in their descriptions of Gaul's trance-like state when he climbed, they played on the theme without directly referencing it. Comparing a Tour de France rider to a Palaeolithic shaman was probably a bit much, even for *L'Équipe*.

There is a further curious connection between Charly Gaul and the idea of the shamans, who sought to commune with and understand animals because they held the secrets of life; hunting animals because that was essential, but also respecting them. Brief though it was, Gaul's experience in the abattoir must have left a deep impression on him. He frequently brought it up in later interviews, sometimes hidden behind that wry sense of humour. Hunting was also a theme of his life. Throughout the off-season, and after retirement from cycling, he enjoyed hunting and fishing trips in the Ardennes forests. And when he retired from the world and disappeared into the forest, his constant companion was a dog called Pocki. In a story that has been retold so many times over the years it has probably lost its original shape, Gaul told a journalist that he enjoyed feeding the deer and birds that came to visit him at his hut. He needed no other company.

Stage 7

TO ITALY AND TO COFFEE

Italy emerged from the Second World War a fractured and humbled nation. Industry had been nearly destroyed, unemployment was high and the Italian lire was close to collapse. Recovery was not helped by political tensions, as the various factions that had made the war so bitter vied for peacetime power. Yet although Italian society was fraught with these structural challenges, the rituals of everyday life survived. And perhaps it seemed more important than ever to hold on to the little things. Like a morning espresso. Since the sixteenth century, when the first Italian coffee was brewed in Venice, the country has been crazy about the black stuff. Coffee, and the lore surrounding it, has been integral to Italian culture.

In 1945 Carlo Ernesto Valente opened a coffee machine factory in Milan, calling his new company *Fabbrica Apparecchiature Electro Meccaniche e Affini* (the Electro-Mechanical and Associated Equipment Factory), and because the signwriter charged by the letter, the name was shortened to its initials or Faema. The company began life producing heaters and accessories for train carriages, but Valente soon saw an opportunity in coffee. While practically every Italian partook of a daily espresso or three, there was little industrial development in the way the coffee was made.

As the post-war economy found its feet and richer countries

talked of conquering space, Faema designed and built a series of machines inspired by the names of the planets. There was the Saturno, a large machine for busy cafés; Marte, a futuristic machine with hydro-compressed infusion; and Venere, a compact model for smaller cafés and sports clubs. Underpinning the range was a business strategy of establishing regional offices around the country. Faema machines became easily accessible for café owners across Italy and the brand shone as a market leader. Valente's vision was clear and progressive. Every factory and office in his expanding empire understood that the company had only one rule: continuous modernisation. Any technical development, he said, must improve the experience of using a Faema machine and, most importantly, the resulting cup.

Shrewdly, Valente invested in marketing, focusing on Italy and Latin America, and bike racing was a central part of his strategy. In 1955 he created the Faema-Guerra cycling team, joining forces with Learco Guerra, winner of the 1934 Giro d'Italia. Known during his career as the 'Human Locomotive', Guerra was one of Italy's most successful riders during the mid-1930s. His victories were used as propaganda by Mussolini's fascist regime. On retirement in 1944 he moved into team management. The deal with Faema gave him the budget to recruit a serious squad. After a modest opening season in 1955, Guerra went on a shopping spree.

Charly Gaul's success in the 1955 Tour de France meant that he was in demand for the lucrative post-Tour criteriums. Given the choice of preparing for the Road Race World Championship in Italy at the end of August – a race of almost 300 kilometres – or driving thousands of kilometres to ride exhibition races across northern Europe, Gaul chose the latter. From afar, this might seem a mercenary decision. Later in his career some commentators accused Gaul of being obsessed with money, yet riding the criteriums was very much an integral part of the business model of professional cycling at the time. If you did well at the Tour, you were expected to show up, smile and race (or at least pretend to race). No one begrudged the riders an opportunity to earn; it was part of the reward for enduring the Tour de France. Furthermore, despite his bronze medal in Solingen, Gaul knew that the possibility of winning the rainbow jersey was slim, no matter how hilly the course. The Road Race World Championship always followed the same format – many laps of a circuit of 15–20 kilometres, usually with a hill in the middle. Gaul liked hills, but he preferred mountains and the World Championship never finished at the top of the hill. His climbing ability was therefore only moderately helpful and he didn't have many other tools to employ.

Another result of Gaul's new-found fame was that his salary expectations increased significantly. Terrot's sports director, Pierre Dion, was unable to persuade the sponsor's board of directors to increase his budget to keep Gaul and reluctantly he had to release him from his contract.

'What we have sown, now others will reap,' Dion said to Alphonse Risch,[33] the secretary of UC Dippach, at a farewell dinner in Dijon. Dion's father, also involved in managing the team, was so upset at losing their protégé that he couldn't say goodbye personally to Gaul and instead passed a message via his son.

That autumn, as Gaul took a short break before starting his cyclo-cross season, there were two serious offers on the table, the Cilo-Saint-Raphaël team and Faema-Guerra. Risch, acting as a mediator in the negotiations, advised Gaul to sign with the Italian team. The Swiss Cilo-Saint-Raphaël outfit was already home to Hugo Koblet and Italian star Pasquale Fornara, and Risch suspected that Gaul would have been expected to work for these two older riders. He knew that Gaul was never going to enjoy being a domestique. At Faema-Guerra his protégé would enjoy much more freedom to lead the team and pursue victories. The canny Guerra knew that he had

to make Gaul feel at home and signed two more Luxembourgers –
Willy Kemp and Marcel Ernzer – to support his new star.

At the end of 1955, Charly received the award for Best Athlete of
the Year from Luxembourg's sports minister, Victor Bodson, and
although he may have found the prize-giving ceremony stressful,
it must have been a proud moment for Charly, Georgette and their
families.

The 1956 World Cyclo-cross Championships took place in
Mühlenbach, just a few kilometres north of Pfaffenthal, where Gaul
had been born. Gaul was highly motivated to perform in front of
his home crowd, but his preparation for the coming road season
compromised his cyclo-cross speed and he was up against specialists
in the discipline, whose entire year was focused on this one day. The
winner was Frenchman André Dufraisse, taking his third world title
in a row. Gaul finished a creditable fifth.

Three weeks later he headed to Italy for the classic single-day race,
Milan-San Remo. While Gaul was never likely to trouble the front
of the race on a course that better suited rouleurs and sprinters, it
was important for him to get used to racing in Italy and to show off
his new red Faema jersey, plus 300 kilometres at race pace was good
for the legs. After Milan–San Remo he rode a series of races in Italy,
including Rome–Naples–Rome, a short-stage race, which, despite its
southerly location, was run off in heavy rain. Gaul was often at the
front of the race, so much so that his new team manager Guerra had
to tell him off for tactical naïveté. It was clear, though, that his form
was coming good – he finished third in the final classification. The
Italian fans, the passionate tifosi, welcomed their adopted son. The
feeling was mutual; for Charly that spring was the beginning of a
lifelong love of all things Italian.

Charly and Federico Bahamontes climb the Stelvio,
Giro d'Italia, 1956

Stage 8

SNOW ANGEL

Friday 8 June 1956: Charly is alone in the lead of the Giro d'Italia. He's been on his bike for eight hours, during which time it has not stopped raining. Every muscle in his body is screaming in protest. Crystals of ice cling to his sodden gloves and he can no longer feel his feet. The road rears up for the last meaningful climb of the race. He has no idea how far ahead of the others he is, but he senses it is a big gap. In the valley, Guerra, his team manager, came alongside to tell him that riders were getting off their bikes and climbing into the cars of spectators. That they were crying. This is your moment, Guerra had shouted. This is when you show everyone what you're made of.

But Charly is too cold to care about any of that and his team car has disappeared. Photographers zoom past on motorbikes, throwing spray in his face. Spectators stamp their feet and issue great clouds of steam as they shout his name: 'Vai, Charly, vai!' The rain turns to sleet then to snow. His tyres swish onwards. Beyond the pain, through the blizzard, he knows what awaits at the summit – la maglia rosa, the precious pink jersey awarded to the race leader. Keep turning the pedals, Charly tells himself. That's all that matters. The snow thickens. Huge flakes land on his lips, his eyelashes. His body stiffens. Every revolution of the pedals feels harder than the last.

Cycling is a pig of a sport, he thinks. They put us out here to kill us. To sacrifice us. Well, fuck them.

Ahead he sees a cluster of spectators. On a day like this that means a café nearby. If he could only get warm, just for a couple of minutes, then he will be able to continue up the mountain. That's only reasonable, isn't it? The circus needs its performers, but they have to be alive! Charly reaches down and flicks out his toe-strap. Behind the crowd he spies a little restaurant, a glowing cave dug into the sopping, awful mountainside. The spectators call to him as he comes to a halt, but he can't talk. He can only lean his bike against the wall of the restaurant and stagger inside. There's a fire, huge jars of pasta, pictures on the wall. He takes in his surroundings without being able to process what he sees. His body is shutting down. They sit him down and put a blanket around his shoulders. Someone guides a cup of hot coffee into his hands.

As he begins to feel the warmth of the liquid move into his bloodstream, there's a commotion at the door. Guerra, the old bastard, bursts in. His eyes are wide with panic and Charly expects him to start shouting, but when he sees the state of his rider, Guerra slows down, comes to crouch in front of Charly.

'Take your time, Charly,' he says. 'We're going to take care of you.'

The team soigneur takes the coffee from Charly's hands and places it on the floor. Then, gently, pulls Charly's sodden jersey over his head. His undershirt comes off, too. Charly still cannot talk. He is conscious of the number of questions he could be asking about the race, but then he really doesn't care. Guerra plonks a bowl of warm water down beside his chair, and together he and the soigneur rub down Charly's body. The warm cloths bring life back to his muscles. He can feel their pain, which is better than feeling nothing at all. They dry him with a towel, then tug a fresh jersey on to his shoulders, put the cup of coffee back in his hands.

'There we go. That's it, Charly, eh? Good as new,' says Guerra.

Charly gives him a sarcastic eye-roll and his manager grins, relieved to have brought his star back from the brink. Charly doesn't need to ask what comes next. He gets to his feet, Guerra's warm hands under his elbows, and makes his way back to his bike. Guerra holds the handlebars and tightens his toe-strap once his cleat has locked into the pedal. The snow has not abated. The spectators are clapping, but on their faces there is horror.

'How far to the top?' he asks Guerra, before setting off.

'Not far, Charly, not far,' comes the too-vague answer.

In the mid-1950s, the organisers of the Giro d'Italia, the second most important 'grand tour' after the Tour de France, had a problem. For a decade their race had been defined by the rivalry between Fausto Coppi and Gino Bartali. The nation followed their battles in the newspapers and by the roadside, and the two men's lives came to symbolise the division that Italy felt in those post-war years – Bartali representing the Catholic, agrarian south and Coppi the modernising, industrial and scientific north. Supported by a range of bit-players, such as the pugilistic Fiorenzo Magni, Coppi and Bartali created a golden age of Italian cycling that has never quite been repeated. To a large degree this is because the conditions were so fertile; after the horrors of the Second World War, Italy was glad to immerse itself in sporting entertainment and the connection of the Italian working class to bicycles was strong. Bicycles were fundamental to everyday life – the primary mode of transport in work and leisure. An Italian working in the fields would cycle to work, cycle to the local bar and cycle to the shops. Children cycled to school. The nation read of Coppi and Bartali's exploits in *La Gazzetta dello Sport*. How many mundane bicycle journeys were transformed into heroic mountain raids in the minds of Italian men and women?

By 1956, however, the golden age was drawing to a close. Bartali had retired two years earlier and Fausto Coppi, though still racing, was past his best. The tifosi hoped for, rather than expected, victories from *Il Campionissimo*. And in the wider society, changes were emerging that would have a significant impact on the sport in the coming years – the proliferation of the car at the expense of the bicycle and the growth of television coverage. The organisers of the Giro were alert to the risk. The Coppi–Bartali years had been good for the ecosystem of Italian cycling, but in the business of sport to stand still is to die. Writing in *La Gazzetta dello Sport*, race organiser, Vincenzo Torriani, put the case for change: 'Each year the Giro is born from one inescapable necessity, to identify with the continual evolution of cycling. Each and every one of us has an interest in ensuring that, like any sport wishing to survive, it adequately reflects the context in which it is set. It cannot allow itself to vegetate, nor live on its memories. To do so would represent a sort of fossilisation and that would be dangerous . . .'

Strong words. Unfortunately for Torriani the ability of any race organiser to effect change is limited. Cycling is a love affair between the riders and the fans; race organisers are just the hoteliers who provide the backdrop. Treacherous new climbs can be found, stages shortened or lengthened, but the riders make the race and the fans make their judgement.

For the 1956 edition, Torriani's team decided to mix it up. Instead of the epic eight-hour stages that had characterised the race during Coppi's best years, the race was now composed of shorter stages, including a sequence of time trials. The route was supposed to promote speed over endurance, but neither the riders nor the fans were inspired by the vision. A sprinter, Alessandro Fantini, led the race for a week before handing the maglia rosa to Pasquale Fornara after the individual time trial at Lucca. Fornara was a good rider – the year before he had finished fourth in the Tour de France, beaten to a podium spot by Charly Gaul – but he was not Fausto Coppi and, as if to underline this point, the biggest talking point of the first week had been Coppi's withdrawal after stage 6 with a back injury. As the race headed into its third and final week, it was generally perceived to have been a failure. Putting opinions aside, the most important metric told the story – newspaper sales had dived.

Gaul came into the 1956 Giro as one of the favourites, though with a heavy caveat. His revelatory 1955 Tour de France had shown his ability in the high mountains, but it had also shown his weaknesses – tactical naïveté, susceptibility to extreme heat and an apparent inability to remain focused every day for three weeks. Moreover, his form was unclear. Gaul did not like the classic one-day races held in Belgium and France during April (for good reason – his lightweight frame was not suited to riding across cobblestones), so the fans had yet to see him at the front of a major race in the 1956 season. Could this exciting new climbing talent step up to take on that most complicated sporting challenge – a grand tour victory?

By the middle of the third week the question persisted. Gaul had started the race cautiously after the Faema team doctor had diagnosed low blood pressure and prescribed medication. Whether or not Gaul actually felt any physical weakness is unclear, but by the end of the first week he seemed to be on fighting form, winning stage 7 through the Matese mountains to Campobasso by over a minute. A week later he won a 3-kilometre hill time trial in Bologna, up to the Madonna di San Luca, narrowly beating fellow climber and friend Federico Bahamontes.

However, he had yet to appear in the top ten overall and three punctures on stage 17, over the giant Stelvio climb, saw him slip back to twenty-fourth place overall, nearly seventeen minutes down on Fornara, who was clinging to a nine-second lead over fellow Italian, Cleto Maule. Gaul must have sensed that his chances of overall victory were falling away with those three punctures; at the finish in Merano he was furious, slamming his bike to the ground and demanding to see his team manager. François Mersch calmed him down, telling Gaul that if he could win tomorrow on Monte Bondone, his Giro objectives would have been met, and he could then focus on the Tour de France. Gaul did calm down, but some of that anger proved useful the next day.

Behind Maule six strong riders, including Nino Defilippis and Jean Brankaert, were grouped at between two and four minutes back. The final mountain stage of the race was set up nicely. Could Fornara hang on? Monte Bondone is one of four peaks on a jagged corrugation running north from the northernmost end of Lake Garda. At over 2,000 metres it is one of the highest mountains in the region and its lopsided peak is covered in snow for most of the year. Nestled in the valley below is the affluent city of Trento, capital of the Trentino-Alto Adige region. During the winter months the area is a mecca for ski enthusiasts, but it doesn't only snow here during the ski season, as the Giro d'Italia was about to discover.

Stage 18 was a brute: 242 kilometres across four major Alpine climbs – the Costalunga, the Passo Rolle, the Brocon and finally Monte Bondone, where the finish line was located. The stage was clearly designed to be the final decisive test and yet surely no amount of climbing could save this forlorn edition of the Giro? The newspapers that morning contained few of the hyperbolic notes that one might expect on such a day. Quite possibly the weary writers had posted their predictions before a freak weather system rolled into the area while the riders, mechanics, managers and everyone else slept.

When Charly Gaul woke the next morning, in a hotel in the spa town of Merano, he was quietly delighted. The temperature had dropped to freezing and an unrelenting rain was falling. Gaul's team, understandably, were appalled.[34] At breakfast they told the team management that they were going to withdraw. With the exception of fellow Luxembourger Marcel Ernzer, with whom Gaul was beginning to develop a friendship that would last his whole career, Gaul did not particularly like his team-mates. With Gaul refusing to share his prize money with them, the feeling was mutual. None of the Faema riders were prepared to ride hard through freezing rain for a leader who didn't show any gratitude. Besides, what was really on offer? Gaul was too far back to challenge for the maglia rosa – the best he could hope for was a stage win.

Gaul likely shared this view. Sixteen minutes was too much to take back on Fornara, a good climber in his own right, but perhaps Gaul could lift himself into the top ten with a strong attacking ride and a stage win was definitely possible. Eventually his team were persuaded to take the start, though it wasn't long before they pulled out, leaving Gaul to fend for himself. On the start line in Merano, Gaul pointed out to Mersch that Fornara was smiling. Gaul liked Fornara; the previous year they had travelled to the post-Tour de France criteriums together in Gaul's Ford Zephyr, sharing the driving. If Fornara was smiling it meant that despite the rain he was confident that he could defend his slim advantage.

On the Costalunga climb Gaul attacked with Bahamontes. The pair were caught on the following descent, so Gaul attacked again on the Passo Rolle. Fornara's smile was long gone. He was suffering under the downpours, and by the summit Gaul had built up a four-minute advantage, but two more punctures cost him six minutes. By the bottom of the Brocon climb Gaul was behind the leading group.

Soaked to the skin, a victim of ill fortune, faced with a long chase back to the leaders he'd previously dropped, Gaul could have been forgiven for giving up. There would be other races and he'd acquitted himself well. No one could have reproached him for riding, rather than racing, into the finish, but that wasn't Gaul's attitude and his steely character came to the fore. That morning he had made up his mind to win, and there were still two mountains to tackle.

That third climb, the Brocon, rises steeply under the shadow of tall pine trees and through pitch-black tunnels. From the lower slopes Gaul began to accelerate. He caught and passed Fornara's group, then set off in pursuit of the two riders now vying for the maglia rosa on the road ahead, Fiorenzo Magni and Nino Defilippis. On the descent of the Brocon, Gaul's brakes were functioning so poorly that he resorted to using his feet to slow himself down on the soaked hairpin bends. When he was able to get alongside his team car, Gaul called out to Guerra to complain about his malfunctioning brakes, to which Guerra helpfully replied, 'It is the water. You'll win like that, Gaul!'

In the valley roads heading towards Trento, with the cold rain driven into his face by a fierce headwind, Gaul powered past Magni and Defilippis. Such was the shock of being caught that Defilippis totally crumbled. If he'd had the strength to stay with Gaul he would have won the Giro, but instead he fell back. Crushed by this sudden turn of events, Defilippis stopped, fell off his bike and had to be carried weeping into his team car.

Charly, meanwhile, was having a semi-serious running feud with his team manager. Approaching Trento, Guerra pulled up and told his young charge that the maglia rosa was a real possibility now. Charly shook his head.

'That's a clumsy cheer,' he shouted back. 'Maglia rosa! That's not possible. Give me something to eat, brake specialist.'

Guerra just shrugged. 'I can't. It is forbidden.'

As Charly powered into Trento he stewed on Guerra's words, starting to get a sense for the chaos unfolding behind him. Riders were strewn across the landscape, most on the verge of quitting the race. Many of those who abandoned later said that concern for their long-term health, their careers, even their lives was the reason for pulling out. Frostbite and hypothermia were very real possibilities.

Leaving Trento Charly spotted the director of the local velodrome, with whom he had been negotiating a contract for three evening appearances after the Giro.

'Bravo, Gaul! Bravo!' called the velodrome director.

'Too late!' Charly called back. 'The contract is now much more expensive!'[35]

As he came to the steep lower slopes of the Monte Bondone, the rain again turned to snow. The temperature had dropped to minus four and the wind whipped the snow into a blizzard. Charly pushed on, maintaining his smooth climbing style while picking a line through the ridges of snow on the road. His red Faema jersey was sodden, his face focused only on forward momentum. The only piece of extra clothing he wore was a red polka dot handkerchief knotted around his neck. Insouciant, pointless. This was not a concession to the weather, this was two fingers raised to it. Behind him the Giro was falling apart. Fornara stopped in Trento and refused to go on. Bahamontes was found huddled in a ditch by a local peasant, who helped the rider to shelter then phoned the race organisers to ask what he should do with this strange creature who doesn't speak Italian? Many years later Bahamontes told a journalist that he had frostbite in his hands and feet, and couldn't use them properly for a month. Other riders dived into a café to drink hot chocolate or to dip their hands into bowls of warm water.

In the midst of the snowstorm Charly Gaul's team manager, former World Champion Learco Guerra, was becoming increasingly panicky. He'd lost sight of Charly some twenty minutes earlier and was now driving up the mountain road, peering through the beating windscreen wipers. In the seminal British cycling magazine, René de Latour wrote, 'By sheer chance, he saw a bike leaning against the wall of a shabby mountain trattoria. "That's Charly's bike!" he exclaimed to his mechanic.' They rushed into the bar and there, sitting on a chair sipping hot coffee, was Gaul, exhausted and so dead to the world that he could hardly speak. After Guerra and his soigneur had rubbed their rider down and pulled a dry jersey on to his shoulders, Gaul resumed his ascent. It didn't take long for him to become cold again.

'I'm dying of cold,' he called to Guerra as he pedalled past groups of fans hardy enough to have themselves ridden up from Trento, who were surely now wondering whether it would be possible to safely descend the mountain once the race had finished.

'Go ahead and die,' replied Guerra, 'but with the maglia rosa.'

We can only speculate as to what Charly thought of his manager's fighting talk, doled out from a heated team car. What did seem to help was a banana, passed to him by a spectator close to the finish. Some sugar, the generosity of a fan, the mere mental distraction of eating, and he knew he was going to make it.

With barely the energy to give a half-hearted victory gesture, Charly crossed the line, came to a halt and fainted. A group of Alpine soldiers picked him up, swaddled him in blankets and carried him to a nearby hut. He couldn't open his mouth, his usual babyface was wrinkled, his hands and feet had turned blue. An hour later, at his hotel, he was still shaking so badly that his clothes had to be cut from his body before he was immersed into a hot bath. He stayed in the bath for half an hour, unable to remember anything of the stage. When he regained some of his senses, Guerra told him he had taken the maglia rosa by three minutes. Gaul reacted by swearing angrily. 'I wish I'd never started bike racing in the first place,' he said.

Incredibly, eight minutes after Gaul, the next rider across the line was Fantini, the sprinter who had led the race in its first week. However, it soon transpired that Fantini had completed much of the stage in a truck. The organisers turned a blind eye, knowing that if they disqualified everyone who cheated that day, Gaul would have been riding the last two stages with only the hardman Fiorenzo Magni (who fought his way into second place overall that day, despite having a broken collarbone, sustained in an earlier crash) for company.[36]

The next day, Gaul wore the maglia rosa with a three minutes and twenty-seven seconds lead over Magni. Never in the history of the

Giro had such a deficit been turned into a race-winning lead. Only forty-three riders remained. Magni later said that he considered an attack on stage 19 to San Pellegrino, but Gaul was too strong and too attentive. The following day, on the traditional processional stage to Milan, Magni rode up to Gaul, patted him on the back and offered his grudging congratulations. Gaul was about to become only the third non-Italian to win the Giro d'Italia.

Glad of a chance to release their inner hyperbole after an otherwise tedious race, the journalists who witnessed Gaul's triumph at Monte Bondone (and plenty who did not) used words like historic . . . legendary . . . drama. Jacques Goddet, writing in *L'Équipe*, commented, 'We found ourselves in the mountain stages of a prehistoric age . . . the most impressive achievement ever in cycling history. Never had a rider to endure more pain, fear and exhaustion.'

Gaul was lauded for his bravery and style. He was compared to heroes like Fausto Coppi and simultaneously set apart from them. Experienced watchers of the sport saw that he was a unique proposition. At twenty-three most riders were learning their craft, respectful of managers and journalists and race organisers. Gaul's shy manners seemed to belie total self-assurance. Even when he lost time he implied that it was all part of a bigger plan. The way he spoke – calmly, thoughtfully, yet with some force – had shocked Marcel Hansenne in the 1955 Tour de France. The way he shouted at the Trento velodrome director after riding for seven hours through freezing rain showed a witty insolence, not to mention a keen commercial awareness.

Cycling thrives on stories such as Monte Bondone. Journalists constructed a narrative that evening in Trento, typing with still-frozen fingers, and their words have echoed down the years. Practically every online article about Charly Gaul today references the stage to Monte Bondone. It immediately defined him, for better or worse.

A storm like that has never been seen again on the mountain and meteorologists are still baffled by what happened that day in May 1956.

Did Gaul understand, then, how important this one day of racing was to become in his life? There is little insight into his immediate reaction. Mersch's biography records the victory and then simply moves on to the next race of that season, which is likely what occupied Gaul's thoughts, too. After the stress and fatigue of the Giro, heightened by media duties in Milan, Gaul would have been happy to recover at home in Luxembourg, spinning out on some easy rides and turning his attention to the forthcoming Tour de France. He must have derived a weighty satisfaction from his Giro victory. It proved his potential, yet he cannot have known just how important that ride to Monte Bondone would become. Years later he spoke of it, 'having marked my life. It was a source of joy and regret.'

PART TWO

1954

PART TWO

Stage 9

THE LIEUTENANT

Cycling is a peculiar sport in terms of its social structures. Races are won by individuals, yet it is a team sport. At professional level it is impossible to enter a race if you are not part of an officially registered team. As a leader, that team should work for you. As a worker, or domestique (which translates literally as domestic), you give up your own chances of victory to put your leader in a position to win. So the team unit and the interactions within it are incredibly important to building a successful career. The peloton, composed of up to twenty teams, is a workforce. There can be tactical alliances between teams, friendships between individual riders on different teams, even familial relations like the Bobet brothers, and there is a sense of solidarity in the peloton that sometimes pushes back against outside forces, such as race organisers who send the riders down unsafe roads. Beyond the peloton there is the wider ecosystem that it supports – journalists, sponsors, organisers, riders' friends and family, fan clubs.

This mini-society was not, in the 1950s at least, a microcosm of society. It was more analogous to a factory. Women were marginalised, their role reduced to public relations girls waving from the promotional caravan or podium girls kissing the winners on the rostrum. Riders' wives and girlfriends appeared only fleetingly at races, the received thinking being that they were an unwelcome distraction and a drain on their partners' energy, so the world of professional cycling, exemplified best by the Tour de France, was an intricate, ever-moving social structure, composed principally of working-class men who had found a way to avoid the drudgery and danger of the coal mine or the factory floor.

Cycling has always appealed to loners. For a shy teenager cycling means escape; it means precious time alone. The majority of professional cyclists simply love going out on their bike. In those teenage years some, like Gaul, discover an innate talent, which, when combined with a good work ethic, may take them on to greatness. The foundation of the whole sport of cycling is the simple act of going out for a solo training ride; the quietude and freedom from other people.

Gaul embodied many of the quirks of shyness. He valued time spent alone and privacy (after retirement, he particularly hated any perceived invasions of his private space). He felt most comfortable with a small group of close, loyal friends and he could be so taciturn that it annoyed his fellow riders. In the peloton he was known as a man of few words and, when he did speak, it came across as abrasive. This is often the consequence of shyness – forced into speech, feeling self-conscious, the shy man rushes to get his words out, or tries to end the conversation before it has started, giving the false impression of roughness and ill-humour. That is not the intent – he simply does not want to be the focus of attention and seeks to shift that focus elsewhere as quickly as possible. Alongside the many descriptions of Gaul as quiet and rude, however, there are other descriptions of him as cordial, friendly and jokey. Herein is the paradox of the introvert. When he felt like it, Gaul could be good company, so when he disappeared back into his shell it must have been confusing for those who did not know him well.

'Often Charly was called arrogant,' Ernzer said. 'Even labelled as anti-social because he did not show himself in public, because he couldn't handle it, to be the focus of the masses. In the peloton it was very similar, very often happy and always friendly, but he wasn't the type to like talking. Charly Gaul was the typical champion, closed and extremely individualistic.' [37]

Writing during the 1959 Tour de France, journalist René de Latour said, 'We chat in a friendly tone with Charly Gaul, but it is pretty much impossible to form an opinion, because it is hard to believe how his moods change. His suggestions, even if they sound optimistic, always keep something in reserve. He loves the solitude of his room, the twilight, the silence. And when he shares the room with his faithful friend Marcel Ernzer, then Ernzer often replies in his place, trying to keep Charly away from the burden of indiscreet questions.'[38]

This was to become a familiar scene for the journalists following the Tour de France. In 1958, on the eve of the final time trial, journalists Roger Bastide and Jacques Grello visited Charly in his room at the Hotel du Nord in Besançon, hoping for an insight into Charly's plans, hopes, fears. The scene was distracting. Charly, sat on a chair with his head bent forward, was getting his hair trimmed. Clothes were strewn across the room, Marcel Ernzer buzzed about in a grey tracksuit, shaving, tidying, and Dr René Bürger lay sprawled across one of the beds.

Gaul's physical presence – or lack of it – surprised Grello, who later wrote: 'His legs are slender, beautiful, surprisingly smooth, his arms are frail, thin and his torso narrow. On his neck, frankly thin, hangs a small gold chain which disappears in the indentation of the undershirt. Thus posed, stooped, white feet in sandals, with his modest grey shorts, he looks fragile and sad as an under-nourished student who would have his hair cut by a friend because he cannot afford the hairdresser.'[39]

Bastide talked about what he had seen in the race so far and slid in questions to Charly, who remained silent. Dr Bürger answered every question on his behalf. Sometimes Charly would give a little smile, as if to confirm the answer his doctor gave, but he never raised his head or met the journalists' eyes.[40]

The extreme physical and mental highs and lows of professional cycling, plus the sport's tactical nuances, added further layers of complexity to a rider's relationship with the press. Any rider who spoke openly to the press risked his race tactics, or details of his physical health, being printed in the next morning's newspapers. If his primary school report is worth noting, Gaul was an intelligent man whose shyness held him back from saying what was going through his mind. Indeed, it seems he was a man who lived to a large degree in his own head. Cycling, perhaps, helped him to process his thoughts. Or simply leave them behind at the front door.

Just as Gaul valued his childhood friends Roby Maas and François Mersch, at Faema-Guerra he began to develop a close friendship with Marcel Ernzer. Born in Esch-sur-Alzette, six years before Gaul, Ernzer had turned professional for Terrot in 1949 after representing Luxembourg at the 1948 Olympics in London. A talented rider in his own right, Ernzer was not a domestique for the first part of his career. In 1954 he took a commanding solo victory at the one-day monument Liège-Bastogne-Liège, 236 kilometres across the Belgian Ardennes hills, which were still strewn with debris from the Battle of the Bulge. Ernzer also won the Luxembourg National Road Race title three times and the Tour de Luxembourg in 1951. He may not have had the panache of Charly Gaul, but Marcel Ernzer was a solid professional and arguably the best rider that Luxembourg had produced since Nicolas Frantz.

When Gaul joined Ernzer at Terrot in 1953, the two men established a rapport (Ernzer was said to be an appreciative audience for Gaul's jokes) and at that year's Dauphiné Libéré the older man was stunned to see how Gaul rode in the mountains: 'As I saw how Charly cracked top riders like Géminiani, Robic, without inhibitions and left behind Teisseire (his team leader), I was so impressed that since that Dauphiné I was convinced he would become one of the world's greats of cycling.[41] Speaking in retirement, Ernzer said that Gaul had been told by manager Pierre Dion to let the team captain Teisseire win that 1953 Dauphiné. On the Iseran climb Gaul could have taken flight, but pulled back because victory would secure Teisseire a place on the French national team for the Tour de France.

While he was impressed with the young climber and joker, at Terrot Marcel Ernzer still had his own ambitions. As far as possible he rode for himself and the pair sometimes raced against each other. In 1955, the year of Gaul's breakthrough at the Tour de France, twenty-nine-year-old Ernzer was considering an early retirement when Gaul confided his imminent departure to a new team. Wouldn't Ernzer like to come to either Cilo-Saint-Raphaël or Faema-Guerra? Gaul drew Ernzer close and made him, along with another sympathetic Luxembourg rider, Willy Kemp, part of the deal. Buy Gaul and you buy Ernzer and Kemp as well.

For Marcel Ernzer this was both a reinvention and reinvigoration. He focused solely on looking after Charly. The two men became virtually inseparable, sharing a room at races and often training together at home in Luxembourg. Ernzer protected Gaul, kept him out of the wind, gave him bottles and food, and gave him his wheel when Gaul punctured. He even helped Gaul open his love letters from fans. Gaul trusted Ernzer and confided in him all his worries, plans and hopes. Gaul's support, of course, went beyond Ernzer, and Faema-Guerra was a strong, organised team, but this special, loyal bond with his countryman was invaluable to Gaul as he attacked the world's toughest races.

Two weeks after his Giro victory Gaul won his first Tour de Luxembourg, cheered on by a wildly partisan crowd. A stage win on a hilly day in the Ardennes showed that he had carried his form through from the Giro. A few days before the Tour de France he won

the Luxembourg Road Race National Championship, too, giving him
the honour of wearing the National Champion's jersey – a fetching
red, white and blue tricolour – in the upcoming Tour de France. The
championship race, in Differdange, close to the French border, was
perceived as something of a hassle by Gaul and his compatriots; the
last thing they wanted a few days before the Tour was an intense,
single-day race, especially one without much prize money. Gaul
won alone by five minutes, Ernzer came in second. One suspects
the result was agreed between the riders before the peloton had even
rolled out of the start.

After the Giro, colour images of Gaul appeared in cycling magazines across Europe. Here was a new kind of fame for Charly, visual
and intense. Emerging from the snow in his red Faema jersey, with
piercing blue eyes and still soft, baby-faced features, Gaul fitted his
nickname. When he wasn't wearing a cap, his James Dean quiff
remained unruffled; his hairdresser must have known what brand of
hair cream could withstand wind, rain and snow. And while amateur
cyclists studied his position and equipment to see what enabled such
climbing prowess, many others simply liked the way he looked. The
Faema office began to get dozens of fan letters every week, which
they duly forwarded on. Sharing a bedroom when away at races, Gaul
and Ernzer would open these stacks of letters together and giggle
at the many indecent proposals. Some were so sexually explicit that
Ernzer told journalists it was enough to put him off women for life.

The Tour de France came too quickly for Gaul in 1956. He arrived
at the start in Reims tired, both physically and mentally, from the
Giro d'Italia and the subsequent weeks of celebrations. Gaul was,
theoretically at least, the favourite for the Tour de France that year.
For a variety of reasons many of his most serious rivals did not start
the race, and Bobet, Kübler, Koblet, Robic and Coppi all chose to miss
it. The French pair of Raymond Poulidor and Jacques Anquetil, who

were to light up the race in the early 60s, were not yet old enough to challenge for the yellow jersey and not selected for the French national or regional teams. It looked like a golden opportunity for Gaul and his friend, the Spanish climber, Federico Bahamontes.

However, the route was easier than in previous years, with considerably less climbing than normal, plus Charly wasn't riding for Faema-Guerra as the Tour de France was still organised in national teams, which brought the usual headache for Luxembourg. In 1956 three foreigners were recruited to make up the team of ten – the Portuguese rider, Antonio Barbosa, the Italian, Aldo Bolzan (who became a naturalised Luxembourger in 1960) and the pioneering Brian Robinson, Britain's first Tour de France finisher.

On the opening flat stages across northern France and Belgium, Gaul lost big chunks of time. Despite winning – to everybody's surprise – a short time trial on the motor racing circuit at Rouen, by stage 6 he was nearly half an hour behind, a huge deficit to make up. It was the familiar Charly Gaul story: an almost pathological inability to focus on racing in the first week because the terrain didn't suit him, justified to journalists and team-mates by the prospect of mountains in the second week. How infuriating it must have been for his team-mates that their star rider had to attack in the mountains simply to get back on terms with the leaders of the race. Everyone saw this dynamic playing out, but no one (with the possible exception of Marcel Ernzer) quite understood it.

Unity within the Luxembourg Mixed team was further compromised by the lack of clarity about prize money allocation. Robinson, joining Nicolas Frantz's motley crew for the first time, expected there to be a meeting before the first stage, but none was arranged. When another rider brought up the subject at dinner a few days into the race, Frantz waved the question away. Robinson deduced that he was expected to work for Gaul, but would not necessarily be paid for his efforts.

Friend and fellow climber Federico Bahamontes was equally ill-equipped to protect his own interests on the flat stages, so the Tour de France headed south from Brittany with a rare sense of being rudderless. There were no star riders taking grip of the race. No one could quite predict what would happen in the Pyrénées. Even if Gaul and Bahamontes took flight, would they really get themselves back in contention?

The race became even more confusing on stage 7, 244 kilometres down the Atlantic coast from Lorient to Angers. The peloton split in two, with thirty-one riders finishing over eighteen minutes ahead. The front group contained Roger Walkowiak, a French rider of Polish heritage, riding for the North-East/Centre regional team. Walkowiak was a solid professional rider, but he was hardly a cycling celebrity. In 1955, after a strong showing at the Dauphiné Libéré, Louison Bobet had called for Walkowiak to be included in the French national team, but the selectors disagreed and consigned him to the regional team. In 1956, however, Walkowiak had ridden a canny first week, slipping into two breakaways and putting himself near the top of the general classification. When the stage 7 split occurred, he was the best-placed rider overall and in Angers he pulled on the yellow jersey.

The journalists were not kind. Walkowiak was dismissed as a journeyman, an opportunist. The typically hyperbolic front page of L'Équipe the next morning focused on the 'Waterloo' of the French national team. Antoine Blondin described Walkowiak as a modest rider unworthy of leading the great race. Walkowiak was hurt by the coverage of his greatest performance. On stage 10 he deliberately lost the yellow jersey, not wanting the pressure of wearing it for two weeks, but remained in touch with his principal rivals and, surprising everyone with his climbing legs, took the jersey back in the Alps. The penultimate stage rolled through the mountains of the Auvergne to Walkowiak's home city of Montluçon, where he received a rapturous welcome. Heading north on the final, monster stage of

331 kilometres from Montluçon to Paris (in that era the Tour organisers had not thought of making transfers by train or car) Walkowiak fended off multiple attacks from compatriot Gilbert Bauvin, who was desperate to defend the honour of the French national team.

Walkowiak's fighting performance, spurred on in no small part by the press criticism, eventually won *L'Équipe* around. Antoine Blondin and others praised Walkowiak's courage, although as an official sponsor of the Tour it was in *L'Équipe*'s commercial interests to celebrate the race winner, whatever the writers really thought. Other newspapers continued to denigrate Walkowiak's achievement and to win '*à la Walkowiak*' became a well-known term in French society, meaning to take an easy or undeserved victory.

After retiring in 1960 Walkowiak returned to the Montluçon Dunlop rubber factory where he had worked during his amateur career. He also tried his hand at farming, then at running a petrol station. None of it fulfilled him and the bitterness he felt towards the Parisian media only deepened over the years. He refused to do any interviews until 1985. In the last years of his life he spoke movingly to journalists, now more sympathetic to his story, of the impact on his life of that unique Tour de France. Like Charly Gaul, Walkowiak might seem something of an anomaly in the history of the Tour de France, yet his story is one of many examples of the impact of critical press coverage.

For Gaul, the 1956 Tour de France could be seen as something of a missed opportunity, yet the toll of his Giro d'Italia victory, not least that momentous day to Monte Bondone, combined with the strange way the Tour unfolded, meant that he was not fully focused on winning the yellow jersey. Only breaking out of his apparent indifference in the Alps, Gaul took an impressive solo victory on stage 18 to Turin, but even then he was upstaged by Walkowiak, who put in a fine performance to take back the yellow jersey on the same day. That win, plus a long break the day before on the mountainous roads to Grenoble, also gave Gaul the King of the Mountains classification. Two stage wins, thirteenth overall and the King of the Mountains award was a satisfactory result, but no more. He never said so publicly, but it seems likely Gaul gave up on winning that Tour in its first week.

Nevertheless 1956 had been a successful year for Charly. At just twenty-three he had graduated to winning a grand tour. The Giro d'Italia may not have had the prestige of the Tour de France, but everyone who understood cycling knew that it was just as tough, and the manner of his victory, the image of him being carried away, frozen, on the top of Monte Bondone, was already etched into cycling's history. Charly Gaul was famous – and that brought its own problems.

Charly and Georgette Schmit, 1956, with members of Georgette's family

Stage 10

CHARACTER DEVELOPMENT

All professional sports are a blend of business and entertainment. Early in the genesis of the Tour de France, its organisers at *L'Auto* allowed riders to be sponsored. As well as the obvious benefit of bringing more money into the sport, the sponsors became a tool for identifying riders. A fan standing on the roadside, perhaps a little worse for wear, faced with a pack of skinny, dusty racers, might just be able to pick out individuals by looking for their team colours and sponsors' logos. Over the decades cycling sponsorship has become more sophisticated and omni-present. Now every surface of the Tour de France is sponsored. The cycling fan accepts this, even cheerfully embraces it, as part of the event's history. The brands that stand out, though, are the team sponsors. Whether it's a flooring manufacturer or a national lottery, the team sponsors take on a curious quasi-identity. Faema-Guerra was a team and within the sport its reputation was shaped by its riders, its manager, its way of operating. Yet Faema was a manufacturer of coffee machines, with its own corporate identity. When a company gets involved in sport it has to accept that its brand is now in the hands of a dozen young men whose principal goal in life is to win a yellow jersey.

For some companies the experience can be transformative. The Italian bike manufacturer Bianchi has a long heritage in the sport and still trades on its association with Fausto Coppi. Mapei, a producer of chemical products for the building industry, would never have achieved its public profile without the incredibly successful cycling team it sponsored during the 1990s. Similarly, the furniture retailer that sponsored Marco Pantani, Mercatone Uno, experienced huge sales growth on the back of their star's exploits. Not only did Pantani place their name on television screens in front of millions of viewers (most of whom were outside Italy and therefore didn't have a way of buying Mercatone Uno products), he also imbued their brand with his own panache. For a cycling team, winning is always the objective, but if victory is only the end point of a mechanised process – as Team Sky showed – it feels hollow and therefore forgettable. To win with style, or even to lose with style, this is what sticks in the memory.

When Marco Pantani returned to racing in 1997 after recovering from a serious accident that nearly ended his career, he had a new look. Or, we might say nowadays, a new brand. With a bandana tied over his bald head, an earring and a goatee beard Pantani became 'Il Pirata' – the Pirate. He even had a logo designed in the style of a skull and crossbones, with his head for the skull and two cutlasses replacing the bones. There is some debate about who thought of the new nickname and how intentionally it came about, but Pantani himself embraced it from the start. He knew that all great cycling heroes have great nicknames. The Pirate was perfect because it fitted his swashbuckling attacks and the way he stole victories from much more organised, well-funded teams. Eddy Merckx was known as the Cannibal for his insatiable appetite for success, Coppi was the Heron for his long legs and grace, Laurent Fignon was the Professor for his intellectualism, Bernard Hinault was the Badger for his pugnacious attitude, Tom Simpson was Major Tom for his Englishness, Hugo Koblet was the Pédaleur de Charme for his style both on and off the bike . . . the list goes on. Pantani understood that a strong nickname becomes a brand and that could elevate his identity beyond his team, beyond his nationality, even beyond his race results. As long as he had the swagger and the charisma, he could live up to the ridiculousness of his nickname. Other riders, less brand-conscious or just not bothered about creating a brand, merely tolerated the nicknames given to them by team-mates or the press. Besides, nicknames are only for team leaders. Domestiques are lucky if their names are remembered at all.

Pantani's path through cycling took him a long way – emotionally, financially and morally – from his origins. He may have shared Charly Gaul's mistrust of journalists, but Pantani loved being a celebrity and all that came with it. Allegations of using performance-enhancing drugs blighted his career and sent him into a depression, which turned him to cocaine. Unable to save himself, he spiralled tragically downwards until, on Valentine's Day 2004, he was found dead in a hotel room in Rimini. He had died of acute cocaine poisoning, alone.

Throughout his career Pantani looked up to Charly Gaul. Both men were climbers, physically very alike, capable of stunning attacks in the high mountains. In later life Gaul met Pantani and the two men became friends. Gaul was able to offer a little fatherly advice to the talented, but wayward, Italian. Sadly, Gaul could not save him from his fate. Pantani certainly would have been aware of Gaul's nickname of the Angel of the Mountains. Did he, perhaps, want to emulate his hero's fame?

Charly Gaul was not as knowing as Pantani. He did not create his nickname, he did not think of himself as a brand (though he was acutely aware of his earning potential and short riding career), and he did not pursue the trappings of celebrity like Pantani. Instead of being in a nightclub surrounded by young women and bottles of champagne, Gaul preferred to be at home in Bettembourg with Georgette, listening to records and pottering around the garden.

He may not have been interested in creating a public persona, but that is not to say that Charly Gaul did not have a strong sense of his own identity. Throughout his career, with meticulous handwriting, he signed his name 'Gaully', combining his surname and the end of his first name. In the 1959 Giro d'Italia he wore a pair of white gloves embroidered with 'GAUL' in black across the knuckles. This may have been a slightly half-hearted attempt to promote his own personal brand in the way that seemed to come so easily to other riders – towards the end of their careers Louison Bobet and Raphaël Géminiani both contrived to sponsor their own teams so that they could ride with their name emblazoned on their chest. Charly's 1959 gloves never appeared again. Perhaps he lost them, perhaps he felt embarrassed at what, for him, seemed to be blatant self-promotion. He did not like the show-business side of cycling. Wasn't it enough for him to race to the best of his ability, to fulfil his contracts?

Some writers have pointed out that Charly had a taste for expensive clothes, particularly Italian suits, and fast cars. His hair was always immaculate. There are several photos of him running a comb through it after a race. He seemed aware of his looks and their effect on the fans, especially female fans, but it would not be reasonable to say that Charly was vain. As a young man from a modest background, thrust into the limelight and paid a significant amount of money, it is entirely understandable to expend a little effort on one's appearance. Cycling is a dangerous, dusty, muddy sport. Dressing well in the evening after a day's racing is comparable to a factory worker who wants to wear a clean shirt for dinner, and looking presentable is part of being professional, representing one's sponsors.

Gaul's face contributed a great deal to the development of his myth. As a youth his features were soft and cherubic; it seemed impossible that such a child could endure such a tough sport. This look of innocence perhaps brought out the parental instinct in cycling fans, even in some of the grizzled reporters following the races. As he aged his face sharpened. In some photos he still looks angelic, but in others he looks more angular, with a prominent jaw and cheek bones, and always there are those blue eyes, usually described as icy or cold. Even in photographs, at the remove of seventy years, they show a vibrancy beyond the usual concentration of a professional sportsman. They seem to say, here is someone who lives his life intensely, who *thinks* intensely.

Eventually, of course, time and the brutality of cycling took their toll. By his mid-thirties his face was heavier, tired. At twenty he looked fifteen; at thirty he looked closer to forty. In the much-recycled short biographies of his life that appear in cycling magazines and websites, Gaul's weight after retirement is often referred to. This is wholly unfair. Yes, Charly had a sweet tooth and a fairly heavy alcohol habit, and he did put on weight after retirement, but this is far from unusual among former professional cyclists and, in most cases, hardly worth a line of newsprint. If he had been a sprinter the journalists would not have dwelt on the subject. It is only because Charly was a climber, with a slender frame that could defy gravity, that his weight in later years was noted. It is as if the journalists could not quite believe the metamorphosis from angel to mortal being. Or perhaps it so greatly disappointed them that, like bitchy columnists, they wanted to call him 'dumpy'.

Gaul never referenced himself as the Angel of the Mountains. He preferred to let his legs create the myth. Very few journalists had his trust and, as his career developed and he saw the gap between what was written in the newspapers and what he perceived to be true, he became suspicious to the point of paranoid. Only René Bürger and Marcel Ernzer were close to him. Everyone else, perhaps even Georgette, was held at arm's length.

'He is first of all a single man,' Roger Frankeur wrote in *L'Équipe*. 'And as such, he is on guard. He likes the moments when his superiority is admitted, but he hates these collective outbursts which prevail where he has not freely chosen to go . . . If he maintains good relations with many people, he does not grant his friendship easily. He does not forget criticism, nor the humiliating doubts that one has for a long time about one's class, one's character, one's riding style.[42]

If Charly's eyes hinted at an intense interior life, his articulation of his thoughts, at least to anyone outside his closest circle, did not match up. Interviewers found him perplexing. Questions were answered briefly or referred to René Bürger and Marcel Ernzer, while the wry smiles on Charly's face seemed to hint that he wasn't giving away anything even close to the truth. The irony is that Charly's unwillingness to open up to journalists meant they had to create their own version of his identity and, when he read what they wrote, he became even more alienated from the journalists and the world they represented.

In a 2005 lecture, Luxembourg academic Frank Wilhelm said, 'Naked performance needs speech to access a meaningful existence, a social dimension; even the permanently televised image is not enough. As a result, the great sportsman is overwhelmed by the commented event; he no longer belongs to himself. Charly Gaul was, I believe, particularly sensitive to this phenomenon and defended himself a little.[43]

Antoine Blondin was a committed Parisian. He was born in the city in 1922, the son of a poet, and studied philosophy at the Sorbonne. After the war Blondin lived, drank and wrote in Saint-Germain-des-Prés, the literary heart of the city. Existentialist philosopher Jean-Paul Sartre was a friend and Blondin was frequently to be found at Les Deux Magots, the famous café where writers like Sartre and Simone de Beauvoir escaped from the tyranny of the blank page. Blondin's debut novel, *L'Europe Buissonnière* (1949) described his experiences of being forced to work in a German rubber factory during the Second World War, a consequence of the German occupation of France. Further novels published in the 1950s were awarded multiple literary prizes and cemented his reputation, bolstered, too, by his bohemian lifestyle. He was a notoriously heavy drinker and evenings in the Left Bank bars often ended with games of 'bullfighting' with passing cars. He also played games with the authorities and tax avoidance nearly landed him in prison.

Blondin was so committed to Parisian life that he hardly ever left the city, seeing little point in exploring provincial France or beyond, but he made an exception for the Tour de France. Every July between 1954 and 1982 (with one exception, ironically 1958 – the year of Charly Gaul's victory, when Blondin had to stay in Paris to finish a novel) he packed his bags and bravely set out beyond the Périphérique. For each of those Tours he observed the race from a red Peugeot 203, given press car number 101, a vehicle that came to be as famous as the race director's car. Blondin sat in the back, on the right, his *L'Équipe* colleague Pierre Chany on the left. After every stage Blondin avoided the press room, with its incessant typewriter din, opting instead for a nearby bistro or hotel bar. He rarely interviewed riders, but simply recorded his impressions of each day, using a novelist's eye for the telling detail. One of his literary heroes was Albert Londres, one of the founders of investigative journalism. Londres wrote in a personal style about war, colonial abuses, lunatic asylums and many other subjects. Blondin sought to emulate his hero, but instead of a war zone he wrote about the Tour de France, in his precise and humorous style. In longhand, at the bistro table, he put down his daily column, then handed it to an assistant who telegraphed it to *L'Équipe*'s headquarters in Montmartre.

Deadline met, Blondin could settle in for a good night of drinking with his journalist colleagues. Over the years, many anecdotes attached themselves to him. One night, thirsty after a heavy session in the bar, he woke up and reached over for the bottle beside his bed. He took a swig, only to find it was a bottle of ink. Another year, having been served guinea fowl at an official Tour dinner for three nights in a row, he announced, 'If this guinea fowl is going to cover the whole Tour, at least have the decency to give it a race number!'

Much has been written about the Tour de France's eminent role in French culture and national identity. Blondin's heyday coincided with a period that is often portrayed as a kind of golden age of French cycling – Bobet, Poulidor, Anquetil. The Tour had not yet become fully international, television coverage was in its infancy and there was a kind of naïve optimism about the brash commercialism of the whole enterprise. The peloton spinning through charming French countryside on a sunny day in July, past families who have spread a picnic out on the roadside – this is the quintessential image of the Tour. Ideally, there will be some sunflowers in the background. Despite all the changes in wider French and European society that seemed to accelerate through the second half of the twentieth century, the Tour retained this stereotypical image, was held within its honeyed glow and much loved for its nostalgic qualities.

Of course, Blondin's columns played their own significant role in creating the mid-century mythology of the Tour. He elevated its heroes and, without resorting to purple prose, re-established its epic qualities. Even when live radio commentary and then live television coverage gave cycling fans a way to follow the action kilometre by kilometre, Blondin's reflections offered a more human insight into the race. His colleague, Chany, was obliged to report the race in a less idiosyncratic style. Together they made a formidable team.

Above all, though, Blondin loved bike racing. He was clear that, for all its cultural and historical layers of meaning, the Tour de France was nothing without its racers. He was skilled at writing pen portraits of the riders, but other journalists worked harder to gain the trust of individual riders. While Roger Frankeur was trying to get access to Charly Gaul's hotel room, Blondin was in the bar getting drunk. Blondin, then, never quite got beyond the pen portrait. One of his favourite riders was Tom Simpson. Blondin played a role in helping Simpson create the image of an eccentric Englishman who became European through cycling. Simpson would arrive at races in a bowler hat, carrying an umbrella, looking like he was walking to work in the City of London. Blondin hinted at Simpson's upper-class credentials, perpetuating the stereotypical image Simpson wanted, but he knew it was a myth; Simpson was as working class as Charly Gaul or Fausto Coppi.

Charly Gaul was not so easy to characterise. Even those who rode alongside him struggled to penetrate his motives. Jean Bobet, writing about Gaul's talent, said, 'Its spring is secret, its performance incomprehensible. He drags with him a kind of fragility and insecurity that make us fear both for the man and for the rider.[34]

In some ways Gaul's nickname was a gift to writers – it was memorable, hinted at mythological connections and could be used in a variety of contexts, but Charly himself did little to endorse it. He did not dress up for his role as 'Major Tom' Simpson did. He did not refer to himself as an angel, and the nickname was so far away from his day-to-day behaviour as to be almost a joke, so, even to the best writers of the Tour de France, Charly Gaul remained something of an enigma.

A YEAR NOT FORGOTTEN

By the beginning of 1957 Charly Gaul was firmly established as one of the stars of the sport. He was the defending Giro d'Italia champion, and in the Tour de France he had a third place, two mountain classification awards and four stage wins. And he was still only twenty-four. His ascendancy had not been without problematic moments, but, on the whole, he had yet to face any significant crises. That was all to change in 1957.

The year started with some bad omens. Having taken a holiday over Christmas and the New Year, Charly signed up for a cyclo-cross race in Albizzate, Italy. It looked like a good proposition – he could pocket some start money, wave to his Italian fans and spend some time with Learco Guerra planning the season ahead. However, while training on the course before the race, Charly fell hard and sustained a shoulder injury that would keep him out of both the Luxembourg Cyclo-cross Championships and the World Championships.

The bad luck continued at the Grand Prix de la Forteresse, a new event on the calendar and a race designed for Charly. His friend and later biographer, François Mersch, dreamt up the concept: a one-day medley race around the ancient fortress of Luxembourg City, climbing and descending the steep cobbled lanes that connect the old town on the cliff to the newer areas below. The race consisted of four stages – two very short road races up and down the 700 metres of the steep hill and two equally short time trials. These were Charly's streets and on race day thousands of Luxembourgers crowded the narrow pavements to get a glimpse of their hero. The race was billed as a duel between Charly and Federico Bahamontes. The Spaniard put himself out of contention in the first race by using a gear that was too high. Charly won the first three races, but in the finale a puncture forced him to pull out. This left Marcel Ernzer to defend Luxembourg's honour, but he was powerless to contain a late attack by Brian Robinson, whose win was received with polite applause from the thousands of fans lining the Brettenweg climb.

The 1956 Tour de Luxembourg had been something of a lap of honour for Gaul following his Giro d'Italia triumph. In 1957, however, Gaul's home race (which was disproportionately important to him because of his patriotism) had moved to a new date in early May. This made it a perfect warm-up for the Giro and Gaul came into it feeling his form was good, but the competition was stiff; in particular from the Saint-Raphaël – Géminiani team, which sent many of its strongest riders, including Roger Rivière, Brian Robinson and Gérard Saint. Gaul got off to a good start by winning the stage 2 time trial at Differdange, in a thunderstorm, taking the race leadership. But his race unwound very quickly on the long and hilly third stage to Diekirch. Saint put in a long-range attack and Gaul missed the moment to jump on his wheel. The Saint-Raphaël Géminiani team then sat stolidly behind Gaul and Ernzer, while they battled in vain to reduce the gap. Eventually, exhausted, they gave up. Saint finished fifteen minutes ahead. In Diekirch, where Charly's uncle Jean-Pierre lived and very much home turf, the crowds booed and whistled at Charly. Some even spat on him as he passed.

Gaul was traumatised by the experience; the shock of experiencing that reaction stayed with him for his whole life. These were his own people and less than a year earlier they had been adulatory. He went from hero to villain so suddenly and so unfairly. What happened on that stage to Diekirch was just part of bike racing. Disappointing, but part of the game. The riders all knew that. So why would his supporters turn on him? Was their love so fickle? The next day, still in shock, Charly pulled out after just 10 kilometres.

The fiasco of the 1957 Tour de Luxembourg illustrates how important Charly's performances were to his country's sense of itself. His narrative, that of plucky underdog, fitted perfectly with his national identity. Luxembourg, like the rest of Europe, was rebuilding its national identity after the horrors of the Second World War. Along with runner Josy Barthel, who won the 1,500 metres at the 1952 Helsinki Olympics (still Luxembourg's only gold medal at the Games), Charly was an emblem of recovery, of resilience, of youthful optimism.

His (perceived) failure on the stage to Diekirch was blown out of all proportion by the Luxembourg press, who showed the sort of eagerness to cut a national hero down to size that we are more used to seeing from British tabloids. Even heavyweight intellectual commentators chimed in. Alphonse Arend was a teacher, and a literary and cultural critic for the *Luxemburger Wort*. Sport was not his usual topic, but even he could not resist piling on the criticism of Gaul. 'The recent Tour de Luxembourg ended with a twist that some consider a scandal: the abandonment of Charly Gaul,' he wrote. 'Suddenly, the idol fell into ruins, and its most fanatical worshipers trampled on the fallen god. This presumptuous young man who had dared to declare himself victor even before the fight, here he is who pitifully lays down his arms, without fighting, without saving his honour. This, the public does not forgive ... The masses can't stand an idol disappointing them, deceiving them ... Never, here and elsewhere, has a sportsman exercised such a fascination on the masses. His young age, the brilliance of his exploits, the candour and arrogance of both his language and his behaviour, all this makes this frail adolescent a sort of mythical being, a winged angel.'[45]

Arend's argument, made at some length, was that Gaul had admitted defeat far too easily. A true hero, he thought, would always fight to the bitter end. It was a hopelessly idealistic way to look at sport – a professional athlete knows when to admit defeat and save his energy for another day – and yet Arend's argument did illuminate the outrageous response of the fans beside the road. They booed and whistled at Gaul because they inherently agreed that a hero, *their hero*, should indeed fight every battle. Perhaps the memory of Luxembourg's capitulation to Germany simmered under this attitude.

However, the article was not universally endorsed by the readers of *Luxemburger Wort*. There was such a backlash that Arend was forced to use another column to defend himself. He was surprised, too, when his entire Latin class stood up 'as one man' to protest about what they saw as the unreasonable moral expectation that their teacher had placed on Gaul.

Another voice of youth to defend Charly was a young woman who published an open letter in the *d'Lëtzebuerger Land* on 2 August 1957. She gave her name only as Marie-Rose: 'Everyone demands exceptional results, record times; whether it is windy, raining, snowing or so scorching hot that the road tar melts, the crowd applauds only superhuman efforts, superhuman records never before reached, over infinite distances, in deadly conditions . . . Charly is a young man and we like him, the young people, he is one of us: with his beautiful childish smile; he has and will have resounding successes and setbacks . . . Charly is one of us because we know the faults of our youth in him: he has impulses, he has inconsistency, carelessness; he likes to let himself be lulled by his successes. He knows how to laugh frankly and cry in secret, like us young people.[46]

Cycling is, in theory at least, so simple, but in reality it is deeply complex. Take the unwritten rules bound up in the tradition of the sport.

Young riders learn them early and rise through the ranks already observing them. If the professional peloton is a micro-society, as many journalists have noted, its morality system applies to a very specific universe. The basic tenet of this morality system is not to take advantage of another's misfortune or basic human need. So, do not attack while your rival is feeding or urinating, or when he has had a mechanical failure or a crash.

This mutual understanding among members of the peloton developed as soon as cycling coalesced into an organised sport in the first half of the twentieth century, and it is easy to see why. When a group of men are being asked to ride for seven hours through the Alps in all kinds of weather, they form a collective view about how best to protect their fundamental needs. Like industrial-era working-class men, the riders looked out for each other as they faced abominable conditions. Survival came before competition. Indeed, since the Tour's inception in 1903 there had been a strong political element to the event, which at times has bubbled up into open hostility between the riders and the organisers. The narrative of the Tour in its first 25 years was celebratory – the riders were giants of the road, examples of resilience and mental fortitude – but in the 1930s the debate became more edgy. Riders openly rebelled against what they saw as the draconian rules imposed by the organisers L'Auto. The phrase '*forçats de la route*' became widely used to describe the Tour peloton. Translated as 'convict-labourers of the road', the term moved the perception of the Tour into a darker place. L'Auto did not help itself by continuing to portray the race as a 'civilising process that transformed its uncouth contestants into honourable, disciplined 'pedal workers' – worthy of emulation by their lower-class fans.[47]

Not surprising, then, that the riders organised their own code of conduct to mitigate the conditions they were being made to endure. Naturally, though, all systems of ethics are open to question, especially when fame and money are at stake. Cycling's unwritten rules are fun because they give us those moments when we sit forward on our armchairs and gasp at some ethical transgression, like attacking through the feed zone, even though it seems that we are increasingly seeing the rules ignored – racing a bike doesn't seem such a feat of endurance anymore or, more likely, perhaps the pressure on riders is so great that they feel the risk of getting a rollicking from their elders is worth it.

It would be convenient to call this a modern phenomenon, somehow connected to a broader breakdown in social respect, but in truth the code has always been flouted. Ask any ex-rider and they will invariably shrug a degree of ambivalence about when the 'rules' might be broken. Indeed, it was easier to get away with it when the media gaze wasn't as all-enveloping as it is today.

Having been forced out of the 1955 Tour de France because of surgery, a race that, given the course and the field, he would otherwise have expected to win, Louison Bobet came to the start of the 1957 Giro d'Italia in Milan fully intent on winning the maglia rosa. Italy's grand tour was one of the few gaps in his palmares, but he was no longer the supremely confident rider he had been in the early 50s and the race didn't go as he'd hoped.

Charly Gaul, smarting from his Tour de Luxembourg experience, also came to the Giro highly motivated. And he started strongly – stage 2 was a hilly 28-kilometre time trial, finishing uphill to Bosco Chiesanuova, just outside Verona. In front of 45,000 spectators Gaul won the stage, one minute and fifteen seconds ahead of fourth-placed Bobet, but thanks to being in a breakaway the day before, the Frenchman found himself in the maglia rosa by half a minute. A great start, but with twenty stages to go in a field dominated by Italian teams, it was much too soon to speculate on the outcome. Displaying over-confidence in his strength, and that of his team, Bobet decided to defend the jersey.

Over the next two weeks a draining battle ensued between Bobet's

Mercier – France squad and the Italian teams, led by Gastone Nencini, Nino Defilippis, Ercole Baldini and Pasquale Fornara. The racing was fast and unpredictable, and the tifosi played their part by shoving their compatriots up the hills, then throwing punches at the French riders. The strain of defending his lead began to take its toll on Bobet. He was nervy. He didn't sleep well. As usual it was his brother, Jean, who took the brunt. 'At Verona, however, Louison landed me with a crisis; he had started thinking,' Jean later wrote sardonically. 'At eleven o'clock in the evening he dragged me outside, saying, "I can't sleep and it'll do us good to walk."'

Like Gaul, Jean Bobet loved Italy. Unlike Gaul, indeed unlike most riders, he was an avid reader and never went to a stage race without a carefully selected pile of books. In the preceding days he had been reading up on Verona's history and had noted that the team hotel was close to the *Casa di Giulietta*, so he steered his overthinking brother towards the *Via Cappello* and, underneath Juliet's balcony, he gave Louison a summary of Shakespeare's play. The blood-soaked tragedy did little to calm Louison's nerves.[48]

In Loreto, a week into the race, Bobet announced to the press that he would not compete in that year's Tour de France because he would not be able to sufficiently recover from the Giro. Though his pride and the enmity he felt towards Gaul would never have allowed him to admit it, he had probably learnt a great deal from Gaul's weak transition from the 1956 Giro to the Tour de France. The news took everyone, including his brother, by surprise. Bobet was reproached by his team-mates, the French national selector and the usually loyal French media. One article accused him of 'cerebral fragility'.

After Bobet lost the pink jersey to Defilippis on stage 8 to Napoli, the Frenchman devised a plan with his Mercier – France team that showed the lengths he was prepared to go to in the name of victory. One of the unwritten rules of racing is that the peloton rides calmly through the feeding stations to allow everyone to grab a musette of food and drink. Once the food has been shoved into a jersey pocket, racing is resumed. It is essentially like agreeing that every factory worker has the right to a tea-break.

As in the 1955 Tour de France, Bobet ordered his team to attack. The Italian teams noticed that his team were carrying extra food in their pockets and were vigilant to the attack. Gaul, coasting along further back in the peloton, missed this nuance and was taken by surprise. A desperate chase ensued. Ernzer dragged Gaul along the valley roads so that when they arrived at the foot of the Radicofani climb he was only forty seconds behind his main rivals. Gaul swept past those Italians who had been trying to hang on to the French team, and by the summit he had caught Bobet and Géminiani. Whether any words of reprimand were exchanged isn't known.

Bobet had to wait until the long stage 12 time trial at Forte dei Marmi, on the Ligurian coast, to take the maglia rosa back. Gaul also put in a strong performance and was hovering behind Bobet at fifty-five seconds, with the biggest mountain stages yet to come.

The next day's stage, from Marmi to Genoa, had only one major climb, the Passo del Bracco. Seeing Gaul as the principal threat to their leader and knowing of his susceptibility to attacks on the flatter roads, the Mercier – France team launched a surprise offensive. Gaul was two minutes behind when the race hit the Bracco climb, but by the top he was able to draw alongside the Frenchman, pat him on the shoulder and say, 'It is no use running away. As you can see I'm still King of the Mountains.'[39] Bobet relinquished the maglia rosa the next day, allowing his team-mate Antonin Rolland into a breakaway and into the lead of the race.

Stage 15, from Saint-Vincent to the fortified Swiss hill-top town of Sion, marked the start of the decisive part of the race. The stage was short – only 134 kilometres – and took the peloton up the fearsome Grand-Saint-Bernard climb. The French were worried about Charly. The way he had nullified their attacks with apparent ease showed he was on his best climbing form. If he attacked Bobet with all his force on the Grand-Saint-Bernard, the Giro could slip beyond Lousion's grip. The only tactic open to them was a repeat of what they'd already tried; an early attack to put Charly under pressure before the road headed upwards. As soon as the race rolled out of its first neutralised kilometres, the French attacked. By 27 kilometres, Bobet, Rolland and Nencini had one minute and twenty seconds on Gaul. It was not enough. On the first ramps of the Saint-Bernard, Gaul counter-attacked and began picking off all the groups of riders spread across the road. He caught the leaders, waited for a short time, then put in a merciless acceleration. Bobet didn't even try to stay with him. At the summit Gaul led by one minute and thirty seconds, but on the descent, on broken and gravel-strewn roads, he punctured and the others caught him. They stayed together into Sion where Bobet sprinted to a stage win ahead of Nencini and Gaul. Bobet moved back into the maglia rosa, with the Italian at fifteen seconds and the Luxembourger at fifty-five seconds. It was clear that the Giro would be decided between these three.

The yo-yo battle continued the next day, the final day in the Alps, to Campo dei Fiori, just outside Varese. After some tentative early moves by the French team, a large breakaway with no threat to Gaul's or Bobet's position was allowed to go clear. Behind, the peloton called a temporary truce as they endured cold rain showers and poorly surfaced mountain roads. According to Jean Bobet, as the finishing climb grew closer, 'Gaul, excited as always by the bad weather, started gesticulating and twitching, unable to keep still. I shared my concern with my friend Marcel Ernzer, Gaul's team-mate and confidante, and the good Marcel replied: "You know, Jean, everyone's twitchy today and Charly gets like that more than anyone when there's a war on."'[30] Not the most reassuring reply from Jean's perspective.

The Campo dei Fiori is a short, steep climb, but after hundreds of kilometres riding tempo in the peloton, in cold conditions, the sudden exertion was particularly brutal. The foot of the climb was packed with spectators, leaving only a narrow path for the riders. Charly put himself in a good position and without warning he shot out of the front of the group. The French team scrambled to keep their leader close, but Gaul was too strong. One by one he reeled in the members of the early breakaway group. By the finish only one man, Alfredo Sabbadin, eluded him. Gaul finished second and took a usefully big chunk of time over his rivals. Behind there was an unfolding controversy. Initially, Bobet and Nencini rode together to limit their losses. At one corner Bobet was a few metres off the back of Nencini's wheel; at the next corner the Italian was out of sight. Bobet was baffled – he had not changed his rhythm or blown up. The French technical director, following in a team car and standing up through the sun-roof, later explained that Nencini had been shoved by so many spectators that he was catapulted up the climb, away from Bobet, who, being French, had of course received no shoves at all. At the top of the climb Nencini finished only eleven seconds ahead of Bobet, but the French team, sure that Nencini would otherwise have finished behind Bobet, put in a complaint and Nencini received a twenty-second penalty.

The French riders were furious. At dinner that evening Géminiani fumed about how he was dropped by Italian riders getting pushed by spectators, while other spectators tried to drag him backwards. 'I demand reimbursement from Italian social security for my pump,' Géminiani told his team-mates, 'which I had to break over the head of an idiot who grabbed my saddle.'[31] Big Gem's tale made his comrades laugh, though the bitterness lingered.

As the race came to its rest day on the shores of Lake Como, Gaul was in pink, fifty-six seconds ahead of Nencini and one minute and seventeen seconds ahead of Bobet. With three stages in the Dolomites, then a flat run-in to Milan, the race was Gaul's to lose. As on any other rest day he had a massage, did a short easy spin with his team-mates, then spoke to the press. While the journalists and fans could never wholeheartedly predict what Gaul might do next – they had learnt that much – there was an expectation of more attacks from the maglia rosa in the coming days. Perhaps something spectacular was about to happen, just as it had a year ago in the snow. Here, Charly made a significant mistake. He told the press that the race was already won. Tomorrow, on Monte Bondone, he would decide just how much time to take on his rivals. Compared with the usual non-committal remarks that riders made in press conferences these were strong words. Bobet, himself a vain and arrogant man, took them as supremely vain and arrogant, and, after the humiliation on Campo dei Fiori, he was quick to anger.

The next morning the peloton rolled out of Como for the 242-kilometre stage to the scene of Gaul's greatest victory. He was in the maglia rosa and feeling good. The French team were looking for an excuse to work him over. The incident that followed started innocuously, but then escalated to such a point that it became one of the defining moments in Gaul's cycling career. Midway through the stage, Bobet and his whole team stopped by the roadside to relieve themselves. Nencini also stopped. Gaul rode past, then stopped a little farther on for the same reason. The French riders remounted and rode past Gaul, who made an indecent gesture at them with, as Raphaël Géminiani lyrically put it, 'his organ of virility'. It may have seemed a good idea at the time, but Charly Gaul was soon cursing his own bravado. Bobet shouted at Nencini and his own team to ride hard. Géminiani powered through to the front, shouting 'We'll show you a pee-pee party, ma chéri!'[52]

Gaul gave chase and held the gap at a few seconds for a while, but without team firepower and with few friends in the peloton, his fate was sealed. After a furious chase for 100 kilometres through the valleys, Gaul cracked on the climb to Monte Bondone. A year earlier, he had soloed through the snow on this mountain to a legendary stage win and the maglia rosa. Now, he would lose more than eight minutes to Bobet, putting him out of contention. One can only imagine the stream of bile that must have spewed from his lips that evening. He swore revenge, telling Bobet the next day, 'Remember, I was a butcher. I know how to use a knife. I will bleed you all. I will open your stomach.'[33]

Bobet knew that Gaul had worked in a slaughterhouse in Luxembourg before turning professional, though it is not known how seriously he took the threat. Gaul's ire was further fuelled when he found out that other members of the peloton had been calling him 'Cher Pi-Pi', a neat pun which translates as 'Dear Pee' and 'Costly Pee'.

The next morning, on a 199-kilometre stage from Trento to Levico Terme, Gaul was intent on revenge. Bobet was now sitting second overall, just nineteen seconds behind Nencini. On the Passo Rolle descent, Nencini punctured, changed a wheel, then took stupefying risks downhill to bridge back to Bobet and the other leaders. Nencini was the fastest descender of his day; it would be Nencini that Roger Rivière was trying to follow in the 1960 Tour de France when the French star crashed on the descent of the Col de Perjuret, breaking his back and ending his career.

On the brink of the biggest result of his career, Nencini must have thought his race was cursed when he punctured again. Bobet and Géminiani didn't wait, seeing an opportunity to take back those nineteen seconds. Nencini changed his wheel and started chasing, then saw ahead the familiar red and white Faema-Guerra jersey, worn by a small rider spinning the pedals with his characteristic ease. It was Gaul, who had dropped back from the Bobet group to pace Nencini back to them. Gaul's knives, that famous day, were his legs.

Not only did Gaul bring Nencini up to the group, he also clipped off at the finish to win the stage. Nencini's lead was safe and, with the two remaining stages over less arduous terrain, he was able to bring home the win for his Chlorodont team and, more importantly, for Italy. Bobet finished in second, still trailing by those tantalising nineteen seconds. Ercole Baldini was third, almost six minutes back, and in fourth was defending champion Gaul.

Despite winning the Giro and the 1960 Tour de France, Nencini never quite became a household name. Early in his career, the raw talent of this man from Barberino di Mugello, near Florence, was recognised by Fausto Coppi and Fiorenzo Magni. He was known for his integrity and stubbornness, and for his Tuscan pride. On the bike, he was a strong all-arounder. In the 1960 Tour he won overall without winning any stages, but, one might argue, the crash of favourite Rivière, an excellent time trialist who was poised to attack Nencini's lead a few days later in the stage 19 race against the clock, has become the defining memory of the contest.

Not that Nencini seems to have been too worried about his level of celebrity. He lived by his principles, raced hard, smoked a few cigarettes, drank some red wine every evening and enjoyed the romantic benefits of being a pro cyclist. After retirement he took up painting, opened a bike shop and spent time with his family, until he died of cancer at the age of forty-nine. Compared with the egoism and spitefulness of the bigger stars around him, Nencini was humble and modest, but he wasn't stupid. When it suited him, Bobet was his ally; the next day, Gaul was his friend. If the 1957 Giro d'Italia is remembered for an indecent gesture at the roadside, it was Nencini who took the winner's trophy home to Tuscany.

With Learco Guerra (centre) and Federico Bahamontes

Stage 12

BEER AND CABBAGES

While Nencini celebrated his unexpected victory and Louison Bobet went home to Brittany to stew, Charly prepared for the Tour de France. Physically he was in great shape and, unlike 1956, this year's route was difficult enough to give him a strong chance – if only he could get to the mountains in touch with the leaders. Along with Bahamontes and the young French hope Jacques Anquetil, who had broken the hour record earlier in the year, Gaul was favourite for the race. The mental battle of the Giro, especially the humiliation of the Monte Bondone stage, had been draining, but he had finished the race with good legs and, when he arrived in Nantes for the usual pre-Tour interviews and cursory medical check, Charly was in good spirits. Again, though, his team was weak. Two Portuguese, one German and one Briton, Brian Robinson, joined forces with six Luxembourgers to make up the Luxembourg Mixed team. In the weeks before the Tour Gaul had requested to join the Dutch team – on what grounds is not clear – and was firmly refused by the UCI.

After the speculation, the awkward television appearances, the careful interviews with reporters, the riders were happy to depart from Nantes on the morning of 27 June. The first stage took them north to Granville and was a predictable affair, won in a sprint by the Frenchman André Darrigade. Gaul finished comfortably in the main group.

The first day had been hot and sunny, and much of the talk in the peloton was about the developing heatwave. A handful of riders were happy with temperatures over 30 degrees Celsius, but most were anxious. Racing for six or seven hours under a blazing mid-summer sun could undo even the fittest rider. In Granville the next morning, the riders prepared for another furnace-like day. Willy Kemp put cabbage leaves under his cotton cap – a time-honoured practice supposed to keep the head cool. Charly was messing about with ice, sharing jokes with reporters, but underneath his humour and bravado, there was real concern. He detested riding in very hot conditions and here, on the plains of northern France, there would be no shade and no cool altitude.

Once a breakaway of thirteen riders had escaped, the peloton settled in for the long ride north. Around them the journalists, team managers and mechanics lolled about in cars, shirtless. Dozens of bottles of water were handed up to the riders and either consumed greedily or poured over heads. The Tour's official doctor, Dr Dumas, was alerted that Charly Gaul was at the back of the peloton and not looking good.

Charly, with Marcel Ernzer and Willy Kemp alongside him, was indeed suffering. For many kilometres his senses had become dull, exhaustion flooding his body. Now his head was throbbing, he was slowing down, muttering about giving up this awful job, about going to live in the countryside with Georgette . . .

Ernzer and Kemp tried to focus him on pedalling. It will pass, they told him. Kemp gave him a segment of orange to suck on, but it only gave Charly nausea. Dr Dumas gave him some pills, which seemed to relieve his misery for a time. Kemp repeatedly went back to Nicolas Frantz's team car to get fresh bottles, pouring them down the neck of his stricken leader. Charly stared longingly at the verge of the road – one of those long, straight featureless roads that characterise northern France. 'I just want to lie down in the grass and go to sleep,' he said. 'Get me a beer,' Gaul instructed Kemp, and his domestique duly returned a few minutes later with an open can. Gaul took three sips and was promptly sick.[54]

'I give up,' he said. Gaul pulled over to the side of the road, but Ernzer wouldn't accept defeat so easily. He coaxed Charly back on to his bike and they pedalled onwards. In the next village a spectator threw a bucket of ice-cold water into Gaul's face, which revived him briefly. Even suffering from heatstroke Gaul pedalled with his famed suppleness.

Twenty kilometres later Gaul and the four riders with him got a time-check; they were thirty minutes behind the peloton. That year the Tour organisers had tightened the time limit rule to 8% of the winner's time, which meant that Gaul's group would likely be eliminated from the race, even if they were to reach Caen.

Antoine Blondin wrote in *L'Équipe*: 'Each carries his cross: that of Charly Gaul, in gold and tiny, dangles around his neck. It seemed to weigh a hundred kilos and he dragged his head in a pendulum nod in which he said no and no each pedal stroke.'[55]

Again, Charly stopped. 'It's over,' he said and this time no one argued. Gaul, Kemp and Ernzer climbed into the broom wagon, which had been crawling along behind them for two hours. In the wagon, Charly gazed silently at the road ahead. The Swiss rider Alcide Vaucher was now the last rider on the road and he was refusing to give up, despite being hopelessly outside the time limit. The broom wagon was obliged to stay behind him all the way to Caen if necessary. Gaul stared at the rider ahead. 'The bicycle is over for me,'[56] he said, although no one else in the wagon believed he was serious, it was just the trauma of exiting the Tour; the shame of the broom wagon. The other riders in the van saw Gaul's pain and tried to sympathise. The French rider, Raymond Elena, related how

Géminiani had told one of Elena's team-mates how formidable Gaul had been at the Giro and that Gaul could be unbeatable at the Tour. Charly just looked at Elena, then slowly turned his head back to the road ahead and the battling, deluded Vaucher.

In Caen the riders retrieved their bikes from the roof of the broom wagon and rolled to their hotels, where a disappointed Nicolas Frantz was waiting, along with a gaggle of journalists who wanted to hear what had gone so wrong. In a feature in the British *Sporting Cyclist* magazine in February 1959, René de Latour described the moment Charly appeared: 'When Gaul arrived at the hotel he looked alert enough. He wore a sad grin but made no great drama of his misfortunes. "It is this heat that kills me," he whispered. "I just can't stand it. Give me all the rain or cold in the world and I'll master it. But this heat . . ."'[57]

Within a few hours Gaul and his team-mates were on a train to Paris, then home to Luxembourg.

It was Charly Gaul's *annus horribilis*. In 1957 he should have won the Giro and he was capable of winning the Tour de France, but he came away with neither. While Jacques Anquetil set about winning the first of his five Tours, Charly was fishing in Luxembourg with Willy Kemp.

Also in 1957, Roland Barthes published *Mythologies*, although it seems unlikely Gaul was aware that he was mentioned in the book. Barthes' description of Gaul's erratic performances – 'sometimes the gods inhabit him and he works wonders; sometimes the gods abandon him, his *leap* is exhausted'[58] – may have been true in previous years, but seems a little harsh when applied to 1957. Crashes and untimely punctures are misfortunes that happen to any rider, heatstroke, too, and even one of Kemp's cabbage leaves probably wouldn't have reduced Charly's susceptibility to the sun.

He is not, of course, blameless. In the Giro d'Italia he was in a winning position. His superiority on the climbs was clear and Bobet was a bundle of raw nerves. All Gaul needed to do was to get to Monte Bondone with his rivals and launch an attack. Then the race would have been truly over. His mistake was to put his confidence into words, public words. Whether or not he intended to goad Bobet, that was the perception. Gaul should have known that Bobet would not laugh it off; he was too vain. By that stage of his career Bobet was a complete racer – he could see multiple ways to attack his rivals, even morally dubious ones such as attacking when the race leader has stopped to relieve himself. Perhaps, by 1957, Bobet was past caring about the moral nuances of cycling.

Gaul's arrogance was as much a weakness as his inability to endure hot weather. Being a shy, inarticulate man, when that arrogance bubbled up to the surface it manifested itself in language that was coarse and usually personal. Cycling is a tough sport. Its combatants may be skinny, but they are hard men and a thick streak of machismo has always run through it, plus a good deal of money rests on races like the Tour de France. Most professional cyclists in the 1950s were working-class men; cycling was their route to a financially comfortable life and they weren't going to let that be taken away from them without a fight. By 1957, Gaul already felt that the Luxembourg public were turning away from him. His failures that year brought criticism rather than sympathy. Some felt that his new-found wealth, which manifested itself in the fast cars he drove around Luxembourg City, was alienating him from his fans. It is a familiar story – working-class boy finds a sporting route out of poverty, is cheered on his ascent, then turned on by the people he has (materially) left behind.

In January 1958 the journalist Roger Bastide came to Bettembourg to interview Charly. The resulting three-page spread appeared in the *L'Équipe*, complete with photographs of Charly 'relaxing' at home with Georgette and Willy Kemp. There is a photo of Charly outside his spacious, newly built house, with his equally spacious new car. Another photo shows him flicking through his record collection.

Bastide was charmed by Georgette when she opened the door to him, describing her outfit and hairstyle at some length. She clearly felt the need to defend Charly from the start, telling the reporter how nice and gentle he is, and had been so ever since she met him aged sixteen. The interview itself was tense, with Bastide probing on the failures of 1957 and Charly bristling. Bastide, for balance, also spoke to Kemp and, separately, to Jang Goldschmidt. The latter's view of his prodigy confirmed what others have said about his early career – that his immaturity and avarice was short-sighted: 'I think Charly is very self-interested. His love of money made him make some mistakes. You have to know how to reward the services rendered.'[59] Considering Charly invited Bastide into his home, the headline of the resulting article seems a little unkind: 'Charly Gaul – Irresolute, but greedy, changing and yet tenacious. Even in his country, he is no longer an idol.'

If his weaknesses hollowed out his popularity during his career, over the following half-century they have come to play a significant role in his myth. The Luxembourgish academic Frank Wilhelm, who has written extensively about Charly Gaul's career says,

'The rider whom we admired for his astounding exploits could also frighten us with his graceless days, his abandonments, his depression. It is this vulnerable, deeply human side of the Angel of the Mountain that seems to me to be the very basis of the myth that he unwittingly engendered, without perhaps realising it. It is this side, precisely, which is missing in certain champions of today . . . rationalist, perfectionist and for that a little icy.'[60]

THE DONKEY

After fishing trips and contract races filled the remainder of the 1957 season, Gaul set about getting a solid winter's preparation for the following year. Now he had two motivations – revenge on Louison Bobet and the French team, and proving himself at the Tour de France.

His winter training did not differ from previous years, but there seemed to be a revitalised attitude in his racing. On 1 December he won a major cyclo-cross race in Kopstal, a small town not far from where he had grown up, beating the new German sensation, Rolf Wolfshohl. Another victory came in Hesperingen in early January, where Wolfshohl pushed Gaul all the way to the finishing straight, but could not overcome the Luxembourger in the sprint. The 20-year-old German – who would go on to take three Cyclo-cross World Championship titles – took his revenge a week later in the snowy Grand Prix Necchi race in Dommeldange. However, while Wolfshohl and the other 'cross specialists were building up to the World Championships in France at the end of February, Gaul's attention reverted to road racing and on 5 February he drove south to the Italian riviera town of Varazze for a training camp with his Faema team.

Today's early season races have proliferated to Spain, Majorca and the Middle East, made accessible by easy air travel. In the 1950s the focal point of the early road racing season was the south of France. Overlooking Toulon, Mont Faron is a rocky crag with a peak at 584 metres. Throughout the 50s and 60s a hill-climb time trial up the narrow and steep road to the summit was the trad-itional curtain-raiser for the European road racing season. The race attracted a good field and had many notable winners in Anquetil, Simpson, Bahamontes and Poulidor, yet retained a relaxed atmos-phere. Performing well on Mont Faron showed you had good form, but it was still very early in the season. In the 1958 edition Gaul gave a glimpse of just how good his winter training had been when he won the hill climb by twenty-three seconds.

The good legs then took him to victories in the second edition of the Grand Prix de la Forteresse, where he beat Louison Bobet in front of an enthusiastic home crowd, and another mountain time trial, this time at Sallanches in the French Alps. By April his form started to wane, as was natural. At the Flèche Wallonne, a semi-classic that finished in Liège after 235 hilly kilometres through the Belgian Ardennes, he came in tenth. These races were valuable training ahead of his third Giro d'Italia, which started in Milan on 18 May.

Gaul's attitude to that 1958 Giro was rather circumspect. He was ever-present at the front of the race, especially in the mountains, yet he held back from his trademark blistering attacks and there were to be no solo heroics either. In the first serious uphill finish at the wonderfully named Superga, Gaul and Bahamontes went head to head and the Luxembourger had to concede to the Spaniard, losing twenty-seven seconds in the final few kilometres. Even on stage 5, from Turin to Mondovì, run off in heavy rain over a series of moun-tain passes, Gaul held back, staying in the group of favourites while an opportunist breakaway by Alfredo Sabbadin took the honours. Gaul's only stage victory came in the 12-kilometre uphill time trial in San Marino, a useful morale-booster for Gaul and something to cheer about for his fans, but not enough to give him the maglia rosa. The Italian Ercole Baldini proved the revelation of that Giro, dominating the other time trials and climbing well enough to protect his overall lead. After the first day in the Dolomites Gaul resigned himself to defending third place overall. In Milan Baldini took the overall victory from Jean Brankaert and Gaul, just over six minutes behind. Happily for Gaul, the man he beat to the final podium spot was Louison Bobet.

That year's Giro d'Italia seemed to be an experiment of sorts. For the first time in his career Gaul showed the kind of consistency that (so prevailing opinion stated) is required to win a grand tour. He was only briefly outside the top ten and he managed to avoid disasters – crashes, punctures, illness and sudden physical collapses. Was this just good luck or evidence of a new maturity in his approach? Gaul and his team were tight-lipped. His reward was a third place, and for the first time in three years he came out of the Giro feeling physically strong and – arguably more important – mentally fresh, ready for the true challenge of the year.

After his dominant victory in the 1957 Tour de France, Jacques Anquetil was the natural leader of the French team twelve months later. Still only twenty-four, Anquetil was not yet the darling of the French public, although their allegiances were beginning to shift from Louison Bobet, who was clearly past his best. Anquetil, a builder's son from Normandy who had beaten Fausto Coppi's hour record in 1956, was good-looking, blond and a stylish presence, both on and off the bike. In June 1958 he had yet to fully win the affections of cycling fans (arguably he never did due to his rather aloof demeanour), but he – or at least his entourage – was in a strong position to influence the selection of the French team that would support him at the Tour.

Understandably, Anquetil did not want to share team leadership with Bobet, but the French team selector Marcel Bidot insisted that the three-time champion be in the team as deselection would have meant humiliation for the man who had restored French national pride only a few years earlier. Instead, the man to pay the price for Anquetil's rising star was Raphaël Géminiani. Despite his years of loyal work for Bobet and the fact that he was in the best form of his life, Big Gem (or Top Gun as he was also known in the peloton) was bumped off the national team and forced to ride for the regional Centre-Midi team.

At 33 he knew that this Tour would be one of his last chances to compete for victory rather than work for someone else, so Géminiani was furious and, when Géminiani was furious, he didn't just quietly seethe or issue muttered threats like Charly Gaul did. In the 1952 Tour de France, after a stage to Namur in Belgium, his compatriot and team-mate Jean Robic decided to hold a press conference in the bath. Robic told the bemused reporters gathered around his tub how clever he had been during the stage, feigning exhaustion so as not to do any work, which had forced Géminiani to wear himself out, to the detriment of Gem's long-term chances of success. Hearing this from the back of the room, Géminiani pushed past the reporters and held Robic under the bath water until their team manager pulled him off. A year later his temper surfaced again at the Tour de France when he and Bobet had a row at the dinner table, ending in Géminiani tipping his plate of food over Bobet's head. Bobet reportedly left the table crying.

In 1958, excluded from the national squad, Géminiani's fury burnt deep. On the start line in Brussels he was intent on revenge and his first attack came before the race had even begun. As the riders were presented to the Belgian fans and the press, Géminiani was 'given' a donkey. Wearing a tracksuit and slippers, with his new team around him, a grinning Géminiani picked up the startled animal. One of the photographers asked him what he would call his new pet. 'Marcel,' replied Géminiani, 'because he is stupid and stubborn.'

There were no selection problems for Charly Gaul. Indeed, six months earlier he had received the pleasing news that, for the first time, his Luxembourg team was to be combined with a Dutch team. The 1958 Tour was experimenting with twelve-man teams and its director, Jacques Goddet, recognising that neither the Netherlands nor Luxembourg could field that many riders, had facilitated a negotiation between the two cycling federations. An agreement was reached and ratified by the UCI; the Dutch were to have eight riders, Luxembourg four. The Dutch Federation insisted on their man Kees Pellenaers being the technical director of the team, but Pellenaers resigned his position after a row about which Dutch riders should be selected. The Luxembourg Cycling Federation seized their opportunity, bringing in Jang Goldschmidt as technical director. At thirty-four, Goldschmidt was the youngest technical director in the race.

Gaul still had his Luxembourgish domestiques – Marcel Ernzer, Aldo Bolzan and Jempy Schmitz – but now he could also call on the services of eight solid Dutch riders. Lacking a star of their own, the Dutch rouleurs were happy to protect Gaul on the flat, windy days, to bring him food and bottles, and to chase down breakaways if required. The principal objective for the team was to get Charly to the Pyrénées with as little time lost as possible. There were no language problems, or riders with their own agenda, problems that had held the Luxembourg team back in the past. In another sign that he was maturing in his outlook, or at least listening to those around him, Gaul agreed to share his winnings with the Dutch riders.

That year's Tour started from the site of the Brussels World's Fair on 26 June, with the newly built Atomium building, a Modernist tribute to scientific progress, as backdrop. Ahead of the riders lay twenty-four stages totalling 4319 kilometres, circumnavigating the country in an anti-clockwise direction. For reasons no one could quite fathom, the organisers had omitted rest days altogether – the previous year there had been two. Perhaps there were just too many French towns eager to pay for a stage start or finish. To further ratchet up the pressure on the riders, live television pictures were to be broadcast on mountain stages for the first time.

After a Belgian first stage to Ghent, predictably won by French sprinter André Darrigade, the race headed west to Dunkirk, dipped south to Versailles, then resumed its journey across Normandy and into Brittany. The stage from Versailles to Caen was the first skirmish in the overall classification battle. The French team split the peloton with a blistering attack. Gaul and the Belgian Jean Brankaert lost two minutes. Anquetil was pleased with the gap, but cautioned against celebrating too early. Two minutes was nothing compared with what Gaul could take back in the mountains, he said.

The following day, along the northern coast of Brittany to Saint-Brieuc, Big Gem began to take his revenge on the French team. His aggression forced clear a group of twelve riders. Perhaps not seeing their former team-mate as a danger, or tired from the previous day, the French team did not mount a serious chase. The breakaway finished ten minutes ahead of the peloton. Having already won the stage to Dunkirk, Gaul's Dutch team-mate Gerrit Voorting now took the yellow jersey. Even more pleasing for Gaul were the signs of sour relations between the French national and regional teams; it was possible that Géminiani could become an unlikely ally in Gaul's bid to dethrone Anquetil.

Two days later, after Brian Robinson won Britain's first ever Tour de France stage in Brest (Robinson crossed the line in second after being pushed into the barriers by Arigo Padovan, but the race jury relegated Padovan and awarded Robinson the stage win), the riders landed in the town of Châteaulin for the first major rendezvous in the overall race, a 46-kilometre time trial. Everyone was waiting for a sign of Anquetil's form. In the team hotel the night before Jang Goldschmidt expressed his confidence that Charly would take victory. Charly himself wasn't so sure and bet Goldschmidt a bottle of sparkling wine that he would lose. The next morning, despite the heavy rain, Gaul still felt nervous and unsure of himself. Even as he was tightening his toe-straps on the start line, Goldschmidt was talking quietly in his ear, telling him how much the course suited him, how strong he was.[61]

For the first kilometre Gaul struggled to get into his rhythm, but fortunately the climb was soon upon him and he started to stamp more meaningfully on the pedals. Over the top he was already bringing into sight those who had started in front of him. From the car behind, Goldschmidt yelled words of encouragement at key moments. After that initial climb the course kept rolling on roads not dissimilar to those he grew up on in Luxembourg. Confidence and motivation high, he caught rider after rider, astonishing the roadside fans with the way he launched himself at the small hills along the route. In the final kilometres he began to think victory might be possible. Back in Châteaulin he flew across the line to record one hour, seven minutes and twelve seconds. It was fast, but would it be enough?

Jang Goldschmidt had managed to commandeer a nearby farm-house for his rider to have a shower and a rest. As Charly pulled on dry clothes he told Goldschmidt that he had felt so good he could have ridden for another hundred kilometres. Charly then sat astride an upstairs window, his leg dangling out, wearing a dressing gown and a sheepish grin while he waited for the rest of the field to arrive. He watched rider after rider come in, all failing to beat his mark. Then came Anquetil, time trial specialist and hour record holder. He crossed the line seven seconds short. A narrow margin, but a big psychological blow to the defending champion's confidence and Gaul received another sixty seconds as a bonus for winning the stage.

Anquetil, amazed, told the press that he never would have expected
Gaul to beat him, quickly adding that he had not been aware of how
close the race was, to imply that it was a lack of information rather
than poor legs that lost him the race. Raphaël Géminiani and Bobet
finished over two minutes down. Charly had comprehensively lost
his bet.

That evening as the team celebrated at dinner (Voorting had
narrowly held on to the yellow jersey to make it a doubly successful
day), those who knew Charly noticed a change in his attitude. He
was surprised by the victory, but took from it a huge amount of
confidence. Despite performing well in time trials in the past, he
had always doubted his abilities in the discipline. Now he had beaten
Jacques Anquetil, and everyone else, on a long time trial in the Tour.
In one day, his friend Mersch observed, he went from doubt to near-
arrogance. Not that anyone minded – you have to be arrogant to win
the Tour de France.

After the adrenaline of victory it was back to work the next day,
with another long stage south, from Quimper to Saint-Nazaire, to
shake out the legs. The peloton were grateful for a tailwind and the
return of sunshine. A large breakaway group was allowed some
freedom and only when it had got twelve minutes ahead did the
peloton wake up and put in a half-hearted chase. Voorting, spinning
along in yellow, was sanguine about losing his jersey. He'd expected
to lose the lead in Châteaulin, so an extra day was a bonus. That the
Dutch-Luxembourg team chose not to expend energy on a chase to
save the maillot jaune was a further signal that they had only one
objective in the race – to get Gaul into that same jersey.

The next three days were relatively uneventful. Goddet wrote
that the anticipated 'war on Gaul did not arrive.' Géminiani showed
himself near the front of the race, but seemed to be biding his time
for a revenge served cold, and the French national team did not
put in the kind of ambush attacks that had hurt Gaul in the past.

Tactics under Anquetil's leadership were more tentative than under Bobet's and, although the latter was still in the team, he held back from dictating the plans. The race, and Charly, arrived safely at the foot of the Pyrénées.

The first day in the mountains from Dax to Pau crossed the Col d'Aubisque. André Darrigade started the day in the yellow jersey, but he knew it would be his last. Gleeful to be back in the mountains, Bahamontes attacked on the Aubisque and danced away from the group of favourites. Again Gaul demonstrated his singularity of purpose by not chasing Bahamontes or points in the King of the Mountains prize and instead he patiently watched his rivals. On the upper slopes of the Aubisque he put in a series of short surges to test those around him. Bobet and Anquetil cracked first. Of the big-name French riders, Raphaël Géminiani stayed closest to Gaul; at the snowbound summit Big Gem was a minute down on Gaul. The descent to Pau nullified all the work the climbers had done. With the road covered in slush and stones, the lightweight climbers and those who weren't prepared to risk their lives took the descent slowly. Bahamontes and Gaul were reeled in and the group of favourites reformed. Two inconsequential riders slipped away.

In Pau, Anquetil's team-mate Louis Bergaud took the stage and Raphaël Géminiani took over the race lead, with the Italian Vito Favero only three seconds behind him. For the big man from Clermont-Ferrand this was a joyous moment; in his eleventh Tour de France, it was Géminiani's first yellow jersey. Marcel Bidot and his donkey were beginning to get worried, but – as the cliché goes – it was still a long way to Paris. That evening in Pau, Gaul was happy with the day's work. He had not gained any time, but his attacks on the Aubisque had showed him who had good legs and who didn't. And, if nothing else, he'd survived two punctures earlier in the day and that treacherous descent. Sometimes in the Tour, just surviving the day is a triumph.

The following day's stage was short, at only 129 kilometres, but punchy, taking the race over the Col d'Aspin and the Col de Peyresourde. Bahamontes attacked once more, jumping clear on the Col d'Aspin, and this time his attack stuck. With an impressive solo ride he rode to victory in Luchon nearly two minutes clear of a chasing group led home by Favero. The Italian's second place earned him a thirty-second bonus, taking him into the yellow jersey.

The Pyrénées had given the spectators some interesting skirmishes, but the race had failed to fully ignite. Bahamontes, in his element and close to the border of his homeland, was the star. Behind him the other favourites had been watchful and careful. By not taking the initiative, the French opened themselves up to speculations about weakness and division as a team. In reality, though, they were, like Gaul, simply playing a waiting game. The two Pyrenean stages were not hard enough to make a big difference – the first had only one major climb, the second was too short to create big time gaps – and ahead of them all was an appointment with a far more frightening climb.

In the Mont Ventoux time-trial, Tour de France, 1958

Stage 14

RETURN TO VENTOUX

Provence in July is rarely cool. Heat lies thickly across the landscape. Luxurious for the holidaymaker, malevolent for a professional cyclist. Charly never really adapted to riding in the heat, though it could also be said that he never really tried. He could have gone to training camps in southern Europe, he could have tried to learn techniques from those who liked the heat, but in his stubbornness – and with a hint of the martyr – he just endured it.

After three flat stages across the south of France, during which no ambushes were laid and with no significant changes to the general classification, the Tour returned to Mont Ventoux. Stage 18 was to be a 21-kilometre mountain time trial, climbing the Giant of Provence. The riders were nervous. Many, including Gaul, had suffered on Ventoux in 1955, when Kübler lost his mind and Malléjac nearly died. The intense effort of a mountain time trial combined with the asphyxiating heat of the upper slopes was a daunting prospect.

When the Tour de France route had been presented to the press in Paris the previous autumn, the organisers said that this stage was a gift from them to Charly Gaul.[62] If so, it was a gift that the recipient was rather ambivalent about. While it offered him an opportunity to take time on his rivals, Gaul had a healthy respect for the mountain. This was a different sort of climb to any other in bike racing. It seemed to have its own will. Like a mythical beast, Ventoux could not be tamed by any human. Anger the beast and it might unleash devastating powers upon you – cauldron-like heat, winds so strong they could whip rocks across the road and a gradient that seemed to steepen with every hairpin bend. At best, the lonely climber could hope to strike a deal with the beast to pass across its domain unscathed.

Anquetil had been dreading this day since the announcement of the route, grumbling about the unfairness of the fact that he was inevitably going to lose a hill climb to Gaul, then be criticised by the newspapers for losing a time trial. Now it was here. At noon, the first rider set off from Bédoin. One by one, spaced at intervals of two minutes, they left the start gate. Only the purest climbers showed any enthusiasm. Charly sat quietly in the shade of a tree, waiting for his allotted time. He had warmed up his legs, tested the gears on his bike. He knew how to manage his nerves and now he just wanted to get going.

In the first kilometres he was relieved to find that his legs still felt as good as they had earlier in the Tour, and the encouragement of the crowd, plus the shouts of Goldschmidt from the car behind, spurred him on. Knowing this could be a defining moment in the career of their hero, a small army of fans had travelled from Luxembourg to cheer him on. They joined 100,000 other spectators, who all paid for the privilege of trudging up the mountain. Soon, however, any sense of exhilaration evaporated into the heat. This was to be a duel. Charly against the mountain. He was on his own. No one could help him. Goldschmidt and the eighteen-year-old team mechanic, Mario Ottusi, stopped shouting. The crowd – two thick bands of people – were immaterial. Charly had tunnel vision. He feared the mountain and he feared the heat. Later, he told friends that his mind was empty but for the repeated phrase: 'Keep pedalling, keep pedalling, do not faint.'

On the bare upper slopes he caught and passed Bobet, who had started two minutes before him, but even this symbolic revenge did not give him a boost. His suffering was too much; defeating a rival was nothing compared with the battle he was having with the mountain. Two kilometres from the finish he nearly crumbled. Up there he was utterly alone – no crowds, no shade, no trees, just a frail being exposed to the elements. His legs felt weak, his mind was gripped by fear of physical collapse and (the heat can do strange things to the mind) he felt enormously hungry. Now his maturity and experience played their part. Still telling himself to just keep pedalling, he backed off the pace a little. Then, approaching the final kilometre, he could see the fans at the finish, calling his name and beckoning him home. Goldschmidt, too, came back to life and began yelling from the car. The pain was nearly over. Charly stamped on the pedals, emptying himself now, and with his last scraps of energy sprinted up the finishing straight.

With a time of one hour, two minutes and nine seconds, Gaul won the stage. Bahamontes came closest, just thirty-one seconds back. Further down the standings the time gaps were considerable. Anquetil lost four minutes on Gaul. Bobet and Géminiani, five. Gaul's time was so fast that it stood as the record for a Mont Ventoux ascent for forty-one years, until broken by Jonathan Vaughters in the 1999 Dauphiné. Vaughters time trialled up the mountain in fifty-six minutes and fifty seconds, and Gaul was there to see his record fall. Interviewed later that year he said, 'I am glad that my record fell. That's what records are there for – to be beaten. The road is pretty similar, slightly better surfaced, but the equipment is better, too. That is bound to have an effect. I can remember that, like today, it was very hot and I was worried about that because I didn't respond well to the heat.'[63]

Predictably, the newspapers eulogised Gaul's performance. The *Miroir des Sports* said, 'The Luxembourger climbed a step above his main opponents. They seemed heavy compared to his airy ease. Bobet was as if rooted to the spot when he overtook him; Anquetil seemed motionless and Géminiani, grimacing, gave the impression of suffering a thousand deaths. And the whole caravan went into ecstasies, to marvel at the grace of this angel or this elf who dominated Mont Ventoux as if playing.'

Gaul himself was more humble. He was exhausted, happy with the result, relieved to have overcome the beast, but he knew he had been close to a terrible collapse, plus he had not yet won the Tour de France. Indeed, that evening he was still nearly four minutes behind Géminiani, who had retaken the yellow jersey.

Alongside his snowy ride to Monte Bondone, the 1958 Ventoux stage was to become one of the defining moments in Gaul's career. His climbing prowess was such that simply winning on a major mountain climb wasn't sufficiently memorable; for Gaul it had to have an epic quality, something of defying the gods. He ascended through fire and ice when others bowed down, and this more than anything is the foundation of his myth.

After epic battles with the gods, it was back to more prosaic obstacles the next day. The stage from Carpentras to Gap was neither long nor especially mountainous – its climbs were the foothills of the Alps, rather than the high mountains themselves. The weather was warm again, but that morning Charly declared himself fit and ready for whatever lay ahead. Checking his bike before the race, he discovered a cut on his front tyre. This was strange because the tyres were new, never ridden. Charly asked Ottusi to change the tyre and set off with the rest of the peloton, thinking nothing more of it.

But 50 kilometres into the stage, with the peloton peacefully rolling along, Charly noticed that his front chainring was loose. He stopped at the roadside. Marcel Ernzer handed over his bike, telling Charly that he had to get back into the peloton as quickly as possible. Ernzer waited for the team car to deliver him a new bike. In the team car a horrified Ottusi set about fixing the loose nuts on Charly's chainring, so he could give the bike back. What on earth was going on? Ottusi had thoroughly checked Gaul's bike earlier that morning.

Meanwhile, Géminiani, that veteran of the French national team with all its underhand tactics of the past, saw an opportunity. He launched a blistering attack, taking with him Vito Favero, and the Belgian pair, Jef Planckaert and Jan Adriaensens. Jacques Anquetil and Gastone Nencini saw the danger of this move and jumped across. Bobet, however, stayed in the second group, watching for Charly's return. Just before the Col de Perty Charly did make it back into Bobet's group, but he was still riding Ernzer's bike, which was too big for him. Worse, he was alone, without team-mates, completely isolated.

The reason for Bobet not going ahead with Anquetil was unclear, though Charly grew convinced that he had deliberately stayed behind to disrupt Charly's chase. This theory seemed to be borne out when Bobet, seeing that Ernzer was still behind the group, raised the pace just enough to keep Ernzer from making it back, while not reducing the gap to the leading group.

Furious, Charly yelled at Goldschmidt, 'Where is Marcel?' The answer was insistent: 'He's coming, he's coming.' Eventually, though, Goldschmidt had to admit to his embattled leader that Marcel was not coming. He was stuck in the peloton, falling further behind. 'I must have my own bike,' Charly shouted back. Ottusi had repaired the loose chainring and now got the bike ready for a swift change, but every time Charly slowed down at the back of the group, Bobet and his allies sprinted away, forcing Charly to abort the bike change. It was clear that stopping would mean losing contact with the group and losing even more time. On the first ramps of the Col de Perty, Bobet was then impertinent enough to suggest that Charly could now use his climbing ability to attack and chase after Géminiani and Anquetil. Charly, understandably, told him to fuck off.

On the descent of the second climb of the day, the Col de Foureyssasse, tired and riding on an unfamiliar bike, Charly crashed, banging his knee and hip. Totally dispirited as he examined his wounds with a pained expression, it seemed for a minute or two that he would pull out of the race. Goldschmidt coaxed him back on to his bike and persuaded him to get to the stage finish at least. When he did get there, battered and bitterly disappointed, he was more than ten minutes behind.

The previous evening, after her husband's victory atop Mont Ventoux, Georgette had called Charly to tell him that she would meet him in Gap the next day. Described by *L'Équipe* in the typical language of the day as a 'beautiful blonde in a white blouse and navy skirt' Georgette watched Charly struggling in, well behind Anquetil. Amid the post-finish melee she kissed her husband and put on a brave smile, but a tear also rolled down her cheek. 'It is a shame,' she told reporters after Charly had ridden off to get changed, 'but everything can change tomorrow. The race is so changeable. And Charly is very good.'[64]

That evening few others shared Georgette's belief in her husband. All the heroism on Mont Ventoux seemed to have been undone by a mechanical problem and the cruel tactics of professional bike racing. That evening in Gap the team tried to dissect how Charly had been left so isolated on what should have been a relatively straightforward stage. More than fifteen minutes down overall now, it looked like Charly's bid to win the Tour would have to wait yet another year.

Among Gaul's entourage there was talk of sabotage, particularly from Ernzer. The cut in the tyre, discovered that morning, was the width of a knife blade. The tyre was brand new, so the incision could not have come from being ridden on a previous stage. And was it a coincidence that Gaul's chainring bolts also came loose, just over an hour into the stage? No specific accusations were made, though, and the speculation was likely fuelled by the bitterness that Ernzer felt about how the day had played out. His friend had been betrayed in the most cynical way and, after giving up his bike, Ernzer had been unable to shepherd Charly back to the front of the race as he would have wished. It must also have been hard for Ernzer to accept that Gaul was so hated by the French team that they would break all the unwritten rules of professional cycling to make sure he lost. As the race headed for the high Alps, the Dutch-Luxembourg team was bowed.

On paper the next day's stage, from Gap to Briançon, looked to be where the Tour de France would be decided. As on previous occasions, the Col d'Izoard lay before the fast descent into Briançon. This was Bobet's terrain, where his own legend had been forged. Could Anquetil now take over the mantle?

On the Col du Vars an early group of escapees, none of whom mattered in the overall classification, got away. Of the favourites only Bahamontes gave chase. Anquetil, Favero, Bobet and Nencini watched each other. Gaul was still feeling stiff in his hip and knee from yesterday's crash and was content to follow the others. This was to be one of Bahamontes's famous long solo breaks; he caught and passed the early leaders on the Izoard and dived into Briançon to take the stage. By staying with the group of favourites Gaul managed to climb two places overall, to sixth, but he was still over sixteen minutes down. Ahead lay just three serious stages before the usual processional ride into Paris: 237 kilometres across the Alps from Briançon to Aix-les-Bains, a flat stage into Besançon, then a 75-kilometre time trial around the city of Dijon. The Tour de France was nearly over. For Charly to come back from a sixteen-minute deficit was impossible.

Stage 15

OUT OF THE DARKNESS

'The weather greatly affected Charly,' said his friend and team-mate Willy Kemp. 'The heat didn't make him sick, but it did put him to sleep. His attitude changed from moment to moment as soon as it looked like rain. In rain and storms he started singing and whistling, which finished off more than one opponent.'[65]

Gaul's love for cold and wet conditions has often been celebrated, but rarely analysed. His doctor, Dr René Bürger, advanced the theory – now debunked by science but still held by some endurance athletes – that there is more oxygen in the air when it rains and that Gaul's ability to process that oxygen was greater than his rivals. We'll never know the physiology of Gaul's performances, but even if he did have a small natural advantage over his rivals, it does not explain the attitude Kemp describes. Most cyclists endure the extreme weather conditions their sport puts them through – heat, cold, rain, strong winds. It is part of the sport. Aspiring cyclists grow up outdoors, learning how to protect themselves from the elements and how to minimise the suffering. In Gaul's day there were cabbage leaves for intense heat, and for wet days, cumbersome plasticky jackets that were neither rainproof nor breathable, meaning the rider got soaked in sweat and, eventually, soaked by the rain. Most riders chose to discard their rain jackets once the racing got serious, if they bothered wearing them at all. Géminiani famously dismissed rain jackets as being 'for tourists', preferring instead to smother his body with a mixture of olive oil and a heat rub called Algipan.[66] Even today, technical cycling clothing will only keep you dry for so long; ride for long enough in the rain and sooner or later you will be wet. Then you get cold and the body begins to ask why it's being put through this.

Growing up in Luxembourg, though, Gaul had more need for a rain jacket than for cabbage leaves. With around 180 days of rain per annum (compared with, for example, 125 days in Bobet's Brittany) Gaul's home town is one of the wetter parts of northern Europe. If we assume that Gaul and Louison Bobet put in roughly the same number of training hours on the bike, then the former could have ridden nearly a third more in the rain. The performance of elite athletes in specific conditions is dependent upon how much practice they have in those conditions.

So, Gaul was used to riding in the cold and wet, certainly more so than riders like Bahamontes, who came from Toledo, just south of Madrid. For Gaul a rainy day was akin to a home advantage. His other big advantage was his personality. As an introvert Gaul drew strength, even happiness, from being on his own.

In modern English the word stoicism has come to mean withstanding pain or trouble without complaint or showing emotion. Gaul's physiological advantage, gained from regularly riding in the rain, became a psychological advantage. At the foot of Monte Bondone, despite being wet and freezing, he was cheerful enough to joke with his team manager and the velodrome owner at the roadside. This was not just the good humour of someone about to take a big victory. In a sport that demands a high degree of stoicism from its competitors, Gaul seems to have had a much higher threshold for suffering and – crucially – suffering alone, so much so that it verged on masochistic. Perhaps he derived a certain amount of pleasure from putting himself through it.

While others grumbled along in the peloton, he was alone in the hills, under the deluge, showing the superiority of his will-power. Based on his arguments with other riders, such as Bobet, it is tempting to think that he was constantly cursing others, bitter and proud, lauding his own toughness, but this is too simplistic and it does not chime with the fuller picture of the man. In later life, whenever he spoke of his most momentous days on the bike, he referred mainly to the more mundane aspects – his equipment, the course, the weather. Aside from race tactics, his mind was largely on the job at hand – riding as fast as possible.

Part of being a professional cyclist is being able to concentrate on the physical act of pedalling – total focus – but riding alone for many hours through the heavy rain, thinking only of the road, of his body, of gear ratios and food intake was a focus of a higher level. Faced with such conditions, most riders huddle in groups, staying close to their colleagues for moral support. Not Charly. At such moments he could go into hyperfocus, the psychological phenomenon in which individuals lose themselves in a task for an extended period, being totally absorbed to the point that they are unaware of anything else around them. Hyperfocus is a relatively new idea and is closely linked with attention deficit hyperactivity disorder (ADHD). One hypothesis is that hyperfocus is a kind of psychological legacy of our ancient past as hunter-gatherers. The hunter needed hyperfocus in order to perform when out hunting, but the rest of the time he could be distracted, restless, impatient. American psychotherapist Thom Hartmann posits that those with ADHD can be characterised as hunters in a farmers' society.[67]

Academic study into the prevalence of ADHD in elite athletes is limited and there are no scientific analyses of the links between

ADHD and professional cycling. What has been proven, however, is that exercise helps to alleviate some of the symptoms of ADHD. Only in the past few years have psychologists begun to identify that ADHD is significantly higher among elite athletes than the general population.[68] Partly this could be because sport is attractive to young people with ADHD – compared with studying at school and college, sport gives them an intense physical outlet, a fast-moving and challenging environment. It is important, too, that sport provides a structured environment, enabling young people with ADHD to focus and perform. The 1989 Tour de France winner, Greg LeMond, self-diagnosed his own ADHD many years after his cycling career had ended. It was, he said, revelatory: 'ADD [attention deficit disorder – an older term for ADHD] was just getting out in the news and the teachers recommended for one of my kids to go see a doctor for ADD. While they were getting examined I read this twenty-question questionnaire and I had every one of them, and now I look back and I laugh about it, because it explains a lot of stuff.'[69]

Some commentators have pointed out that many of the symptoms of ADHD – usually perceived negatively – prove to be assets in elite sport. American psychiatrist Dale Archer, writing in *Forbes* in 2014, noted, '. . . there are many strengths linked to ADHD which, leveraged properly, can lead to success in multiple areas of life. These advantages can include: an ability to multitask, a propensity to thrive in situations of chaos, creativity, non-linear thinking, an adventurous spirit, resilience, high energy, risk taking, calm under pressure, and the capacity for hyper focus in something that fascinates you.'[70]

All of these qualities are helpful to a man trying to win a bike race, at least the way Charly Gaul liked to win bike races. There is no evidence that Charly Gaul had ADHD; indeed the condition was only formally recognised by most European countries in the late

1980s. Taking into account the way he conducted himself within the peloton and with the press, we might speculate that Gaul was mildly autistic. The symptoms of autism and ADHD are frequently hard to separate.[71] Getting anxious about social situations, finding it hard to understand what others are thinking or feeling, seeming blunt or rude without intending to – these are all symptoms of autism in adults. One could also argue that they are also just symptoms of introversion.

We have seen Gaul's behaviour so know something of his personality. It was integral to his success and to his later troubles. We can, of course, only speculate about his mental health. We cannot diagnose him posthumously. And yet, like LeMond, looking at Charly Gaul from this perspective does explain a great deal. Individuals with ADHD are easily bored (flat Tour stages) and thrive on pressure, crisis and deadlines (mountain stages deep into a grand tour); individuals with ADHD are prescribed medical-grade amphetamines to raise their dopamine levels and improve focus; individuals with ADHD have a stronger than average fear of failure, and use that fear to motivate themselves to extraordinary acts (Monte Bondone, Aix-les-Bains).

Zeno, the founder of the ancient Greek stoic school of philosophy, would have been proud of Gaul's resilience and stoicism. Gaul did not, however, quite detach himself from the baubles of society's approval as Zeno would have wanted. He enjoyed the money and status that success brought. Like many professional athletes from a working-class background who make a lot of money, he liked to spend his salary on fast cars and expensive Italian clothes. And when the fame turned darker, when he felt the public turn against him, it broke his heart.

François Mersch was part of Charly's entourage during the 1958 Tour de France and witnessed the highs and lows of his friend's emotions. He later wrote: 'After the so-called Black Monday Charly's morale sunk so low that in the first hours after arriving at Gap he was crushed, convinced that finally he had lost the Tour. And yet he didn't abandon; there was something still in his subconscious telling him the race could take another turn.'[72]

The journalist Roger Frankeur, one of the few that Charly trusted and confided in, came to Charly's hotel room that Monday evening and at the end of their conversation, as he turned to leave, Frankeur said to Charly, 'If I understand the way you're looking at me Charly, then I think you haven't yet admitted defeat. Isn't there something else you can do?'[73]

These were powerful words for Charly, kindling hope in the face of defeat. He respected Frankeur's opinion, and the Frenchman, in turn, seemed to have a knack of saying the right thing at the right time. After the infamous stage to Monte Bondone in the 1956 Giro, Frankeur had found Gaul and Ernzer shivering in a mountain chalet near the finish, still in sodden racing clothing. He told Charly that he'd catch a cold if he stayed there any longer, gave Charly his coat and helped him over to the Faema team car, where he exhorted the driver to take his riders to their hotel in Trento and get them into warm baths. As the car pulled away, Frankeur shouted, 'You'll win tomorrow, Charly!'[74]

However, for all the positive words of those around him, there was plenty of criticism, too. The French press delighted in what they saw as Charly's defeat at the hands of Bobet and Anquetil. It didn't matter that Big Gem was in the yellow jersey – a Frenchman was leading the race, with another (Anquetil) in third. Once out of the Alps, a long time trial at Dijon lay in store and Vito Favero, sandwiched in second place, was only four minutes ahead of Anquetil. Could a French one-two in Paris be possible?

Gaul felt humiliated by the press coverage, and suspected, too, that many of the riders in the peloton were laughing at him. The 'sabotage' of his bike, the cynical French tactics, Bobet's ironic words on the Col de Porte and now the newspapers making fun of him – it all fuelled a growing rage.

Celebrating his 1958 Tour de France victory, Parc des Princes, Paris

Stage 16

THE DELUGE

It is the morning of Wednesday 16 July. Charly wakes up in a hotel room in Briançon. He has slept well and feels rested and refreshed. Such a feeling at the end of a grand tour is enough in itself to make a professional cyclist happy. He finds, too, when he gets out of bed, that his knee is no longer hurting, which makes him even more cheerful. Marcel Ernzer is pleased to see his friend in such high spirits as they head down to breakfast. Indeed, Charly is in such a good mood that his team-mates notice it, too, and later, at the end of one of the most famous days in Tour de France history, they will remark on it to journalists.

Charly's friend François Mersch describes the scene.[75] Jang Goldschmidt comes into the room and takes Charly out to the hotel terrace. At an altitude of 1,300 metres, Briançon is the highest city in France. The terrace affords the two men a stunning Alpine panorama. Already the sun is high and warm. It looks like it will be a lovely day. They gaze out to the high peaks.

'Look Charly,' says Jang. 'Do you see that haze over the Lautaret and the Galibier? Today is the day for you.'

'That's fog,' Charly replies.

'I think it is rain,' says Jang. 'Today you'll have the conditions you love. That's if your knee doesn't hold you back.'

'My knee is fine.'

At this, Jang turns to Charly, beaming. 'Charly, you have to win this stage! Five passes and probably some rain. You have to attack.'

But Charly is more cautious. 'For the time being, the sun is still shining, but I'll definitely try something today.'

Whatever the weather, he knows it is going to be a long day in the saddle: 219 kilometres with a quintet of climbs: the Lautaret, Luitel, Porte, Cucheron and Granier. These are not the most famous climbs in the Tour. They do not have the dramatic landscape of the Col d'Izoard or Mont Ventoux, nor the history of the Col du Tourmalet, but the riders know that none are easy and the cumulative effect of five in one day, coming after nearly 4,000 kilometres of hard-fought racing, is significant.

The Tour, a travelling village, converges on the central square in Briançon, a fortified town that reminds Charly of his own capital city. As the sun rises the heat becomes thick. A rumour goes around the peloton that the locals are saying there will be thunderstorms. Perhaps Jang was right. Or lucky. At nine Charly swings his leg over his bike and makes his way to the start line. The peloton rolls out of town and takes the valley road, north-west, towards the Col du Lautaret. Under the shadow of jagged peaks on both sides, the road gradually begins to climb.

A peculiar apathy seems to spread through the riders. They are hot, exhausted from three weeks of racing without a rest day, mindful of the seven hours ahead. Besides, no one is seriously thinking that Géminiani will not still be wearing the yellow jersey in Aix-les-Bains. Top Gun has nearly four minutes on Favero and nearly eight minutes on Anquetil. Even with the long time trial to Dijon, it seems highly unlikely Anquetil will make that sort of time back. No one else is in contention. Gaul is in sixth place, at sixteen minutes. Bahamontes is one place behind, at nineteen minutes. Even if the two climbers attack, it would only be for the consolation of a stage win. In the middle of the peloton, Charly bides his time.

The Lautaret is a slow grind of a climb. The peloton takes it slowly, still loosening their legs. Near the top, at the Café de la Ferme, a junction gives the option of heading up to the Col du Galibier, one of the Tour's truly iconic (and toughest) climbs. Today, though, the race is sticking to the lower pass. As he crosses the summit Charly feels the first drops of rain on his face. By the time they reach Le Bourg-d'Oisans, where the first feeding station is located, it is raining hard. A small group of opportunists have gone clear, hunting for intermediate prizes and the – albeit remote – possibility of competing for the stage.

The climb of Luitel Chamrousse is approaching. Goldschmidt yells at Charly to attack at the bottom of the climb, knowing that his rider has good legs, that conditions are perfect, but that Charly also needs a bit of confidence to make the leap. Ernzer understands this too. As the peloton approaches the climb he rides alongside his leader and leans close.

'Are you going to attack?' he says.

'Certainly,' says Charly.

'I can see that you are in good form,' says Ernzer. 'Today you will accomplish a great feat.'

Now Charly believes in himself. Today he will win the stage in such a way that it will be remembered for years – a way that will silence his critics. He thinks of the scores he has to settle. His anger surges, usefully.

On the narrow, twisting lane that sends the riders hurtling into the Luitel climb, Gaul finds himself next to Bobet. He can't help himself.

'You're ready, Monsieur Bobet? I'll give you a chance. I'll attack on the climb and I'll even tell you which hairpin. You want to win the Tour more than I do? Easy. Come with me. I've told you what you need to know.'

Bobet, however, does not rise to the taunt. Just gives a wry smile. 'You better go without me,' he says. 'I'm not feeling too good today.'

So Charly attacks. He sprints, out of the saddle, through the first section of the climb, and when he does take a moment to look behind he can see a group of four, including Bahamontes, attempting to give chase. Bobet is some distance further back, riding alongside Géminiani and Anquetil. Charly is both heartened and slightly disappointed. Do the French not consider him a serious threat? Are they really that indifferent to his attack? He stamps on the pedals again. The road carves through a dense pine forest; a longer, steeper version of the Croix de Chaubouret, the climb that he utilised to win the Circuit des Six Provinces in 1954, the climb which earned him his nickname. When Charly next looks over his shoulder he finds Bahamontes clinging to his back wheel, his face contorted with the effort of doing so. This is good, he thinks. Always useful to have another rider to share the workload, especially in the valleys, but when he next looks back to check on Bahamontes, the Spaniard is gone. Charly is alone again. At the summit Goldschmidt pulls alongside and yells that he has three minutes on Anquetil and five minutes on Géminiani. Everyone else is scattered across the mountainside.

On the descent, plunging through the rain and fog, Charly punctures. Ottusi changes the wheel quickly and Jang pushes him off again. Having descended into Grenoble, he picks up more food from a feeding station, which is a relief because his jersey pockets are empty and on such long, cold days he needs a lot of fuel. He stuffs some sugar cubes into his mouth and the rest into his pockets. Two riders from the early breakaway group have latched on to Charly's wheel now, but they must know their time at the front will end. Within a few minutes of starting the Col de Porte climb, Charly dances away from them. He has with him only the Netherlands/Luxembourg team car, one police motorcyclist and one press photographer riding pillion on a motorcycle. The other photographers have chosen to stay behind to capture the battle between Anquetil and Géminiani; the battle – they think – for the yellow jersey.

Goldschmidt, clad in a raincoat with a white cotton cap turned backwards on his head, just like his star rider, has assumed his usual position, standing on the passenger seat and leaning over the windscreen of the white convertible Citroen 203. The rain is so heavy that water runs down his face.

'You're alone in the front now, Charly,' Goldschmidt shouts.

Charly just nods. He knows that. He also knows that now is the time to concentrate, to go deep into his reserves to extend his lead. The Porte is a second category climb, difficult enough that anyone suffering can lose a lot of time. He keeps spinning the pedals, weaving his bike through the mud and stones being washed on to the road. Like him, the groups of spectators who have braved the weather to stand up here among the dripping trees have their faces lowered to the ground. The rain is a deluge now. Whenever Charly tries to eat something he gets a mouthful of rainwater, too, and has to spit the food out. The spectators, having even less information about the race than Charly, are amazed to see him out in front alone. As he approaches they peer at him. Is it really Charly Gaul? Is that possible?

Over the top of the Porte, down the descent, with streams rushing down the road with him, and on to the next climb. Here, on the Cucheron, Charly is relentless. His style is still faultless. Near the top he sprints hard, out of the saddle, as if chased by demons. Or Louison Bobet. The landscape around him – if he had the time to admire it – is an exaggerated version of the Ardennes: deep river valleys, forested hills, verdant meadows. It would be pretty on a different day. Now, though, an early afternoon in July, it is nearly dark. The headlights from the Tour's vehicles beam yellow across glistening roads and thunder rolls through the low cloud.

The last climb of the day, the Col du Granier, lies close to Aix-les-Bains. Charly sets about the climb with no loss of power or will. A lone journalist on a motorbike comes past and raises ten fingers. What on earth does that mean? The journalist shouts, 'To Géminiani.' Ten minutes to Gem? Can that really be true? Further up the climb another journalist speeds past, trying to get to the finish line before Charly, shouting 'Twelve minutes!' as he does so. Goldschmidt confirms: 'Charly tonight you could be in yellow!'

Astonished as he is, Charly has little time to think about what must be happening behind. At the summit of the Granier he forces down a ham sandwich then drops into Aix-les-Bains, taking as many risks as he dares. If he is close to the jersey, as crazy as that seems, every second is vital. Through the darkness, through sheets of rain and deep puddles on the road, he ploughs along the final few flat kilometres. Thousands of spectators line the streets, huddled under umbrellas. The finish line is barely visible in the darkness and the chaos of spectators, vehicles, race officials. Charly sprints towards the photographers' flashlights and comes to a juddering halt. He shakes the raindrops from his body, then the ever-present, ever-protective Goldschmidt drapes a coat around his shoulders.

'Are you tired Charly?' Jang asks.

'No, I feel fine,' his man replies.

The throng of journalists press in on Charly, but Goldschmidt is a burly, no-nonsense sort of man and he guides Charly away, fending off tape recorders pushed into his rider's face. Georgette is close, too, her petite frame dwarfed by one of her husband's rain jackets, her blonde hair under a sodden white headscarf. Now she can finally give her Charly the victor's kiss that she had first intended at Gap.

'In the rain, Charly has been able to give his all,' she tells *L'Équipe*, and adds, laughing, 'And to think, when he is at home he doesn't want to go out shooting when it rains!'

For Anquetil, Géminiani and Bobet, that day's storm was both literal and figurative. Although Anquetil dropped Géminiani on the

Luitel, and looked to be setting himself up for a crack at taking yellow, he began to fade on the Porte. Géminiani had broken a pedal earlier on the climb, but now began to find his rhythm. Helped by the Italian duo Favero and Nencini, and fuelled by anger that the French national team seemed to be riding against him, which in turn was helping Gaul, Big Gem caught and passed Anquetil. On the Cucheron Anquetil was able to limit the damage, staying within a minute of the Géminiani group. One climb later, under the apocalyptic storm, both riders fell apart. Big Gem was dropped by his domestique Jean Dotto and began to cry. The 1956 winner, Walkowiak, had to physically push Anquetil to the top. Anquetil later said, 'From the first hairpins of the Col de Porte, I thought I'd gone mad. I was diminished by 60 per cent. Why? I wish I knew. It was as if my lungs were stuffed with cotton wool. I was suffocating.'[76]

By the top of the climb Géminiani was twelve minutes down, Anquetil was seventeen and Bobet was even further back, and things didn't get any better for Anquetil. By the finish line he was a broken man, coughing up blood, exhausted and some twenty-three minutes down. Bobet finished three minutes ahead of him. The Italian Favero had cleverly used the French in-fighting to jump up the overall standings. By finishing third, ten minutes behind Gaul, Favero became the new yellow jersey, though his lead over Géminiani was a mere thirty-nine seconds.

When he finished, Géminiani fell into the arms of former winner, André Leducq. British writer Charlie Woods relates how Leducq 'prevailed upon the driver of the Le Parisien car to give them a lift to the hotel. In the back seat the exhausted rider began to sob on Leducq's shoulder, but after a while pulled himself together. "What about Favero?" he enquired. "Thirty-nine seconds up," came the ready reply. This cheered him; he might have lost the yellow jersey, but he could get it back in the time trial. Victory was still possible. Emboldened, Gem enquired of Gaul, "How much did Charly pull back – was it five minutes?" There was an uneasy silence. Everyone stared ahead. Eventually it fell to the photographer in the front seat to mutter the dreadful news out of the side of his mouth: "Fourteen minutes, fifteen including the bonus . . ." A pitiful moan tore through the Big Gem's stricken frame and he buried his head once more in Leducq's shoulder. "That's it then," he said, sniffing pathetically, "Charly's won the Tour."[77]

As Géminiani was leaving for his hotel, Bobet was talking to reporters and he was in a reflective mood. 'Charly is a rider like no other . . . Margins like that do not occur nowadays, they hark back to the pre-war Tours, which makes me think that Charly's one of those old-style road men mysteriously reborn amongst us. Either that or he's not human at all, more of a supernatural being.'[78]

Gaul's ride through the rain-soaked Chartreuse Mountains stunned the race. L'Équipe portrayed it as a massacre. Jacques Goddet wrote: 'Angel or star, we do not know what word to use . . . Let's agree that Charly Gaul does not belong to our kind, having found a way, after so much waste and mess, to get back into position to win the Tour from which, in the morning, he was excluded.'[79]

Three stages remained and Gaul was not actually leading the race – he was still one minute and seven seconds behind Favero – but everyone was convinced that the Tour was his. With such form and confidence, who could hope to beat him in the time trial from Besançon to Dijon? Anquetil, on paper the best time triallist in the race, had been beaten by Gaul in both previous tests at Châteaulin and Ventoux. Besides, seven hours in the cold Alpine rain made the Frenchman ill. He was taken to hospital in Besançon, where chest X-rays diagnosed a pulmonary infection. Dr Dumas and Bidot told him that he would have to leave the race.

'What a disaster, I'm taking everyone into this disaster,' Anquetil groaned. Despairing of his situation and not totally lucid, Anquetil thought it was the end of his career; that he would end up as a kind of young invalid, shuffling pathetically around his home village. That night in his hospital bed, 'He had a nightmare about a phantom cyclist made up of raindrops. Every time Anquetil approached him, he would melt away, only to reappear several hundred yards further down the road. He had, of course, the sad face and modest smile of Charly Gaul.'[80]

On the flatter roads from Aix-les-Bains to Besançon, with sunny weather restored, the remaining riders were grateful for a chance to recover. Gaul was attentive to possible attacks, but none of the contenders for the overall classification tried anything. The time trial was now the only rendezvous. Resting, as far as that is possible on a 237-kilometre stage, was the top priority.

After the doubts and nerves of the previous time trials, Gaul and his entourage were remarkably relaxed before the start in Besançon. Goldschmidt laughed and joked with Gaul and Ottusi. Charly declared himself ready for the 71 kilometres ahead. He started calmly. It was another day of fine weather and the course was not as challenging as Châteaulin. Spinning through the pastoral landscape of forests and fields east of Dijon, a few kilometres in he began to find his rhythm, upping the pace and crouching low over the handlebars. On the road ahead he could see the support vehicles for another rider. Goldschmidt shouted encouragement from the car. After nearly an hour on the bike, Gaul sprinted up a small hill then, dropping down the other side, saw the Frenchman, Bergaud, ahead and another rider, Dotto. Two scalps at the same time. Gaul swept past both riders, but then heard a terrible sound. A photographer's motorbike swerved and collided with both Dotto and Bergaud, bringing all three down in a tangle of metal and bodies. The crash was made worse by the speed at which they were travelling. Badly injured, Dotto left the race in an ambulance. It was a narrow escape for Gaul and perhaps a sign that luck was finally on his side.

In Dijon he raced into the stadium in front of thousands of fans, stopping the clock at one hour, forty minutes and twenty-seven seconds. Goldschmidt gave him a bottle of water and a cold sponge. A bouquet of flowers was thrust into his hands, even though he had not yet officially won, and microphones were held under his nose. There was a short, tense wait, Charly surrounded by his supporters, all sweating under the hot sun. Then the result was announced. Charly had won the stage and taken the yellow jersey. Goldschmidt was overjoyed, Charly's supporters celebrated and everyone wanted to shake Charly's hand. Charly himself, though, felt more relieved than anything else. As the yellow jersey was pulled over his shoulders, for the first time in his career, he was smiling, yet François Mersch noted, too, the distant look in his friend's eyes. This was the moment that Charly had long dreamt of, the culmination of a decade of work. Did it feel just a little unreal?

While today's Tour de France final stage is processional and mercifully short, starting in mid-afternoon in a suburb of Paris, in the 1950s the final stage was more ambiguous in its purpose. Due to the nature of the Parisian cityscape, the stage usually ended in a sprint, but the unwritten rule that no one attacked the yellow jersey was considerably blurrier than it is today.

The evening before his coronation, Charly's elation turned to anxiety. Stage 24, the final stage, would take the peloton from Dijon to the Parc des Princes, a velodrome in the 16th arrondissement – some 320 kilometres. Mario Ottusi was bawled out when he suggested that tomorrow might be an easy day in which he could relax a little. 'The Tour is not over,' Charly shouted. 'It won't be over until the day I stop riding. And even then, I will have to tweak my bike so that I can hang it in my living room.'[81]

With Favero and Géminiani both more than three minutes behind, it seemed unlikely that Gaul's position would be threatened by a serious attack. Had Géminiani been racing on the French national team with Bobet, Gaul might have had cause to worry about an early ambush, but Géminiani's South-West regional team was not strong enough to cause that degree of chaos, even if their leader had instructed it. Géminiani knew the Tour was lost in Aix-les-Bains, when the *Le Parisien* photographer had told him Gaul's winning margin. He had grieved then, comforted by André Leducq, and by the last stage he was beginning to come to terms with third place.

So if racing tactics did not threaten Gaul, the principal worry was a crash or a mechanical at an inopportune moment. For the first hour of the stage, Gaul, now so easy for the crowds to spot in his bright yellow jersey, rode very cautiously and deliberately. His team-mates surrounded him, constantly checking he was safe and well-supplied with food and water.

After the first feeding station a press photographer on a motorbike came alongside Charly and called out for a photo of the first three in the general classification. Favero and Géminiani rode on either side of Charly and put their arms over his shoulders. Charly grinned, for this was the moment that his rivals were finally admitting defeat for everyone to see. He had won the Tour de France, though there were still four more hours on the bike.

In the outskirts of Paris the speed picked up. Charly ordered his team to ride on the front and chase down anyone who tried to escape, no matter how far down on the overall classification they were. Two riders, Marcel Ernzer and Jempy Schmitz, stayed with Charly, a little further back in the line. These were nervous moments. A mechanical problem now could spell disaster. Favero would not be compelled to wait for him and the peloton was moving so fast that a chase back would be near-impossible. Finally, the flamme rouge was overhead. One kilometre to go. The peloton snaked into the grounds of the Parc des Princes and through a tunnel, bursting out into the sunlight and the cheers of an estimated 40,000 fans. Charly took the turns slowly, letting himself drift back in the group. The peloton streamed around the concrete banking, lining up for a big sprint to decide the stage winner. Ominously, even in those final moments of a three-week race and Charly's hard-earned victory, there was still time for tragedy.

As the sprinters wound up their biggest gears on the last half-lap of the track, the *secrétaire-général* of the velodrome, a seventy-year-old man called Constant Wouters, had spotted some photographers standing too close to the side of the finishing straight. Believing them to be a danger to the riders, Wouters ran across the grass to remonstrate with them, but by putting himself behind the photographers, Wouters did not see the oncoming riders and the oncoming riders did not see him. The photographers, all experienced at dodging sprinters in such situations, got out of the way. Wouters did not have time. André Darrigade, flying down the inside of the track towards a stage win, hit Wouters. Both men fell heavily. Darrigade was able to limp across the line and go to the medical room for treatment. Wouters was not so fortunate. He was rushed to hospital, where he died eleven days later.

Hearing of the severity of the accident, Charly made sure to find Darrigade and, as a token, give him one of his winner's bouquets. Speaking fifty years later, Darrigade remembered: 'Charly spoke rarely. Some said he was anti-social but with me he has always been perfectly friendly. I am thinking, for example, of the 1958 Tour de France, which he won. When I arrived at the Parc des Princes, I was in a good position to win the coveted final stage. But there the park gardener [Wouters, the velodrome's *secrétaire-général*], finding that the photographers were approaching too close to the track, wanted to push them aside. He stepped on to the track as I appeared. The collision was incredibly violent and the gardener lost his life. As for me, groggy, I received first aid in the infirmary. When I returned to the lawn of the Parc, I was pleasantly surprised to see Gaul come towards me and offer me his winner's bouquet, with which I did the lap of honour. That eased my grief and pain a little.'[82]

For Charly, there was one final twist to the day's racing. When he came to a halt in the Parc des Princes and handed his bike to Ottusi, they discovered a crack in his frame near the handlebar stem. Charly had ridden 320 kilometres from Dijon on a broken bike. If the crack had widened the front end of his bike would have disintegrated, sending him sprawling to the road, but this detail was soon swallowed up by the celebrations.

There were many laps of honour – on a different bike – with his loyal team-mates and the final yellow jersey was presented amid a huge crowd of dignitaries, friends and family, followed by hours of photographs and interviews. Georgette was there, though she hardly got a chance to speak to her husband. Charly's mother had not received an invitation to the ceremonies and some charming of the *gendarmes* by her niece, Maggy, was required to get Catherine to her son. The oddities of the official ceremony included Charly being given a kir royale cocktail and being kissed for the photographers by the famous prima ballerina Ludmilla Tchérina. Charly smiled bravely through it all, slightly dazed, but still looking boyish, cherubic, handsome. Among all the thousands of column inches that described Gaul's triumph, perhaps Robert Chapatte summed it up best: 'What more can be said? Charly won the Tour in the style of [Fausto] Coppi. In four key stages. Isn't that the biggest compliment?'[83]

Stage 17

ONE SINGLE DAY

The evening before the final stage to Paris, when thoughts turned to the traditional post-Tour parties, Gaul said that he just wanted to go and get a good night's sleep. A few days later, when faced with a punishing schedule of thirty criterium races throughout August (having shared his winnings with his team as promised, he felt obliged to sign up for the fee-paying races to cash in on his victory), Charly grumbled to a journalist that all that racing would not leave him much time to see his garden again, listen to his records, stroll around his house.

Taken out of context this comment could sound rather ungrateful, but it is just the honest thoughts of a true introvert, someone for whom being with others is draining. As well as the physical and mental challenge, the Tour de France can be a social challenge. The riders are always surrounded by others – managers, mechanics, soigneurs, journalists, photographers, doctors, race officials. To save money, the riders always share a room. Meals are taken as a team. Everywhere the riders go thousands of fans crowd in, trying to feel part of the experience. For a star rider, even before television and phone cameras became ubiquitous, the spotlight was constant. Being an introvert in such a setting must be doubly exhausting because there is such little space to be alone. Some have noted Charly's love of the evenings, when he could lie quietly in his hotel room and think, and little wonder, because from the moment he awoke on any given day, he would not have had a chance to be alone until the end of that day. Marcel Ernzer, with whom he shared a room, knew when to let his friend have some peace.

The post-Tour parties were functional rather than hedonistic. There was a reception in the Ajax football stadium in Amsterdam to celebrate the role of the Dutch riders on the team, a parade in Luxembourg City, and celebrations, too, in Gaul's home town of Bettembourg and at his cycling club UC Dippach.

At the end of the season, he was awarded the Trophée Edmond Gentil for the best rider of the year, the most prestigious award in cycling. The panel of judges, chaired by Jacques Goddet, chose Gaul over the Giro winner and World Champion, Ercole Baldini. And while his success in the Tour de France obliged him to attend more functions than ever before, Gaul did not break from his usual winter routine, still putting in a solid block of training combined with cyclo-cross racing. In the first months of 1959 his form was just as promising as it had been twelve months previously.

The forty-second Giro d'Italia started in Milan on 16 May 1959. The riders faced a total distance of 3,657 kilometres over twenty-two stages, but for this edition the organisers had tried to be innovative. At the time, the Giro was a long way behind the Tour de France in prestige. The latter was more international in its field and press coverage, and success there was more coveted by sponsors, so the Giro organisers decided to provoke a more dramatic race. The structure of the Tour de France, which had not changed much in decades, was to have a week or more of flat stages, taking the race from northern France down to either the Alps or the Pyrénées. This was inherently boring for fans because the star riders could hide in the peloton, letting the sprinters take the glory. A case in point was 1958, when Gaul had been anonymous for the first two weeks and only made his winning move with three stages to go. The Giro organisers changed things by moving the mountains to earlier in the race. They hoped that by doing so the favourites would be forced to show their cards early on, perhaps take the maglia rosa and then have to defend it for much longer, making for a more exciting race.

Gaul was now racing for EMI-Guerra, a variation of his former Faema team sponsored by the legendary record label. The riders and staff around Gaul remained the same. The principal change was the switch from Faema's famous red jersey to an equally distinctive blue and white striped jersey. As the reigning Tour de France champion, Gaul came to the Giro as joint favourite with Jacques Anquetil.

The Frenchman was encouraged by a route that included four time trials and tempted by the prestige of becoming the first French winner of the Giro, but he wasn't going to travel to Milan for the chance of prize money alone. Anquetil was as mercenary as any of the other top professionals of the era – he wanted some start money. Initially the organisers refused, saying that the prize money was attractive enough. Behind the scenes, however, a small army of marketing middle men were trying to find a way to pay Anquetil to fly south. Eventually, after a great number of telephone calls between Paris and Milan, a solution was found in the unlikely form of a new Italian brandy company called Fynsec, who wanted some advertising. Now, for a chunky fee, they could have their name emblazoned on Jacques Anquetil's chest. Anquetil and his team were happy to oblige, even if Anquetil was more of a whisky drinker. So 'Maître Jacques' arrived in Milan in good form, good finances and with a strong team. There were other strong contenders at the start, including the ever-present Gastone Nencini, but most journalists predicted a duel between Gaul and Anquetil.

The opening week lived up to the organisers' hopes. On the second day, a 22-kilometre time trial around Salsomaggiore Terme, Anquetil started as favourite. He decided to put a huge gear on his bike – fifty-two teeth on his front chainring and thirteen teeth on the smallest rear sprocket. Before the start, René de Latour inspected Anquetil's bike and noticed the gear. Seeing the journalist, Anquetil came over and swore him to secrecy. The gearing gamble paid off. Anquetil emerged as the strongest, averaging nearly 48 kilometres per hour, beating Ercole Baldini by thirty-nine seconds. Gaul was another minute behind, but was relaxed about losing time – there was a long way to go.

Gaul was also quick to retaliate. The following day's stage finished on the climb to Abetone, a ski resort in Tuscany. A group of twelve riders arrived at the climb in the lead, with Gaul and Anquetil in a second group. Anquetil's team was already depleted – Jean Graczyk was struggling with a stomach ache and André Darrigade injured. At the foot of the climb Gaul launched a stinging attack, riding across the gap to the front group, passing them and continuing alone to the stage win and the maglia rosa. That evening Gaul led the Giro by one minute and eight seconds from Belgian Rik Van Looy and one minute and twenty-seven seconds from Anquetil. The Frenchman was, as usual, quick to find an excuse: 'The fact is that I did not spot Gaul when he went. I am not used to seeing him in an EMI jersey. But it is of no importance, really. I even wonder if it is not better to see him as the race leader. Now he will have to fight to keep his jersey, not me.'[84]

The race proceeded south towards Rome, then Naples, and Charly's EMI team were kept busy chasing down attacks from the Italian teams that felt aggrieved at missing out on early glory and were no doubt getting pressure from their sponsors. At the end of the first week Charly had retained his overall lead, but it had been a tense few days. In Naples, Charly gave an interview to a journalist from *Le Miroir des Sports*: 'Here is Charly Gaul in front of a hearty green salad followed by a steak the size of two hands. Gaul eats diligently, with pleasure: it is always a good sign for me, appetite, he says, tackling the half chicken that follows the steak. Gaul is no longer the sullen boy that we have long known. He exudes the joy of living. His combativeness bursts everywhere, can be read in his shining eyes, expresses itself in his assured words. And yet I'm a little bored to ride so well and so early in the season, he says. it is almost too beautiful . . .'[85]

Gaul's objective for the 1959 season was to win both the Giro d'Italia and the Tour de France. The grand tour double has always been one of the most challenging and elusive feats in cycling. With the two races run in May and July respectively, it is hard to maintain winning form for the whole period; if the Tour was run in September, the riders could allow their condition to dip then build back up again. As Gaul tucked into his steak in that restaurant in Naples, only one rider, Fausto Coppi, had achieved the double. With both races now on his palmares, in different years, for Gaul, winning the double was a logical target – stretching stretching yet theoretically possible.

This is only a moment in time, one evening meal, analysed through the filter of a journalist's report, yet it tells us a great deal about the psychology of Gaul. There he was, leading the Giro d'Italia after a week of racing, in the form of his life, riding in an assured manner, and yet he was worrying about the next race. Underneath the swagger and the icy looks there was a patina of anxiety about Gaul. On the bike, and particularly going uphill, he lived in the moment, felt only the sensations of the road and his body, emptied his conscious mind. He was a hunter, focused, alert to his instincts and his surroundings. Off the bike, though, one senses that he worried a great deal.

The journalist probed Gaul on Anquetil's principal advantage: 'Isn't he superior to you on the flat, that is to say when it is necessary to escape and to exert oneself there sometimes for hours?' 'Yes,' said Charly, 'I'll still give him the right to take three minutes in the 51 kilometres of the last stage against the clock, Turin to Susa, and again because I do not intend to give myself fully. The Giro will be played in the Alpine stage Aosta to Courmayeur, because I do not even count on the Dolomites – too easy for my liking this year. But I know, I will be patient . . . like in the Tour last year.'

Stage 8, a mountain time trial on the slopes of Mount Vesuvius, offered him an opportunity to extend his lead as insurance against further losses in the flat Turin to Susa time trial. The road to the jagged crown of the volcano snakes back and forth across a wild landscape amid lush and, in places, charred vegetation, although at only 8 kilometres, the test was short but wickedly steep. As the rider placed second on the overall classification, Anquetil would start one minute ahead of Gaul, a situation that made the Frenchman nervous. He knew how much the climb suited Gaul and was desperate to avoid the ignominy of being caught. True to form, the two men used different gears – Charly went low, Anquetil high. In the first 2 kilometres, over a rough, cobbled road, Anquetil used his bigger gear to good effect, gaining a few seconds on Gaul, but once Gaul got into his rhythm he began to chase down his rival. Sprinting through the narrow corridor of road left by the fans, Gaul hauled himself up towards Anquetil's back wheel. He did not quite make the catch – another kilometre and it would have been certain – but he took the stage victory by thirty-seven seconds from Guido Boni, with Anquetil at fifty-two seconds.

From Naples the race transferred across the Tyrrhenian Sea to the picturesque volcanic island of Ischia for the third time trial in seven days. This time the course was more to Anquetil's liking – 31 kilometres of narrow, rolling roads around the island. He was surprised, however, to be beaten by nearly a minute by the Sicilian rider, Antonino Catalano. Gaul only lost twenty-two seconds and remained comfortably in the maglia rosa.

After two relatively uneventful days, the race headed north along the Adriatic coast towards the seaside town of Rimini. There the Giro would have its only rest day. In this first act of the drama, however, there was one last shock awaiting the maglia rosa. A few kilometres from the finish in Rimini a rider crashed in front of Charly, sending him to the ground. Flushed with adrenaline, he was able to quickly remount and chase back into the peloton. When the adrenaline subsided after the stage, Charly was besieged by aches and a painful road rash, a frustrating way to finish an otherwise successful ten days. On the rest day he did not go out for his usual training spin, instead staying in bed for most of the day.

Gaul had one minute and fifty seconds on Anquetil and had been defending his jersey admirably. It seemed that the erratic performances of a few years earlier were a thing of the past; Gaul was now a more confident, more commanding figure. In grand tours, however, as Gaul knew from bitter experience, things can change quickly. The race was heading north, towards the Dolomites. This was Gaul's favourite terrain, but he also knew that he would come under heavy attack.

Anquetil came out of the rest day fighting. The next day, – a hilly stage to San Marino – should have suited Gaul, but he was still suffering pain from the Rimini crash and was unable to follow Anquetil when he put in a surprise attack on the flat roads before the final climb. Abruptly all but half a minute of Gaul's lead was wiped out. He was furious, though not with Anquetil. On the steep climb to San Marino the fans had been pushing Italian riders, but not the man in the maglia rosa. 'They think I can climb well enough,' he grumbled.[86]

Gaul took back another eleven seconds on the stage 15 to Rovereto, but on stage 15 to Bolzano, the Luxembourger's race began to fall apart. Over 198 kilometres, with three major climbs of the Brocon, Rolle and Costalunga, on roads familiar to Gaul from his 1956 epic to Monte Bondone, the stage should have been the backdrop for him to re-establish his authority in the race. But Gaul seemed diffident and nervous, staying in the pack of favourites as they climbed into the thick fog that lay across the mountains that day. With one long time trial remaining, Anquetil was content to finish in the same group as Gaul and maintain the status quo. Then disaster struck for Gaul. Two punctures on the descent of the Costalunga meant a frantic, doomed chase down into Bolzano. Anquetil was the new maglia rosa and Gaul was nearly two minutes down.

The following three stages did not see any changes to the overall classification. Anquetil looked good in pink, while Gaul hovered around the maglia rosa, biding his time, looking for opportunities to go on the offensive. Here, again, was a more mature rider. Rather than rush into attacking Anquetil, he waited for the moment that would pay the highest dividend.

The 51-kilometre time trial from Turin to Susa was not going to be an opportunity for Gaul because it suited Anquetil's rouleur qualities perfectly. Gaul had to focus on limiting his losses. Before the race, with their starting positions reversed from the much shorter Vesuvius test, Anquetil was getting his excuses in early. In an individual time trial a rider who is caught and passed by another rider is supposed to stay well clear of the faster man. Jumping into his slipstream is not allowed.

'I know what's going to happen. I will catch Gaul about the half-way mark, and then will not be able to shake him off my wheel. He will stay there like a leech . . . There is nothing in the Giro regulations as punishment except a 500 lire fine. Charly would pay 500,000 lire to gain a minute on me,'[87] Anquetil told René de Latour. And his prediction was right. Caught after only 22 kilometres, Gaul sat on, or close to, Anquetil's wheel for the remainder of the stage. Only in the final few kilometres did Anquetil manage to draw clear of his 'leech'. To add to the Frenchman's frustration, Gaul was not even reprimanded by the organisers. By the end of the day Gaul was still in second place, three minutes and forty-nine seconds down overall.

The following day was a remarkably short stage, just 100 kilometres from Turin to Saint-Vincent. It was run off at a brutally fast pace, with Alfredo Sabbadin taking a lone victory, but most of the overall contenders were focused on what was still to come. The riders just wanted to get a massage and an early night, for the next day the Giro peloton faced the queen stage of the race – 296 kilometres through the Alps from Aosta to Courmayeur, taking in three huge mountain passes. It was to be the final act of the Giro, after which only the ceremonial run-in to Milan followed.

That evening, however, the Giro's organisers were worried. It was raining in Saint-Vincent and there were reports of snow in the surrounding mountains. At the race headquarters in the Hotel Bilia, a plan was being developed to split the stage in two – a time trial from Aosta to Cervinia and a road stage from Cervinia to Courmayeur. The organisers undoubtedly were anxious to avoid a repeat of the Monte Bondone stage of 1956, after which they were accused of putting riders' lives at risk. Learco Guerra and François Mersch joined journalists from *France-Soir* and *L'Équipe* in the bar of the hotel, as they debated the impact of such a move.

'I do not even dare tell Charly that,' Guerra groaned. 'He will go straight home.' Mersch, ever-confident in his friend and with a couple of drinks inside him, suggested that Charly could take back four minutes on Anquetil in an uphill time trial, which drew much laughter from Robert Chapatte and Pierre Chany.

Every fifteen minutes a member of the organising team came to the bar and tried to make a telephone call to the monastery at the summit of the Grand-Saint-Bernard pass. The calls did not connect and the man banged the receiver against the bar in frustration: 'The monks are supposed to tell us whether it is raining or snowing up there, but I can never get through.'[88]

The journalists agreed that if it was an Italian in the maglia rosa that evening, the organisers would not be trying so hard to keep their queen stage on – it would already have been cancelled. Eventually someone pointed out to the organisers that they did not need to rely on the uncommunicative monks; someone could get in a car and drive up the pass to assess the conditions. This advice was followed and, past midnight, the drinkers in the bar of the Hotel Bilia received the cheering news that it was only raining on the Grand-Saint-Bernard. The stage would go ahead as planned.

Unaware of this melodrama, Charly woke the next morning feeling rested and confident. He was going to attack, that much was certain. Like the previous year's Tour de France, logic dictated that an attack could only give him a stage win. To take back four minutes on Anquetil, who was climbing stronger than ever before, seemed highly unlikely, but then the experience of that biblical stage through the Chartreuse Mountains reminded Gaul that anything was possible. Once he was clear, all he had to do was ride. If those behind him collapsed, he could benefit.

The early kilometres were nervous in the peloton. Everyone knew that attacks were coming, not only from Gaul but also from anyone who still wanted to get something out of this Giro d'Italia. On the Aosta Valley approach to the Grand-Saint-Bernard pass, five riders escaped, of which the best-placed in the general classification was Imerio Massignan, ten minutes down on Anquetil. As the quintet came to the start of climb, which takes 11 kilometres to ascend 854 metres to its summit and an altitude of 2473 metres, they had a forty-second lead. Not for long. Gaul attacked, dancing away from the peloton through the hairpin bends. Italian climbers Ronchini and Battistini held his wheel for a while, but soon dropped back to the group, wary of over-committing themselves so early in a long stage. Gaul himself was also not fully committed, his intention only to soften up his opponents, because even Charly Gaul wouldn't make a race-winning attack with 270 kilometres to go. However, as he glanced over his shoulder on each bend, he saw that his plan was working. Anquetil's maglia rosa was close to the front of the group and he had team-mates with him. They weren't trying to close the gap, but they were working hard.

Between high banks of snow, the majesty of the Alps laid out in a panorama behind him, Gaul stamped on the pedals and caught the five short-lived escapees. Perhaps for a few minutes the five thought they might enjoy a day of glory. Then reality met myth. Gaul swept past them without a word or a look. Only Massignan was able to hold his wheel for a kilometre or so, before giving up and letting Charly fly over the summit alone. On the descent towards the Swiss border, Charly eased up and let a group of twenty ride back up to him. He had tested Anquetil, and himself, and now he would wait for the next skirmish. Anquetil, at this point, was not panicking. He had fully expected Charly to attack and had ridden at his own pace on the climb. The day was all about damage limitation and he had nearly four minutes in hand.

The next climb was the Forclaz, not as high as the Grand-Saint-Bernard, but with gradients that made it a difficult prospect. Charly attacked again, though this too was intended to be a softening blow rather than the knock-out punch. He accelerated hard on the lower slopes and quickly opened a gap. Behind him the main group splintered – now everyone was beginning to suffer. Gaul crossed the summit of the Forclaz with the German climber Hans Junkermann, with Massignan and Battistini not far behind. Anquetil, who was starting to show the pressure, was two minutes down.

Again, the descent saw an easing of the pace. The front of the race regrouped on the valley roads towards Chamonix. The race crossed another border, this time from Switzerland into France. On the lesser climb to Megève, Gaul suffered a puncture, but got a quick wheel change and was back in the leading group of twenty-two riders. This group rolled on through the town of Bourg-Saint-Maurice and now Anquetil had cause to feel more confident. He had survived two big attacks by Gaul and there was only one significant climb left, the Petit-Saint-Bernard. His colleagues began to believe in his chances too; a team-mate rode alongside and said, 'Jacques, now you have the Giro in your pocket!'[89] Anquetil just smiled.

So, there was only one remaining climb and it was a brute. Climbing to an altitude of 2,188 metres over 28 kilometres, the Petit-Saint-Bernard belies its name, and it represented Charly's last – and slim – chance of taking a second Giro d'Italia. Before the village of Bourg-Saint-Maurice four riders had escaped. Nobodies. The group let them go. Charly stayed near the front. Last night in his hotel room he had planned this stage carefully. So far everything had gone to plan; now he had to deliver the coup de grâce. As the peloton left the village the road began to climb. Just after a sharp bend, Charly attacked. Those around Anquetil looked at him and saw only a flinch, as if the attack was a minor wound in itself. He did not respond and neither did anyone else. Here on the lower slopes the road zig-zags up through idyllic cow pastures and Charly opened up a sizeable gap, sweeping around each bend, his legs twirling in his character-istic style.

With that 'infernal rhythm,'[90] Charly set about the climb with total determination. This was the moment he had been waiting for. Beyond the meadows the road straightens out and clings to the shoulder of the mountain, ascending relentlessly. Taken in isolation this was a hard climb, but after seven hours of racing, at the end of a three-week tour, it was torture. Not for Charly. He was in his element. This was where he belonged. As he climbed, the temperature dropped. Then it began to rain. Even better. Twelve kilometres from the summit he caught the four leaders. The strongest climber, Junkermann, latched on to his wheel briefly, but went deep into oxygen debt trying to stay with him and had to let the Luxembourger go. Exhausted, Junkermann practically came to a standstill. At the summit of the Petit-Saint-Bernard Gaul was two minutes ahead of the next rider,

Massignan. Then came Nencini at five minutes, Ronchini at six, with a stricken Anquetil crawling over the top at more than six minutes behind.

There were still 28 kilometres to the finish in Courmayeur, most of it a wet and slippery descent. Those inside Gaul's team car watched nervously as he negotiated bend after bend. He had to go beyond his usual cautious descending style if he was to maintain the gap on Anquetil, who was a better descender and was taking risks to recover time. Massignan smelled blood. If he could get back up to Gaul a stage victory was possible. When the two riders hit the valley road, Massignan was just ten seconds behind. But Gaul did not sit up and wait for the Italian. He knew that there was a short climb in the last five kilometres. There he gave one last hard effort. Massignan fell back. At the finish line Charly grinned as he lifted his arms in victory. Whatever the outcome of the overall race, he knew this was special. He had executed his plan perfectly; the softening-up attacks on the Grand-Saint-Bernard and the Forclaz, then the final blow on the Petit-Saint-Bernard. Up there, alone, he was free; he was showing the world his talent.

The clock at the finish line in Courmayeur ticked on. Anquetil, exhausted and under-fulled because he had not eaten enough during the stage, had lost time on the descent. He finished in eleventh place, nearly ten minutes down. Mobbed by journalists, photographers and fans, Charly pushed away the microphones and told Learco Guerra to take him to his hotel. He did not want to stand on the podium to collect his maglia rosa; he wanted it brought to him in his room. With only the ceremonial stage to Milan remaining, Charly had won his second Giro d'Italia. Anquetil gave no excuses. Yes, he had not eaten enough and, yes, he'd punctured, but ultimately he had not been able to ride at Charly's pace. He was beaten fair and square. Once again a devastating display of climbing virtuosity in the final days of a grand tour had brought overall victory. 'I will win this Giro

d'Italia in one single day,[51] Charly had promised Georgette before
the start in Milan. He was true to his word.

How does an athlete judge when they have reached their peak? After
winning the 1959 Giro d'Italia Charly Gaul was firmly established as
one of the best riders in the world and (though Federico Bahamontes
may have disagreed) the top climber. He was twenty-six years old.
Most professional cyclists find their best form in their late twenties.
Some maintain that form, augmented with the benefits of experience,
into their early thirties. Charly, however, had already reached his
personal summit. Never again would he take victory in a grand tour.

Naturally Charly did not know this at the time, at least in terms
of results. In the summer of 1959 he was climbing up into the mist,
assuming that there were further heights ahead. The reality, however,
was that his descent was about to begin. Charly, Barthes asserted,
had the leap, but occasionally it deserted him and the lights went out,
precipitating those disastrous days that have become just as famous
as the days of soaring speed. And perhaps the leap cannot sustain a
long career; it simply burns out.

Louison Bobet, the professional, the worker, the man with will-
power, won major professional races between 1948 and 1959. By 1959
Bobet was thirty-four years old and no longer the rider he used to
be, but at the end of his career he deployed his resources cleverly,
targeting specific races that he wanted to have on his palmares, and
using all his experience to prevail.

No longer able to summon much enthusiasm for racing, Louison's
brother, Jean, retired shortly before the 1959 Tour de France and
became a journalist for L'Équipe. At the start in Mulhouse he discovered that he was to share a room for three weeks with Antoine
Blondin. While Blondin mused about Jean's apparently seamless
transition to cycling journalist, Jean was probably worrying about
Blondin's infamous drinking capabilities.

So Jean observed his brother from a little more distance than previously and he saw his waning powers. He later wrote, 'That's how it goes. One day, powerless to prevent it, he sees the rear wheel of the rider immediately in front slip away from him. He strains his sinews. Other people cannot see it yet. He sticks at it tenaciously, but the wheel has gone for good. To disguise his weakness he pretends to look back, he has a mouthful of water. But he knows he has become impotent . . . It is over: he will not win again. He is finished, not yet even thirty-five.'[32]

PART THREE

Tour de France, 1958

Stage 18

WAITING FOR THE RAIN

'Gaul has a scheme in mind – to win both the Giro and the Tour in the same year,' wrote René de Latour. 'True he wants the money. But the timid, yet terribly confident Gaul, would also like to join the only other man ever to have brought off that double: Fausto Coppi.'[93]

In the 1959 Tour de France Charly looked, initially, to be riding well. He was careful in the opening stages and limited his losses to Anquetil in the first time trial at Nantes. He waited patiently for the race to arrive in the Pyrénées, and on the first mountain stage, from Bayonne to Bagnères-de-Bigorre, he went on the attack with his usual conspirator, Federico Bahamontes. The pair worked together over the Col du Tourmalet, a climbing super-tandem, showing the race their superiority. The attack also seemed to suggest that Bahamontes was in the hunt for overall victory. The pair were caught by the finish, but it was an ominous sign for everyone else.

Two days later, in a way that was becoming increasingly familiar, everything fell apart for Gaul. The stage from Albi to Aurillac was not supposed to be decisive. The climbs were not huge, the distance not especially long, but a sweltering heat descended on the narrow gorges of the Massif Central and experienced observers of the Tour knew that it was potentially a day for ambushes. The attacks started early and the young French talent, Henry Anglade, went clear in a dangerous-looking group. Anglade was riding for the regional Centre-Midi team, which lacked the firepower of the French national team, but also lacked the in-fighting. The national team was particularly top-heavy that year, with Big Gem (restored to his rightful place after the controversy of 1958), Anquetil, Bobet and Roger Rivière. By this stage it had become apparent that these four were not prepared to work for each other – or indeed for any of their compatriots.

Gaul and his Netherlands/Luxembourg team were forced to follow the moves. Those close to him noted that he seemed worryingly hesitant, dulled by the heat. On the relatively innocuous Montsalvy climb he tried to hold on, then had to give up. By the summit he was ten minutes down on the leaders. Looking pale and pained, Gaul limped on to the finish, eventually losing more than twenty minutes. Bobet finished alongside him, also exhausted, resigned. As the press scrum descended on Gaul, tomorrow's headlines were already predictable – Gaul was a fallen Angel.

Charly's team hotel that evening was in the centre of Aurillac. On his arrival, the hotelier, aware of his celebrity guest's tough day at the office, took Charly aside and offered him the use of a private house he owned in the countryside. You will be able to rest better there, he suggested. Charly asked if the house had a telephone, for he was expecting a call from Georgette. Reassured that it did, he left town in an unmarked black Citroen to avoid the attention of the press photographers. At the hotelier's house, with the heat fading into the evening, he was able to eat, bathe, get a massage. He strolled in the garden and seemed to those with him to be fully recovered, and quite calm about the day's events.

Georgette, when she called, was concerned for her husband's health. She exhorted him to retire from the race. He reassured her that he felt perfectly fine – that that he was not suffering and would recover for the next day. When she reminded him of the disastrous stage to Cherbourg in the 1957 Tour he became annoyed, telling her that it was totally different. In Cherbourg the heat was so bad he could barely stand up, let alone ride. Today, he insisted, he had been able to follow the moves for several hours until, eventually, his legs had become numb. All his power to press on the pedals had evaporated. It was something he could not understand. He didn't have to say it – everyone around him knew what Charly was thinking. Just let it rain for one day in the high mountains and that twenty-minute time loss could be reversed.

Charly's beloved rain did not fall, but, as predicted, he recovered physically, going on the attack with Bahamontes on the first day in the Alps. Renewing their partnership, the duo rode clear of the field with breathtaking ease. Unable to respond and crippled by their in-fighting, the French struggled to organise a chase. Gaul and Bahamontes took their opportunity, sharing the work and each other's food, to ride into Grenoble with a gap of nearly four minutes over the closest riders. In the packed velodrome Gaul outsprinted his companion to take a welcome stage win, while Bahamontes took the yellow jersey.

On the two remaining days in the Alps Gaul's good form continued. He took second place on the stage to Saint-Vincent d'Aoste and third place in Annecy. It was not enough, however, to lift him into the top ten overall. He finished the Tour twelfth, twenty-four minutes down. Had he not lost so much time on the road to Aurillac he would have finished second, though had he been in contention the race may have played out very differently in the Alps.

For Louison Bobet the stage to Aurillac was not an exceptional experience. He knew, by then, what his brother was observing from the relative comfort of a press motorbike – that he was finished as a Tour contender. It was clear from the way he was riding, and it was clear from the way he behaved around other riders. At the start of stage 18 to Saint-Vincent, Valle d'Aosta, with a long, cold day in the mountains ahead, Jean was astonished to see his brother chatting

cordially with Charly Gaul. This confirmed what he already suspected – that Louison was no longer a rider to be feared. The bitter
rivals were now on speaking terms. It was a poignant moment which
illustrated that once the heat of racing was gone, two experienced
professional cyclists could put aside their history and find at least
some common ground.

As soon as the stage started the two men disappeared into the
peloton. While Gaul was at the front of the race, following the moves
and looking for chances to attack, Bobet was at the back from the
start. He was in serious trouble and ahead of him lay the terrible
climb of the Col de l'Iseran, 33 kilometres of unrelenting suffering
that takes a rider to an altitude of 2,770 metres.

'I wondered what on earth was keeping him going forward and, at
the same time, what could possibly stop him,' Jean wrote. 'I caught
up with him on my motorbike, close enough to touch him. He sig-
nalled to me to go away with the unbearable, despairing look of a
drowning man.'[94]

Jean told his motorbike pilot to drive on and did not see his
brother again until the evening. Louison clawed his way up the Col
de l'Iseran and at the summit he stopped, climbed off his bike and
got into a team car. His Tour, and his whole Tour de France career,
was over. Riding along the valley before the climb, far behind the
rest of the race, he already knew this inevitability, yet still he took
on the climb. For a champion, for a proud man, it was perfect symbolism – he wanted to finish at the top.

Since his victory in the 1959 Giro, the organisers of the Vuelta a
España had been trying to persuade him to ride the 1960 Vuelta,
which was to take place in April. Charly was not keen – he wasn't
used to racing in Spain and he feared that the race would blunt his
preparation for the Giro. To put the Vuelta organisers off he told
them he would only ride for what he considered to be an exorbitant

start fee, but the organisers were struggling to attract any other star riders to their race, so they had money to spare. To Charly's shock and dismay, they agreed to his terms and he was obliged to start. Considering his ambivalence, it is not surprising that he was not entirely committed to racing when he arrived in Spain. As well as the unfamiliar roads, the intense heat and the strange food, Gaul and his team were not impressed to find that the stages often turned out to be 30 kilometres longer than the race handbook stated and that after each stage there were lengthy transfers to the hotel.

The race was billed as a showdown between the two greatest climbers in the sport, Gaul and Bahamontes. The latter had won the Tour de France nine months earlier and was now riding for Gaul's former team Faema (though he had a distinctly frosty relationship with the team manager, Bernardo Ruiz – 'We mutually tolerate each other,' the Eagle of Toledo said). If Gaul was known for his silences, Bahamontes had a reputation for bragging and self-aggrandisement. To the Spanish people he was a hero.

On stage 7, starting and finishing in Madrid, Gaul attacked on the Navacerrada climb, bursting past an early breakaway group. Only the Belgian, Frans De Mulder, a classics specialist and former miner, could follow Gaul's pace. The pair plunged into Madrid, where De Mulder won the sprint for the stage. Bahamontes finished nearly five minutes down.

Any building excitement was, however, extinguished the next day. The stage from Guadalajara to Zaragoza was long (264 kilometres), flat and there would be a strong, chilly wind blowing into the riders' faces. The organisers had scheduled a later than usual start and the peloton responded by asking for an extra feed zone. When the organisers refused, the peloton went on strike, riding slowly for the whole stage. They arrived at the Romereda stadium in Zaragoza three hours later than planned, greeted by the whistles of 30,000 fans who had been waiting there all evening. The newspapers dubbed it the 'stage of hunger'. After that the race spluttered along. Bahamontes's attacks proved insufficient to put him back in contention overall, and instead of focusing on the race he instead picked fights with the race organisers and even spectators. On one stage he jumped off his bike and attacked an abusive fan with his pump.

Meanwhile, Gaul and Ernzer waited for as long as seemed polite, then pulled out. The organisers had got their star rider and were probably not amused that he had just used it as a very well-paid training race, but his withdrawal was the least of their problems. At the finish in Bilbao only twenty-four riders were left in the race. The whole tour had been such a disaster that some doubted the Vuelta could carry on. 'The race is over. May God forgive it!' was the head-line in Spanish newspaper, *MARCA*.

A month later, back in the more familiar surroundings of Italy for the Giro, his principal rivals were Jacques Anquetil and Gastone Nencini. For the first two weeks he remained close to both, watching and waiting. Yet when the decisive moment came, a 68-kilometre time trial along the shores of Lake Como to Lecco, Gaul could not compete with the flying Anquetil. Now twenty-six years old, *Monsieur Chrono* was maturing into the rider who would go on to win another four Tours de France. He had always been good against the clock, hence the nickname, but in that long Giro test he was unstoppable, the only rider to complete the course in less than one and a half hours. Fellow time trial specialist, Ercole Baldini, finished nearly one and a half minutes behind. Gaul had a disastrous day. He was caught and passed by Anquetil, and this time he could not hang on in Anquetil's slipstream. He lost more than six minutes.

Following the pattern of recent years, Gaul did come good in the final few days of the race, taking a stage win in Bormio after a sadis-tically hard stage that included the Gavia climb, but the time gaps to his rivals were solid rather than stunning. Behind him Nencini threw down a desperate last-minute challenge to Anquetil's authority, but the Frenchman salvaged his maglia rosa, taking a lead of just twenty-eight seconds into the final stage to Milan. Gaul finished in third.

There was to be no Tour de France for Charly that year. In June he told the Luxembourg Cycling Federation that he was suffering with bronchitis, an after-effect of a cold he had picked up in Spain. Dr Bürger confirmed the diagnosis, though it does seem odd that Gaul was able to race competitively in Italy if he was carrying the illness from the Vuelta. It was, perhaps, as much about exhaustion as a specific illness. Riding two-thirds of the Vuelta and then the Giro was a challenging proposition for any rider; going on to compete in the Tour was possibly a step too far.

Other than a decent seventh place in the Road Race World Championship in Hohenstein, Germany, there were to be no other significant results for Gaul that season. His lacklustre season, which effectively ended in Milan in May, did not prevent him from securing a lucrative new contract for 1961. In October he signed for an Italian team managed by the former Swiss star, Ferdi Kübler, the madman of Ventoux, and sponsored by a pasta manufacturer called Gazzola. Kübler had been observing Gaul's development as a rider and felt that the Luxembourger was maturing into a wise tactician. Gazzola offered Gaul a contract worth one million Luxembourg francs per annum and, once he had brought three domestiques into the deal – Marcel Ernzer, Roger Thull and Aldo Bolzan – he was quick to sign up.

With the benefit of hindsight it looks like an error of judgement on the part of Kübler, who was relatively inexperienced as a team manager. He signed Gaul just at the point when Gaul's career was beginning to fade. At the time, however, Gaul was only twenty-seven years old, and he had won the Giro in 1959 and finished third in 1960. Illnesses often mean top riders have quiet years. Kübler probably expected Gaul to bounce back in 1961. Moreover, cycling teams are not always thinking about results when they buy a rider's services;

with a rider like Charly Gaul publicity was guaranteed, and Gazzola managed to use the deal to negotiate an extensive distribution contract for its products in Luxembourg.

Financially, Gaul was in a very comfortable position. With his new contract and all his earnings to date, the former abattoir worker was able to invest in several properties in Luxembourg and indulge in his taste for fast cars and Italian suits. A Frankfurt evening newspaper reported that he had owned eleven cars in four years. At the time of signing the Gazzola contract he was driving a Mercedes 190 SL. His personal life was more troubled. At the spacious blue and pink house on the outskirts of Bettembourg that he had built for him, Charly and Georgette's marriage was faltering. In the autumn of 1960 they separated.

Further misery came in late February 1961. Returning from a training camp to his empty house, Gaul found that he had been the victim of a burglary. The thieves took a watch, a clock, some items of jewellery and all his trophies, medals and plaques. Gaul confirmed the crime to a reporter from the *Luxemburger Wort* newspaper and, in a shakily emotional voice, told them to offer a large reward for the return of his trophies. No one ever came forward.

On the road Gaul still enjoyed some success in 1961, but by his own standards it was modest. In the Giro d'Italia he finished fourth overall and took victory on the penultimate stage, 275 kilometres to Bormio, crossing three major passes, including the fearsome Stelvio. The Tour de France was a similar story – Gaul finished third overall, taking a solo win in the Alps on the stage to Grenoble, despite a heavy crash on the descent of the Col du Cucheron. The Tour that year was a curiously apathetic affair. After losing the Giro to a relatively unknown rider, Arnaldo Pambianco, Jacques Anquetil was intent on total domination in his home race. He took the yellow jersey on the first day and never relinquished it. Gaul was ever-present at the front of the race, particularly in the mountains, yet lacked the killer blow – or the killer weather – to seriously threaten Anquetil.

Gaul's stage win came on the same roads that had witnessed his stunning 1958 ride through the deluge to Aix-les-Bains, 50 kilometres north of Grenoble, and the journalists covering it were excited by the prospect of a repeat performance. René de Latour described the scene: 'Passing the "middle markers" on a narrow mountain climb is difficult enough. When one eventually arrives among the heads, there is inevitably a barrage of cars, and for some kilometres we had to remain behind, standing on the car seats to see what was going on ahead. Our car-radio, tuned to Radio-Tour, was not on its best behaviour, but suddenly it spluttered back to life for just long enough to tell us that something big was in the air "... *positions au sommet du Col du Granier ... Premier Charly Gaul ...*"[95]

Anquetil might have been dropped, but he was still in control, riding in a small group of the other favourites over the Col du Granier, then on to the Col du Cucheron. Gaul's crash at 80 kilometres per hour on the descent of the Cucheron could have put him out of the race. Instead, bruised, and with his shorts and jersey ripped, he got back on his bike, gingerly completed the descent and set about tackling the Col de Porte. The crowd at the Grenoble velodrome, aware of the drama unfolding in the mountains, waited anxiously for the famous climber. Gaul was still very much a fans' favourite.

'A great roar went up as he entered the track,' wrote De Latour, 'and pedalled round the cement oval. His jersey was torn at the shoulder, his eyes fixed grimly ahead. He crossed the line and became enveloped in the inevitable scrum of journalists and photographers.' It was a courageous victory and it helped secure Gaul's position in the overall classification, but the crash had taken away any chance of significant time gains over Anquetil.

That evening Antoine Blondin sat down to write an especially memorable column. News had come through from America that Ernest Hemingway, the writer, had died. Hemingway, now more famous for his hunting and fishing exploits, was a passionate cycle racing fan from the time he spent in Paris in the 1920s. Interested in cycling as a motif of speed and energy, he had written about the sport in *The Sun Also Rises* (1926), *Death in the Afternoon* (1932) and several short stories. Hemingway was a hero to Blondin and a strong influence. After witnessing Charly Gaul's grim arrival in Grenoble, he composed a column that imagined Hemingway watching the stage:

> *And the ramp was rising, turning the rider into an animal condition. The man who was dragging the pack down was called Gaul. In his own way he is also a matador (the Luxembourg rider had been a butcher boy) whose electric eye flashes, whose skin bristles with goosebumps. The great hunter approached this designated prey, towards which the spectators swung triumphant jets of water. He appreciated the fall which brought Gaul to the ground, before rendering him in bloody rags at the bottom of the descent. He repeated the parable of the Old Man and the Sea which tells us that nothing is certain until the finish line is crossed.*[96]

By the final day of the Tour, Anquetil's lead – at over ten minutes – was looking about as certain as bike racing gets. Gaul, however, was anything but certain about the slender four-second lead he had over third-placed rider, Guido Carlesi. With such a small advantage, Gaul was open to attacks on the final stage, from Tours to Paris. The time for the general classification was to be taken at the entrance to the Parc des Princes velodrome, allowing the sprinters to go off and contest the stage win on the track, while the top overall riders coasted around. In the kilometre before the peloton arrived at the velodrome Carlesi and his team-mates launched an attack. Marcel Ernzer, fully expecting it, leapt after them, thinking Charly was on his wheel, but Gaul nearly collided with another rider, had to check his speed to stay upright and lost touch. As the peloton flew through the velodrome gates there was a gap between the two groups, which the timekeeper recorded as six seconds. Charly was relegated to third within sight of the finishing line.

A small consolation was the cheerful reception he was given by the French crowd inside the Parc des Princes. Throughout the previous three weeks Anquetil had endured booing and whistling from French fans, who objected to his aloof demeanour; before the Tour he had stated that he intended to lead the race from start to finish and that was precisely what he did. Unfortunately, the fans saw this as egotistical and the race as boring. They liked to cheer on an underdog and Charly received the warmth they could not give to their own rider.

Anquetil could never quite win the favour of the French fans. They had loved Louison Bobet, and later they came to love Raymond Poulidor, nicknamed the 'Eternal Second', but Anquetil's principal flaw was perceived to be arrogance and that did not go down well. He was dominant, a perfectionist and he liked the finer things in life, such as champagne. The fans – fuelled by the media – saw this as a repudiation by Anquetil of how a professional cyclist should behave. Perhaps if his tipple of choice had been beer, a more working-class drink, he might have won more friends. There was also a coolness to Anquetil. 'Unlike Bobet,' he once said. 'losing a race doesn't make me ill – I just work out how to get even, which is what I often manage to do.[97]

Even if, in 1961, he no longer quite had the ability to turn a race on its head, Charly Gaul was still a very special rider. He had huge support on the roadside, particularly in Italy, and the other riders knew that on the toughest mountain stages he could drop them all, almost at will. The stage over the snow-banked hairpins of the Stelvio has gone down in Giro history as one of its most iconic. Gaul had learnt a great deal about racing. He no longer won by twenty minutes, but he also no longer lost twenty minutes. He was more measured, more controlled, calmer.

Throughout 1961 his focus on racing was undermined by the interest the tabloids were taking in his love life. As his separation from Georgette became public, so did his affair with a young woman named Nicole Regenwetter. Daughter of the official decorator of the Luxembourg royal court, Regenwetter was several social notches above Gaul. She was a brunette, taller than him (the newspapers delighted in describing how she wore flat shoes when they were together) and eight years younger.

The pair were introduced by mutual friends in 1957, though it is not clear how long it was before the affair began. During the 1961 Tour de France the French tabloid, *Ici Paris*, published a double-page spread interview with Nicole, describing her and Charly as thwarted lovers. As a symbol of their commitment to each other, both wore a single gold ring. It was for Nicole that Charly was riding, according to *Ici Paris*. For their forbidden love, he wanted more than ever to win the Tour. After every stage Charly would telephone Nicole and talk for half an hour about 'everything, except the Tour'. Every morning he received a letter from her. The article went on: 'Nicole suffers for her love. She who belongs to the upper middle class of Luxembourg – her father is the official decorator of the court – she who was always a reserved and obedient young girl, has to face not only the puritanical public opinion of the small capital, but also the severity of a father who had dreamed of another party for his daughter.[98]

Adopting a faux-romantic tone typical of tabloid newspapers at the time, the article went on to describe how Nicole rebelled against her father's wishes, continuing the affair and, when Charly was away racing, travelled every day to Bettembourg to clean his house. She had even had to endure being shouted at in the street by Georgette. Not surprisingly, the article did not dwell on this scene, but it does tell us a great deal. Georgette loved Charly and had been at his side throughout his career. Now, rich and famous, he had taken a lover. A familiar trope, but no less bitter for that. Her separation from Charly in the autumn of 1960 was presumably the culmination of his betrayal, with the realisation that he would never come back to her.

As well as the disapproval of her father and the public shame of an extra-marital affair in a Catholic society, Charly and Nicole had to contend with Luxembourg's severe divorce laws. A couple who wished to divorce were obliged to demonstrate to a court that they had made four serious attempts to reconcile their differences. By the summer of 1961 Charly had refused three times to resume living with Georgette. Another pretence at reconciliation was planned for November, after which he hoped to be allowed his divorce. Even then, Luxembourg law dictated that he would have to wait three years to remarry.

Nicole and Charly could not wait that long. In December 1962 they travelled to Dover, only the second time Charly had been to England, and married in the registry office. The marriage certificate states the witnesses as René de Latour, the renowned cycling journalist, and one Winifred K Spanner.

This chapter of Charly Gaul's life has not been written about in earlier biographies. Both Mersch and Bressler chose not to mention Gaul's second marriage. Both men considered Gaul a friend, and Mersch would have witnessed first-hand the impact of the relationship. Bressler only knew Gaul when the latter came to work at the Ministry of Sport archives, long after his retirement, and there Gaul rarely talked about his personal history. While it is understandable to omit its mention on the grounds that it is irrelevant to winning or losing bike races (though that is debatable – many great riders of the era, including Louison Bobet, named a stable home life as contributing to their success on the road), this controversial marriage does contribute to our overall understanding of Charly Gaul the man.

To what degree the affair affected his cycling performances is unknowable. Georgette fitted the mould of a professional cyclist's wife – she was from a cycling family, loved the sport, supported her husband through tough times, and knew when to talk about cycling and when to hold back. Other than sensationalist articles like the *Ici Paris* piece, information about Nicole Regenwetter is scarce. The truth of her affair and marriage has faded into the past. What seems certain, however, is that the attention of the newspapers was damaging for everyone around the couple. Charly was already suspicious of journalists. Articles that criticised his racing tactics were one thing; articles about his divorce and remarriage must have inspired a much deeper resentment.

Riding for Peugeot, 1963

Stage 19

THE DESCENT

'For a champion it is unbearable not to be first, because the champion knows no half-measures. It is victory or failure. And failure is inadmissible, even for a champion approaching the age limit, for the simple reason that he is still a man in his prime.[99] Jean Bobet was writing about his brother, but the sentiment applies just as well to Charly Gaul, whose last year at the top was 1961. The following year it was clear to everyone, perhaps except Gaul himself, that he was past his best. It must have been a difficult fact to accept. At the start of the 1962 season he had only just turned twenty-nine. The sort of decline Gaul experienced at this age usually happened three or four years later and many riders in the peloton had maintained race-winning strength into their early thirties.

The athlete lives through his body, is finely attuned to it and therefore feels its failure as an early sign of death. And, as Jean Bobet mentions, this stroke of mortality is cruel because at thirty or thirty-five a man is in his prime – or thinks he is. Walking down the street in civilian clothes a professional cyclist looks like a fit young man. Inside, however, he knows that he is already past his best. Age has struck him down. By comparison, writers and artists live in their heads; only the mental slowing of true old age can affect them.

Failure is inevitable for all athletes. It is part of the process, yet harder to accept if it seems to have come too soon or if you have regrets about your career. The thoughtful athlete plans for retirement and comes to terms with what lies ahead. Those who fool themselves into thinking that this is only a temporary dip in form, that a return to the top is possible, are making it harder for themselves. Gaul's results were meagre in 1962. In the Giro d'Italia he was a shadow of his former self. As in previous years the race for the maglia rosa was expected to play out over the final few days in the Dolomites, but stage 14 was hit by snow and rain, and the organisers, learning the lesson from 1956, stopped the race on the lower slopes of the Passo di Rolle. Charly took shelter in a nearby mountain hut and complained to Rik Van Looy that this weather suited him perfectly. There were fifty-seven riders who abandoned that day.

The positioning of the Tour de Luxembourg on the calendar, nestled between the Giro and the Tour de France, was both a blessing and a curse for Charly. If he had a successful Giro and came out of it feeling strong, he could carry the form and the morale through to his home tour, and be treated to a virtual lap of honour of his homeland. If, however, he was feeling weak or sick or the fans were disappointed by his Giro appearance, the Tour de Luxembourg was an ordeal. So it was in 1962. Suffering with a sore throat, he rode listlessly, rarely appearing at the front. The fans booed and whistled at him. Charly, in turn, blamed the press. He stopped talking altogether to Pilo Fonck, a Luxembourg television journalist who had previously been a trusted confidante. The estrangement was to last ten years.

The situation wasn't helped by speculation in the newspapers that Charly wanted to leave Luxembourg for Italy. It was even said that he wanted to take Italian citizenship. This caused such a controversy that he was obliged to put out a tersely worded statement denying the rumour.

The Tour de France held more troubles. *L'Équipe* writer Philippe Brunel later wrote, 'Without knowing it, he was climbing the slope of his own decline. He grumbled as he climbed the Pyrénées and his eyes were flecked with blood.[100] Gaul blamed the lingering sore throat, yet it was clear to everyone that the malaise was deeper. Though his smooth pedalling style remained, the power had gone. His face looked strained, and as he gazed up the mountains to where the leaders rode ahead of him, Charly knew that his best days were over. Marcel Ernzer, now thirty-six years old, had already decided this would be his last Tour de France. Allying himself to Charly Gaul had given his career a second tailwind, for which he was enormously grateful, but now he was ready to hang up his wheels. Like most domestiques, he was unaccustomed to winning races for himself. With Charly no longer in the hunt for victories, Ernzer's role lost its meaning.

He later reflected, 'Getting out in 1962 was tough for us both: for myself, because a new life – a more settled one – began, and for Charly, because he had to get used to the fact that I'm no longer next to him.' Ernzer's farewell Tour de France did not go as planned. A heavy crash on the stage to Saint-Gaudens took him out of the race. He underwent surgery to remove a blood clot and doctors advised him to end his career with immediate effect. After the surgery another fall would have been very dangerous. That evening in Saint-Gaudens, Gaul confided to a journalist that he was scared in the peloton, feeling that the abuse of stimulants combined with fatigue was making riders clumsy.[101]

Apart from being rather self-centred while his friend was undergoing surgery (though it is quite possible the journalist quoted selectively), this comment is somewhat ironic given the rumours of drug abuse that surrounded Gaul for much of his career. Amphetamines were allegedly Gaul's drug of choice and he took so many of these pills that on occasion he was seen to foam at the mouth. Some have speculated that amphetamine abuse was the reason he performed so well in the cold and rain, though there is no evidence to substantiate such a claim; indeed, amphetamines are more commonly associated with reducing body temperature and have been known to cause hypothermia in cold conditions. Amphetamines do, however, lead to psychosis, symptoms of which include delusions of grandeur and paranoia. It is worth noting that, if Gaul did take amphetamines, he was not out of step with the rest of the peloton. While stimulants were theoretically banned in the 50s and 60s, enforcement was lax to the point of conspiratorial. Fausto Coppi admitted using amphetamines to win the 1949 Tour de France. Some, like Louison Bobet, claimed to have never knowingly taken illegal stimulants, though they also never questioned the mysterious small bottles that their soigneurs told them to drink. Doping was as old as bike racing. It was only when Tom Simpson died on Mont Ventoux that the authorities really began to take it seriously.

In 1963, Gaul left Gazzola for the French Peugeot-BP team, but its iconic white jersey with its black checkerboard design did little to lift his form. The team were more focused on the Tour de France than the Giro d'Italia, so Gaul only rode the Tour. He pulled out, exhausted, on stage 15. The spark had definitively been extinguished.

Why did he keep going beyond 1962? Cynically, we might think that it was just for the money. Or was it also because he had not planned for retirement, both practically and emotionally? As early as February 1959, some of the more perceptive cycling writers were predicting that his career would not be a long one. 'Just over twenty-six years of age, Gaul has still a big career ahead of him,' René de Latour wrote in a *Sporting Cyclist* feature, 'but I do not think he will ever become a veteran rider. He likes the sport only for the wealth and comfort it can bring him. His house on the outskirts of the little town of Bettembourg is cosy and well furnished. He has a pretty wife who knows that Charly does not like to talk about his races when he comes home, whether he has won or lost.'[102]

Publicly, Gaul never said why he kept going. Outwardly, at least, he maintained that he still believed he could return to something approaching his best. It seems more likely, in retrospect, that he simply could not face retirement, with its attendant loss of purpose and structure. Since the age of fifteen he had been utterly focused on success in cycling. What else was there to do?

A lifeline materialised in the winter of 1964 when he was approached by a small Belgian team hoping to take a step up. Jules Spagnaerts founded the Libertas bicycle brand in 1919. A former cyclist, Spagnaerts had spent much of the First World War in a German prison camp and he named his fledgling company for the value he held most dear – freedom. The company's logo was a stylised version of the Statue of Liberty. The Libertas brand grew steadily through the first half of the century, with Spagnaerts' sons, Jan and Kamiel, eventually taking over the helm. From 1953 they sponsored a team, though the modest budget restricted them to mainly Flemish races.

Coming into the 1964 season, Jan and Kamiel set about trying to crack the top-flight of racing. They dreamt of a Libertas squad in the Tour de France. To achieve this they would need a co-sponsor. Charly Gaul, without a contract for the upcoming season, seemed like a good opportunity. He was clearly past his best, but still a big name who could win the attention of potential sponsors. On the road, even if he no longer won races, he would be able to mentor the younger riders.

Gaul agreed to ride for Libertas on the condition that he had a guaranteed spot in the team at the Tour de France, but the Spagnaerts brothers' pursuit of co-sponsors proved to be harder than they expected, even with Gaul signed up to the project. For the 1964 season they were unable to secure more investment and missed out on a Tour slot. Gaul, sticking to his terms, rode as an independent during 1964, which meant missing out on the big races.

He did, however, stay loyal to the Spagnaerts brothers and, when they eventually found a co-sponsor in the form of the Belgian Lamot brewery, he signed for the team. Gaul's friend and domestique Roger Thull also signed. In all, the expanded squad had twenty-seven riders, a blend of young Belgian talents and older riders hoping to return to better days. Newly motivated, in the early months of 1965 Gaul put in thousands of kilometres of pre-season training in Luxembourg. After training sessions he often went hunting in the Ardennes forests. For Gaul, as for the new Lamot-Libertas team, everything was focused on the Tour de France and Gaul claimed to be in with a chance of victory, noting that the route of the 1965 Tour was very similar to that of his victorious 1958 edition. Moreover, Jacques Anquetil had already said he planned to skip the Tour that year.

The first step, though, was for Lamot-Libertas to get selected, which presented a major challenge. The Tour was now run with trade teams rather than national teams, but each trade team was registered to a country and the Tour organisers divided the twelve invitations between these nations: France, Italy, Spain, Belgium and the Netherlands. Belgium had three spots and these were already filled. For Lamot-Libertas to get a start they would have to persuade the Tour to open up an additional invitation and the best way to accomplish that was by getting impressive results in the early season races.

The tone of the season, however, was set on a training camp in the south of France. The riders disagreed about how to train together, splitting into different groups. Worse, there was partying in the evening and – a serious transgression in that era – some of the riders brought their wives with them. Throughout the spring, the team's results were mediocre. Despite his optimism and monastic training, Gaul never troubled the front of a major race. Only in the mountainous Tour of the Basque Country did he show a glimmer of his former self, attacking on a climb before being reeled back in. The team were not invited to Milan – San Remo, nor to the Vuelta a España (perhaps the organisers remembered Gaul's previous half-hearted appearance at their race), so the Dauphiné Libéré in June represented the last chance for Lamot-Libertas, and Charly Gaul, to justify an invitation to the Tour.

The headline billing for the race was a duel between arch-rivals Anquetil and Raymond Poulidor. The race started well for Lamot-Libertas, with Belgian Roger Verheyden taking second place on the opening stage, but as soon as the race hit the mountains Verheyden slipped away from the top of the overall classification. Gaul fared little better. After the first mountains stage he was six minutes down on Anquetil. Two stages later, twenty-six minutes down. Any hope of a high overall position was gone. On stage 6 to Grenoble he withdrew from the race. To add further insult, that evening thieves broke into the team truck and stole all the bikes inside.

Driving back to Belgium after this disastrous showing, the manager, Willy Riem, decided that his team simply were not good enough to go to the Tour de France. Even if they could, by some miracle, inveigle an invite, their appearance would inevitably end in embarrassment. By informing the team, its sponsors and the Tour organisers of his decision, Riem effectively ended the Lamot-Libertas team. At the end of the season both sponsors pulled out and the riders' contracts were terminated.

Gaul clung on to his hope of riding the Tour. He spoke to Guillaume Driessens, manager of the Flandria team and an old friend from their shared time at Faema. Driessens offered to bring Gaul into his squad for the Tour, but the authorities quickly pointed out that a mid-season transfer was not allowed.

Speaking later, Driessens said of Charly: 'He wasn't at all that anti-social guy that many newspapers dismissed him as. On the contrary, he was one of the funniest in the field provided the sun left him alone. With the journalists, however, things got a little more complicated. Initially he was good with the press people, though reluctantly, but

they soon began attacking hard, which in turn affected him over time
with a certain dislike towards the media. It was a feast for the eyes
to admire him as he raced ... I was very sorry when I heard in 1965
that he had been fired from where he rode and I would have had him
in my team for the Tour ... but unfortunately that was impossible.
He was always a star that audiences wanted to see.[103]

This was the end of the road. The 1965 Tour de France was won by
the stylish first-year professional, Felice Gimondi. A new generation
was taking over. Charly Gaul was at home in Luxembourg, hunting
and fishing. His final race as a professional was at the Niederkorn
track in Luxembourg on 11 August. A month later he competed in
the Luxembourg inter-club championship at Esch-sur-Alzette, where
his team finished third. Charly Gaul's cycling career was over.

Stage 20

RETIRING INTO MYTH

Ten days before Christmas 1961, Jean and Louison Bobet attended a charity gala in Brussels. At nine in the evening the party ended and the brothers began the drive back to Paris. Jean was at the wheel of a black Peugeot 404. Louison, beside him, soon fell asleep. It never became clear what caused the accident. Possibly Jean's concentration lapsed momentarily or he too fell asleep. Near the town of Montry, just east of Paris, the car left the road and crashed into a concrete wall. Jean was thrown through the windscreen and when the car came to a rest in a ditch he found himself sitting on the bonnet. Behind him, Louison was wedged between the dashboard and his seat. 'I am broken, I am broken,' he screamed. After ten minutes a local man discovered the car and called for a doctor. The brothers were taken to hospital in Paris where Jean was found to have a broken leg. Louison had a fractured femur, a fractured ankle and numerous contusions. They were devastating injuries from which there would be no return to racing. Early in 1962, at the age of thirty-seven, Louison announced his retirement.

Given his age, retirement had been on Louison's mind for the past couple of years. Most of his earnings from cycling had been invested in land – he owned a tract of forest in the Jura region – and his financial position was comfortable enough that he did not need to work.

He could have done a few radio and television appearances, appeared at criteriums as a celebrity guest and lived a life of leisure, but that wasn't Louison's style. He wanted to prove himself in business and he applied himself to the commercial world just as diligently as he had to cycling.

After the initial trauma of the car accident, Louison set himself a routine of careful restorative activities. He took regular trips to the Brittany coast where, on the beach at Carnac, he swam in the Atlantic every morning. Along with some gentle cycling and the odd game of tennis, the seawater helped him to recover his strength and he became fascinated by its health benefits. Thalassotherapy, as seawater cures are known, was a relatively new concept in France at the time. When racing in Italy Louison had often enjoyed going to Italian spas, with their sleek white marble, and now he had the idea of establishing a thalassotherapy institute in Brittany. He instructed his notary to sell some of his land and in Port du Crouesty, not far from the beaches where he swam, found a plot that suited his purposes. After negotiations with the Mayor of Quiberon, he was granted permission to build the Louison Bobet Centre. First, however, he had to raise more money and more awareness of thalassotherapy. During 1963 he worked hard to learn the basics of the relevant medicine, plus accounting, marketing and management techniques.

As with so many start-up businesses, Bobet's thalassotherapy centre soon dominated his life. He worked six long days a week. On Sunday mornings he went out for a ride with his brother. The hard work paid off. The institute was such a success that it diversified into a nutrition hotel and Bobet was able to open three other centres in France, as well as advising on thalassotherapy businesses as far afield as Mexico and Florida. The sheer drive, the force of will, that had taken him over the Izoard and Ventoux, that had enabled him to cling on to his yellow jersey despite horrific saddle sores in 1956, now brought him success in a completely different field. His name and wealth helped him get started, but his character did the rest.

If thalassotherapy was his business, Bobet's joy was flying. In 1955, while recovering from perineum surgery, Bobet had studied for his pilot's exam. The local aerodrome adapted one of their planes to allow him to sit more comfortably and he proved to be an excellent pupil. He passed the exam first time, getting a first-class amateur licence, and thereafter he and Jean – a rather nervous navigator – made many trips across the country in Louison's two-seater Jodel D112. He was a competent pilot and usually anyone accompanying him felt safe with him at the controls, though occasionally his ambition got the better of prudence. Jean Bobet wrote about how, 'Once, I landed with him among the cows, on an extremely steep-sloping field in the hills of the Perche region.[104] Raphaël Géminiani took great pleasure in enlarging the stories of Louison's misadventures for comic effect.

Bobet's retirement is something of a counterpoint to that of Charly Gaul. If, throughout their cycling careers, the two men hated each other (let's assume the media reports were not exaggerated), that only accentuates the fact that they were very different personalities and, most likely, did not understand one another. When Bobet retired he wanted a new challenge. He split his life in two: cycling was about achievement through physical endeavour; business was about achievement through intellect. We use the term retirement for professional athletes, but in Bobet's case it would be more accurate to talk about a career switch.

Bobet's approach was unusual. It was more common for former riders to stay in the world they knew – cycling. Team management, either for a professional trade team or as a national coach working for a governing body, was a logical career choice. Such roles were perfect because the former rider could employ all their experience and connections to help younger riders. Raphaël Géminiani became a team owner before he had even finished racing and went on to manage a number of successful riders, including Jacques Anquetil. His larger-than-life personality proved to be an exceptionally good asset for attracting sponsors and corralling his riders. Ferdi Kübler also took to team management when his racing days ended, though ultimately he preferred to spend his days on the golf course or the ski slope.

Manufacturing bicycles, or at least lending your name to badge bicycles made by someone else, was another common retirement business. This tended to work only for star riders whose name was easily recognised by the bicycle-buying public, but for domestiques, famous only in their home town, there was always the safe option of opening a bike shop. While some good analysis has been done that shows the social backgrounds of young men who went on to become professional cyclists, there is little analysis of what professions they went on to take up after their careers. It seems a safe assumption that, even if most men stayed true to their geographical area (as a working-class sport, cycling was always rooted in local communities), their wealth enabled them to choose a different job to that of their fathers. Bobet did not return to the pre-dawn grind of the boulangerie.

Jacques Anquetil did go back to his roots, though his return was very different to his departure. Anquetil's father was a builder from Normandy whose work disappeared when he refused to accept contracts from the occupying Germans in 1941. So Anquetil Senior was forced to join his relatives working on a nearby strawberry farm. Jacques helped out, too, and when the cycling bug bit him, he negotiated a deal with his father whereby he would pay for a new blue Stella racing bike with work harvesting strawberries. After his career, Anquetil returned to the land, only now he owned the land that he farmed and grew oats, barley, wheat and maize. He also had a herd of cows. After wildfires he replanted many hectares of trees.

He was devoted to his vocation, putting in long days on the tractor, throwing himself into the hard life of a farmer, despite the fact that he was making very little money from it. In cycling, he had been focused on financial gain. Farming, his true passion, he did virtually for nothing.

Anquetil's trouble, however, was that he was Jacques Anquetil. Famous, rich, charming. He was continually drawn into a world of glamorous parties and socialising, and the tension between these two very different lifestyles became stressful. He enjoyed dressing up and going to fancy events in Paris with his wife, Janine, but he also enjoyed hunting wild boar on his estate.

In May 1987 he was diagnosed with advanced stomach cancer. Despite surgery and radiotherapy, the cancer did not abate. Six months later he was dead. In the years that followed, in dozens of magazine articles and biographies, those that knew him were asked about the cause of his cancer. This was an unfair question because, as with most cancers, not even his doctors could say with any con- fidence, but many pointed to his prolonged use of amphetamines, citing Bobet and Gastone Nencini as examples of other riders who had taken stimulants during their career, then succumbed to cancer in their fifties. The connection has never been proven conclusively. Anquetil himself disputed this idea, arguing that his use of ampheta- mines was twenty years earlier – would the cancer really have such a gestation period? Instead, his friends pointed to his heavy drinking, particularly of whisky, during the farming years. Others thought that the stress of his complicated love life was to blame. Of course, we will never know.

Adjusting to 'normal' life is difficult for any retired athlete. Many cyclists have talked about the ennui they feel after their career ends: boredom, lethargy, depression. The adrenaline of competition is gone (though living it vicariously as a team manager must be some compensation). The pain, to which cyclists are addicted, is gone. The danger of throwing oneself down a mountain is also gone. To return to ADHD, if a cyclist has used cycling to keep his dopamine levels high, and if he needs the exhilaration of racing just to feel normal, when it is gone he will struggle to be happy. This would also explain why Charly kept racing for as long as he did, even after he knew that he would no longer win races – he needed the dopamine that cycling gave him.

And fame fades quickly. Only Tour de France winners remain celebrities. Other riders disappear from public view, whether they like it or not. Once there were thousands of people lining the roadside and chanting your name. A few years later you are recognised only by a few old-timers with a keen eye.

The loss of status is brutal, as Charly found out even before his career had ended. At the height of their careers professional cyclists are perceived by fans as almost supernatural beings. Not only the fans are in thrall to these men-machines, so are the journalists, the photographers, the team staff, the pretty girls giving out flowers and kisses to the winners, the gendarmes protecting the roads . . . The whole circus of professional cycling huddles, awestruck, around the peloton. When a rider retires they go from star status to anonymity almost overnight. Without a race number on their back, they are nothing. Most professional riders have been talented, and therefore watched and admired, since their teenage years. It must be hard to accept that status had a time limit.

Another reason why retirement from elite sport is so hard is the concept known as tunnel vision. In any sport, getting to the top requires some degree of single-mindedness of purpose. The athlete must be obsessive, driven. There is no sense of perspective, no contingency, no back-up plan. When Anquetil was lying in his hospital bed in Besançon in 1958, thinking that his career was over, he did not see a return to strawberry farming. He saw himself destitute and shambolic. To get to the top of a sport requires intense focus and energy. After retirement, what can compare? Bobet and Anquetil found new vocations. Charly Gaul was not so fortunate.

Bobet and Anquetil both seemed, on the surface, to embrace their new identities (businessman and gentleman farmer respectively), but we cannot know how they saw themselves. Perhaps they always thought of themselves as cyclists, as Tour de France winners, just as the rest of the world did. Charly Gaul's sense of self-worth and status was certainly closely bound to cycling. He took criticism (even the illogical and unfair booing from former fans) very hard and his identity was even more specific, being connected to climbing. He was, after all, the Angel of the Mountains. When that ability ebbed away, when he looked despairingly up a climb to the younger, faster riders ahead, that identity began to disappear.

Winner of the 1947 Tour de France, the first after the Second World War, Jean Robic was a distinctive figure in cycling in the mid-twentieth century. A proud Breton (who was ashamed to admit that he had actually been born in the French Ardennes because his father was working there briefly), Robic moved to Paris in 1940 to work as a cycle mechanic and to pursue a professional racing contract. With the war severely disrupting racing, it took until 1943 for Robic to turn professional, but even then the cycling journalists did not pay him much attention and he was given the unkind nickname of the 'Hobgoblin of the Brittany Moor'.

Pierre Chany wrote, 'He had a face that was speckled like a bitter apple, large ears and a little nervous and muscular body. At the same time proud and stubborn, he detested all those whom nature had made better proportioned and all those whom he considered nature had given a more handsome body. He hated Louison Bobet, accusing him of being a false Breton.[105]

When he arrived on the start line of the 1947 Tour de France, riding for the regional Brittany team, no one considered him even an outside favourite. He won stage 4, then rode strongly in the mountains, gradually moving himself up the general classification until, by the final stage, he was in third place. The Italian Pierre Brambilla was in the yellow jersey and looked assured of victory in Paris. Robic had other ideas. Halfway through the stage he launched a stinging attack on a short hill. Brambilla and one other rider, a Frenchman named Édouard Fachleitner, went with him, but Brambilla quickly fell back, unable to stay with Robic's pace. The duo caught a group that had been ahead of the peloton, of which only one rider, Lucien Teisseire (later Charly Gaul's team leader at Alcyon Dunlop), had the energy to join them. Teisseire and Fachleitner attempted to work Robic over, but he was equal to all their attacks, and once they accepted they were not going to drop him, Robic did a deal with Fachleitner, offering him 100,000 francs in exchange for his work. Behind, the peloton was indecisive. Robic was not a popular figure. Indeed he was frequently bad-tempered and arrogant, but no French team wanted to help an Italian so soon after the war. Brambilla could do nothing, but watch the Tour slip from his fingers. In Paris, Robic and Fachleitner finished nineteen minutes ahead and Robic won the Tour. Fachleitner finished second overall and poor Brambilla third.

Three stories attached themselves to this piece of Tour history. Having promised to bring the yellow jersey home to his new wife, Raymonde, Robic actually gave it to the Sainte-Anned'Auray Church in Morbihan, Brittany. Fachleitner was berated by his team manager for only asking for 100,000 francs to cooperate – and Pierre Brambilla was so disgusted that he buried his bike in his garden. The veracity of this last tale has been challenged, yet it remains part of cycling mythology.

Robic never again seriously challenged for victory in Paris, but he remained a threatening presence at the front of the race throughout the early 50s. Like Charly Gaul, he was a rider who had the potential to disrupt a race, to cause trouble – someone who could not be ignored. He knew nothing other than cycling. He went on racing for professional teams until he was forty years old and even after official retirement he continued racing in amateur events, living off start fees and prize money. His last race was in 1967. He was forty-six.

Adjusting to life after racing proved difficult. Robic took over the running of his family's café, but the business failed. Then his marriage fell apart. Unemployed, he became depressed. He tried other jobs, including refereeing wrestling matches and sitting on a bicycle as part of the Tour de France caravan, but nothing worked out. Eventually an old friend gave him a job to save him from destitution.

In July 1980 Robic went to a party to celebrate Joop Zoetemelk's Tour de France victory. Driving home to Brittany he was involved in a car accident and died, aged fifty-nine. Robic was a pugnacious character whose success came from bloody-minded grit and opportunism. His whole life was built around cycling. Too old to compete, he did not know what else to do. He had not planned ahead by making shrewd investments, nor had he made any influential friends in cycling who might offer him a job.

Hugo Koblet was another rider from Gaul's era whose life ended prematurely and tragically. Koblet won the 1950 Giro d'Italia and the 1951 Tour de France, but after that 1951 victory, at the relatively young age of twenty-seven, his talent went into a decline that, at the time, seemed mysterious. No one could work it out. Koblet was a graceful rider and, just like Gaul, he never lost his pedalling style, just the power behind it. He particularly suffered in the high mountains. The journalists of *L'Équipe* expressed their bewilderment at Koblet's inexplicably fading star. The real reason was sadly mundane and in those days would never have made it into newspaper print – a botched injection of amphetamines had affected his bone marrow and consequently his ability to manufacture red blood cells. The higher the altitude, the weaker he got.

Koblet was famous for carrying a comb in his racing jersey, so that he could style his hair immediately after a race, or even during it. Handsome, charming, easygoing, Koblet was Robic's opposite and yet when he retired he was afflicted with the same problems. Drifting from job to job, Koblet was careless with his money and got into debt. His marriage to a young model, Sonja, broke up. Depressed, confused by the turn his life had taken, he ended up living alone in a small apartment in Zurich.

In November 1964 Koblet was driving along a stretch of road just outside Zurich when his Alfa Romeo left the road and crashed into a pear tree. A witness who lived nearby ran to the crumpled wreck and found Koblet critically injured. 'Just let me die,' Koblet whispered.[106] Four days later, he did. At first it seemed to be an accidental death, but it transpired that Koblet had passed the pear tree, stopped and turned his car, driven back past the tree, turned again, passed the tree a third time, before turning again and driving into it at high speed. Reluctantly, Koblet's friends and family, and the wider cycling world, came to accept that it had been suicide.

The list of former professional cyclists who have suffered in their retirement is long. Depression often results in alcohol abuse, debt and marriage break-ups. Many of the stories describe a tragic downward spiral. Some stories of traumatic lives after retirement, like those of Robic and Koblet, and more recently Jan Ullrich, become part of cycling mythology, but for every famous story of decline there are undoubtedly dozens of other, quieter, unpublicised episodes of depression. Some riders learn to cope with their depression, some are submerged. Occasionally a former rider will open up in a magazine interview. Often this happens when they have come through the other side of their pain, when they feel able to talk about what they have experienced.

Individuals who are vulnerable to depression because of adverse events in their childhood, social factors or genetics can be triggered by high stress situations. Professional cycling, with its pressure, its constant scrutiny, its culture of doping, its obsession with body weight, its continual (and unhealthy) focus on winners versus losers, is not a healthy environment for a vulnerable individual. Charly Gaul may have had a melancholic nature, but he recognised the stress for what it was – a threat to his mental health. During his career he established coping mechanisms – developing his close circle of friends and advisers, holding the press at arm's length and living a quiet life in Bettembourg with Georgette. The coping mechanisms didn't always work, but on the whole they did. He made it through to the end of his career and then, when the stress of being a famous retired cyclist threatened to engulf him, he knew what to do.

The Ardennes

PERGOLA

It is not clear whose idea it was for Charly to open a bar. His parents had been successful innkeepers when he was a child, so perhaps he had fond memories of the business, and his former manager Jang Goldschmidt ran a popular bar near Luxembourg's Grand Palace. It seems likely that Goldschmidt helped to facilitate the distribution deals with drinks companies. For former professional cyclists, opening a bar was also a common way to spend their retirement because they needed little start-up capital and had a neat inbuilt marketing ploy – customers would want to come and be served by a champion, to drink away some time while listening to stories about the good old days, perhaps while watching the Tour de France on a little television in the corner. This business model, however, depended on the former rider being sociable with every punter who walked through the door, no matter how tiresome they were, and the work was not easy – long hours, physical work and the challenge of managing staff.

The Pergola (although everyone called it the Brasserie Charly Gaul) was situated on the Route de Thionville in Bonneweg, close to Luxembourg's main railway station. It was only a few hundred metres from where Charly had trained to be a butcher all those years ago. In September 1967, two years after his last race, Charly and Nicole hosted a party to celebrate its opening, but it soon became apparent that Charly was not cut out for hospitality. He did not want to lean on the zinc, polishing a glass while entertaining the regulars with tall stories. His drinking became more than sociable. Customers started noticing that Charly, quiet and morose, was consuming more than anyone else. Alcohol, as always, was a symptom of a deeper sadness in Charly. A sensitive man, for all his outward bravado on the bike, he felt hurt by the way his career had ended. His fans had turned against him; the people of Luxembourg had turned against him. Rather than lauding his career, at its close they had whistled and booed him when he raced on home roads. Fuelled by the newspapers, adulation turned to rancour.

Charly felt betrayed, too, by the Luxembourg Cycling Federation. Soon after his retirement there were discussions about a role as national coach, which would have been a soft way for Charly to transition to life after racing. Such jobs were often offered to star riders once their racing career was over. The position involved coaching and developing younger riders, selecting the teams for World Championships and managing the teams at those champion-ships. It was a good job for a former rider who wanted to stay in the racing community but did not have the resilience or energy needed to run a trade team, and it was seen as a reward for riders who had brought fame and glory to their country.

Charly was ever attuned to a financial opportunity, but this time he priced himself too high. The Federation could not afford his desired salary and turned him down. It is possible that the Federation was happy to use the salary negotiations as an excuse not to take him on. Charly was hardly suited to being a coach and no one would have wanted young Luxembourg racers to be developed quite in his mould; ten years earlier he had driven Nicolas Frantz to despair by ignoring the tactical advice of the older man. So there was no job. Charly was so upset that he instructed lawyers to contest the decision. When they failed, he put out a press release, written in formal German, to clarify his position. Despite all that he had done for Luxembourg, as he saw it, the Federation had turned its back on him. Denied the opportunity to work in cycling, the bar probably seemed a credible alternative.

In January 1968 there was to be another blow. On a wet Wednesday lunchtime Charly was driving north from Luxembourg City to go hunting with friends. On the road between Dommeldange and Waldhof, on a slick left-hand curve, he lost control of the car, which spun, rolled over into a ditch, hit a concrete reinforcing wall and finally came to a rest on a pathway beside the road. There were several witnesses who had been walking along the pathway and they ran to the wreckage. Charly was alive, but badly injured. An ambulance rushed him to hospital in Luxembourg City, where the doctors diagnosed a trauma to his cranial base, concussion and a broken nose. His life was not in danger, but a graft was required to the base of his skull, a complicated and relatively risky surgery. His convalescence was going to take some time.

This car crash is often omitted from the story of Charly's difficult retirement years, yet, when we add it to the picture already established, it becomes a significant event. Here was a man who felt let down by the world of cycling, the world that had adored him only a few years earlier. Whether or not he had ever liked the idea of owning a bar, by January 1968 he was under no illusions that the enterprise was doomed. He was drinking a lot, his marriage to Nicole was disintegrating and now he was lying in a hospital bed, recovering from multiple serious injuries. It must have seemed as if his whole world was imploding.

It is not uncommon for people to reassess their lives after life-threatening accidents. Perhaps Charly simply thought, to hell with it. Perhaps, as some have suggested, he was clinically depressed. Nevertheless, Charly was strong-willed. He knew what made him happy. Or more pertinently, he knew what made him unhappy. Once he was recovered from his injuries Charly closed the Pergola, left Nicole and disappeared.

If Charly's face played a prominent role in the establishment of his myth, it was nothing compared with Greta Garbo. Indeed, Roland Barthes dedicated a whole chapter of *Mythologies* to analysing the 'extreme beauty' of Garbo's face. Charly has sometimes been referred to as the Garbo of the peloton, though it is unlikely he was ever aware of such references. The comparison seems unlikely, but bears closer inspection.

Today, Garbo is as known for her quip 'I want to be alone,' as she is for her magnetic screen performances. Only, she never quite said that. 'I want to be *let* alone,' is what she said. The additional word makes a lot of difference, implying that she wanted others – reporters, studios, paparazzi, over-zealous fans – not to bother her. She did not want to be alone. Solitude did, however, come to dominate her life, whether she initiated it or not. Born in Sweden in 1905, Garbo moved to Hollywood at the age of twenty, after her performance in a small Swedish film caught the eye of Louis B Mayer, chief executive of Metro-Goldwyn-Mayer. With MGM she made a series of silent films that established her as a star, with 1928's *A Woman of Affairs* making her the studio's highest grossing box office attraction. She was one of the few actresses to successfully move from silent films to talkies, and her career continued successfully until the late 1930s with a string of critically acclaimed films and three Academy Awards nominations. In 1941, however, she retired abruptly from acting and withdrew from the public gaze.

The shift from being one of world's most recognisable and alluring faces, available to anyone across the world via a cinema screen, to 'recluse' seemed shockingly uncompromising. Over the years and decades that followed, film-makers and journalists attempted to coax her back into the world she had left behind, and when she refused the rumours about her lifestyle spiralled. Garbo-spotting became a sport in New York City, where she lived from 1953 until her death in 1990 – she walked through the city streets every day, usually wearing sunglasses, a big floppy hat and a slouchy coat. And here lies the paradox of Garbo's reclusion. She did not disappear to a remote Swedish island. Nor did she lock herself away in a Howard Hughes-style mansion in Beverley Hills. She moved to Manhattan, one of the busiest cities in the world. One might say she was hiding in plain sight, only she was not really hiding. She was only choosing who she wanted to engage with. She had friends and lovers throughout these years.

During her career, even as far back as her first silent films, Garbo did not enjoy the attention that accompanies fame. She shunned studio parties and avoided the press as much as possible. She had a few close friends, but otherwise cut a lonely figure. Living in Beverly Hills, she enjoyed walking alone on the beach, but missed the modesty and melancholy of her native Sweden. 'I have been thinking a lot about Tistad,' the actress wrote in a letter to a friend. 'About summers there when it rains and that marvellous melancholy enfolds us.'[107]

The catalyst for her retirement was a film called *Two-Faced Woman*, a critical flop. Garbo was tired of Hollywood, tired of making films and fighting the demands of the studio. She had plenty of money and decided that she simply wanted another life. Unable to cope with a film star who would not engage with them, the newspapers resorted to wild speculation about her personal life. Garbo never married, though not for a want of proposals. Two male friends each proposed to her three times. She was, however, doomed to an unrequited love. For over sixty years she exchanged letters with the Swedish actress, Mimi Pollak, with whom Garbo had studied in Sweden. Garbo's love for Pollak came to define her life. She had other relationships, but – it would seem from her recently published letters – none as meaningful to her as that love for Pollak. And so she walked the streets of Manhattan, drifting through life, a lonely and enigmatic figure. Numerous attempts were made to entice her back into film-making. She rejected them all.

Garbo came to embody the idea of a recluse in popular culture. Her story was appealing, yet also a little unnerving. It made sense if she was depressed, but if she was not depressed, if she had simply decided to stop making films and live the rest of her life without a clear purpose, that was harder to accept. We subscribe to the idea that our lives are defined by work, by family or usually a combination of both. Louison Bobet ended his cycling career and switched to the world of business. One purpose swapped for another. That is something we can understand and respect because it conforms to our idea that until the onset of old age, we need to have a purpose. Greta Garbo and Charly Gaul both confounded that idea.

Uncomfortable with the idea that people, famous or otherwise, may simply wish to be alone (or let alone), society has tinged solitude with negative connotations. The term 'loner', for example, is often linked to serious criminal behaviour, implying dangerous psychological issues. After he died, some of Charly Gaul's friends felt they had to defend him against the accusation that he had an antisocial personality, the implication being that antisocial was a bad thing, but why is it assumed that being sociable is the standard to which we all must aspire?

There have recently been a handful of books published that celebrate introversion and shyness, and their arguments have had to be defensive because the prevailing societal norm is for extraversion. As Susan Cain points out in her book, *Quiet*, much of the world is designed by extraverts for extraverts. Modern offices, for example, are open plan, a concept that would induce anxiety in an introvert. Fortunately for Charly, the archive of the Luxembourg Ministry of Sport, where he worked from 1989, was not big enough to be made open plan. Other writers, such as Sara Maitland, in her book *How to Be Alone*, have tried to analyse why society seems to feel so uncomfortable about people seeking solitude. Does society have a default setting of community and togetherness? Is the pursuit of solitude somehow self-indulgent and narcissistic? We can detect such undercurrents in the reactions to Charly Gaul and Greta Garbo. The newspapers played to these themes. The implication of the coverage was: how dare they reject the world that made them rich and famous, the world of people, for this self-indulgent, escapist way of living?

Like Garbo, Charly Gaul did not really disappear. When he closed the Pergola he went to stay at a holiday home he owned on the bank of the Sauer river, near the village of Lipperscheid. It was a basic affair, a static caravan without electricity or running water, and Charly could surely have afforded something more comfortable, but that wasn't the point. He wanted to be alone and he wanted a simple life. The mobile home was not the ramshackle wooden hut it has sometimes been portrayed as, nor was it isolated. Charly built a fence around his plot and grew vegetables in an allotment. He also had neighbours – such mobile homes were popular with Luxembourg City dwellers who wanted to escape to nature. It was an idyllic spot, set in a meadow beside the river where he could fish, surrounded by the Ardennes forests, where he walked and hunted.

His 'disappearance' was from public view. No longer did he turn up at bike races as a spectator; no longer did he grant journalists an interview. He still saw friends and family, regularly going hunting with childhood friend, Roby Maas, and the master butcher, Norbert Berg, and he maintained an apartment in the city, splitting his time between there and the mobile home. Rumours began to circulate in Luxembourg that he was living as a wild man in the hills and eventually the cycling media picked up on the idea. They sent journalists to track him down and those that persevered and found him were given short shrift. 'I just want to be left alone,' he told them. 'All that [cycling] is another life, long ago.'[108]

All his life, the natural world had played an important part in Charly's life. He learnt to walk in a farmyard, then grew up in a village dominated by agricultural workers. His family's ancestry was based in the Ardennes valleys and, although his parents' restless career had taken the Gaul family to the city, Charly never disconnected from the landscape of his youth. Cycling gave him the freedom to explore, to map and to memorise that landscape, often alone. During these years of seclusion his constant companion was a dog called Pocki. It made Charly happy to grow his own food, to watch deer come to graze in the meadow close to his home, to hunt and fish nearby. For the first time in twenty years he was out of the spotlight.

Dressed in green hunters' fatigues, Charly walked the forests around his home, watching the wildlife more than hunting it. In May 1974, while walking in his usual hunting ground in Eisenborn, he came across an orphaned baby wild boar in a nest. Its mother had been shot by a hunter. Charly took the baby home, cared for him and named him Muly. In October of the same year, when Muly got sick, Charly took him to a veterinarian who gave Muly an injection. Perhaps the vet was unused to treating wild animals or maybe he made a mistake with the dose. Muly died as a result of that injection and Charly was heartbroken. Afterwards, he swore never again to go hunting for wild animals. Like the hunters of ancient mythology, Charly lived with, and respected, animals in the wild. Hearing of Muly's death, Charly's mother wrote in her diary, 'Charly has a good heart, he cried for his little friend.'[109]

Occasionally a journalist managed to break through. Just before Christmas 1972 the Dutch journalist Jean Nelissen persuaded Charly to go for a drink. His interview, brief but descriptive, appeared in *De Limburger.*

'Charly lives in a flat in Luxembourg. His only companion is a little dachshund, called Pocki. "I am alone," says Charly, "I no longer interact with people. If you have a lot of money, the friends come and the women. Later they all melt away."

Charlie is forty now. Does he not live too pessimistically?

"Maybe," he says, "From nature I've always been a pessimist. I can't laugh if there is nothing to laugh about. And I haven't done anything in the last few years as a reason why I could laugh. I have no children, am not married. I was married. First with Georgette, a blonde. I'm divorced from her. Then I married Nicole, a rich girl from the city of Luxembourg. I left her too. She is now remarried. I have become suspicious, especially in front of women. The women are bad. The women are dying for money."

Charly puts on a hat and walks to a café on the corner of the street. Inside he sits at a table and orders a whisky. The café owner, a big friendly man, greets him exuberantly. Charly pushes the hat on the back of his head and says, "He is one of the few that are still good to me." The innkeeper brings the drink, looks on endearingly as the Angel pours the whiskey down his throat, points to Charly and says, "He was great, before." Charly nods. "That's right," he says, "In the past!"[110]

There is no reason to doubt the veracity of Nelissen's article, but it is only a fragment, one moment in a long expanse of time. By 1972 Charly had been living alone for more than four years, with no contact with the cycling world. The only people he saw were close friends and family, those that knew him best and were accustomed to his moods. This one rather tense conversation is revealing in that he talks about his lack of marriage and children, rather than cycling, as the underlying reasons for his sadness. His relationships to Georgette and Nicole both occurred during his career as a cyclist. He met

Georgette when he was a talented young rider. Then, at the height of his fame, he had an affair with Nicole. Their marriage ended in the dark winter of 1967–68. We can never know what went on inside these marriages, but perhaps the suspicion Charly felt towards those in the wider cycling world – that they wanted something from him, whether it was money, reflected glory or juicy stories – somehow bled into his relationships.

He was an intelligent man, too intelligent to really believe that women pursue men for their money, as he grumbled to Nelissen. Underneath these words we can detect, above all, loneliness. It is interesting, too, that he mentions children. Turning forty, unmarried and childless, that loneliness must have been insufferable. Living quietly in the splendour of the Ardennes countryside gave him a welcome peace after the frenetic and itinerant lifestyle of a professional cyclist. On a deeper level, though, did he think his chances of finding the happiness of family life had vanished?

Stage 22

A NEW TEAM

Alice Koller was an American writer whose career was defined by solitude. If *Walden* by Henry David Thoreau was the original memoir of living in solitude, at one with nature, Koller's *An Unknown Woman* is the twentieth century feminist update. Koller was a talented philosophy student and graduated with a doctorate from Harvard in 1960, but she struggled to settle into a permanent job and two years later she moved to Nantucket Island, off the coast of Massachusetts. There, for three months, she lived in complete isolation, with only a puppy named Logos for company. Later she wrote that during those three months it was necessary for her to ask herself many questions about the way her life had unfolded and what lay ahead for her. The biggest question of all was: should I go on living?

She decided she should, or at least would, go on living, and when she moved to the mainland she wrote her notes up into two books: first *An Unknown Woman* and then *The Stations of Solitude*. Permanence, however, still eluded her. She moved house many times and had many short-term jobs. It took fourteen years of rejections before *An Unknown Woman* found a publisher and became a surprise bestseller. It clearly hit a nerve with the reading public.

Koller's stations of solitude are like train stations – places where we stop as we travel through our lives: 'You reach the first station of solitude the day you ask, "What have I been doing with my life?" From that moment you begin the circuit.'

Solitude is a choice and, if you are prepared to accept the self-examination, a wise choice. The end point of the process is a deep knowledge of yourself and a clear picture of 'the person you wish to be, the life you wish to live … The route toward yourself that you pursue by yourself is your reflective occupation at the first station of solitude. The journey is almost totally one of looking back. When you leave the station you will probably never look back again. There will be no nostalgia for the life you used to live: it belongs to someone you no longer are.'[111]

In his book *Shrinking Violets*, Joe Moran writes, 'The shy are often drawn to the natural world because it seems easier to relate to than people. But at some point they must confront its obstinate otherness, its lack of interest in and refusal to give anything back to them … The fact that nature seeks no relationship with us is both consoling to shy people and not consoling enough, because it will not lessen their loneliness.'[112]

Charly may have thought himself happy in his rural idyll, but his friends knew that – for all his introversion – Charly needed people. One such friend, Norbert Graas, owned a Ford dealership in Kirchberg and conjured up the perfect job for his car-loving friend. Charly would pick up new cars from the dealership and drive them the short distance to Sandweiler, to be registered at the Société Nationale de Contrôle Technique (SNCT), before driving them back. Charly did not need the money – the interest alone on his investments easily covered his simple lifestyle – and yet he took Graas's job, showing that by the mid-70s he was ready for more human interaction.

At the SNCT, Charly met Josée Milbert, an attractive, dark-haired secretary, and the two began a relationship. Norbert Graas's plan was succeeding. Josée was quiet and strong, and she saw the vulnerability in Charly. In July 1977 Charly and Josée married and settled in a rose-coloured bungalow on the Rue de l'Horizon in the village of Itzig, just south of Luxembourg City. Josée presumably refused to live in Charly's mobile home. In the summer of 1978, twenty years after Charly's victory at the Tour de France, the publisher Auto-Revue tracked down Charly at his mobile home and, accompanied by a photographer, presented him with a book commemorating the seventy-fifth anniversary of the first Tour. It is an awkward picture: the publisher in a black three-piece suit, the river and woods in the background, Charly wearing shorts and sandals, his bare torso tanned and strong from years of working outdoors on his vegetable garden. Looking on is Josée, wearing a long summer dress and heavily pregnant.

From the moment of Fabienne Gaul's birth, Charly was a proud and happy father. Photographs of him holding Fabienne as a baby show a man utterly in love. The joy in his face is deep, permanent. He dedicated himself to his family and to his garden. Sometimes he would repair the bicycles of his neighbour's children, but that was as close to cycling as he got.

Gradually, carefully, Josée encouraged him to re-engage with the cycling world. In 1979 he made a rare public appearance at Luxembourg's first National Day of the Bicycle, shaking hands with other older figures from the country's cycling community, and though he looked rather stern in a long overcoat (most of the others wore their old team tracksuits), Charly looked genuinely delighted to see old friends and acquaintances. He was not quite ready to watch cycling on television, though, and he did not even own a bike. Perhaps playing with his daughter seemed like more fun. Journalists were still dispatched without their interviews. He was simply a man enjoying late fatherhood and a marriage that was very different from his previous two. Josée was a young woman who understood him, protected him and coaxed him away from the darker side of introspection.

The image of a fat, scruffy, bearded figure shambling around in a hut in the forest – an image that is perpetuated to this day – was never accurate. Yes, he grew a beard, but it was always neatly trimmed. Yes, he put on weight, but, like a beard, such weight gain was in keeping with many men of his age. As the photographs attest, he was solidly built rather than fat. To compare a man in his forties to his Tour de France-winning self is hardly fair or useful and Charly was never scruffy. He loved clothes too much. Whenever he appeared in public he was smart, even if he was wearing tweedy hunting clothes. Indeed on many occasions after his retirement he appeared in such nice suits that observers were compelled to remark on them. At times he verged on a dandy.

Charly's reclusiveness amounted only to a withdrawal from the public gaze. After the traumas of the late 60s, he followed his instinct. He knew himself well enough to know that he had to be alone, had to return to the world from which he had come. Today we might call it a mental health crisis and perhaps that would be accurate, but it was a crisis that Charly knew how to solve. He cut himself off from what he perceived to be doing him damage – journalists, Nicole, business, cycling – and took up a simpler life. Did he use the silence to process what had happened to him? We will never know.

Nor will we ever know how happy or how depressed he really was during the early 70s. The cycling writers came up with their own sensationalised conclusions. There was a note of bitterness in their descriptions of a wild hermit. How dare a Tour de France winner remove himself from their circle? How dare such a popular rider reject the whole model of the retired professional rider who socialises affably within the sport, who makes himself available for journalists who want a piquant quote or need to fill some pages during the quiet winter months with a retrospective? It was ironic that the very quality cycling writers celebrated in races – that of attacking and riding alone – was now, in retirement, something that they could not understand or endorse.

The end of Charly's estrangement from the press came in 1983 with a chance encounter. On a hot midsummer's day Pilo Fonck was a passenger in a press car during the Tour de Luxembourg. As the car travelled slowly along in the race convoy, ahead of the riders, he gazed out at the fans standing on the verge. He saw a middle-aged man with a grey beard, accompanied by a woman and a young girl, and immediately recognised the man as Charly Gaul. Fonck told the driver to stop, jumped out and re-introduced himself. Would Charly like to do an interview? It was, after all, 25 years since his Tour de France win. To Fonck's surprise, Charly agreed.

The interview focused mainly on Charly's cycling career. Of his retirement Charly said, 'I bought myself a little portable television and I connected it to the battery of my car to watch the Tour de France. When the battery ran down, I called the man at the garage. I had travelled plenty. I told myself, "You're happy here, at peace." There was nothing, but the trees and the water. I passed my days planting vegetables. Deer used to come and eat at the end of my garden. How do I explain what I did? Well, it is difficult to go back into normal society. Today, of course, I laugh about it, but that period was essential: without it, I wouldn't have been able to tackle the final slope, that of old age.'[113]

Here we return to mythology and storytelling. The mythology surrounding his career centred on ascent, on climbing towards heaven, towards God. In 1968 he began a descent – into the earth, into himself – in order to attain a deeper knowledge of life, of himself. In order to attain transcendence, the shaman journeys deep into the earth (this is usually a spiritual journey, though shamans did also literally install themselves in caves) and there he confronts his own death. Only by doing this can the shaman progress to a true ascension to the heavens. When he returns to his community the shaman is in a perilous state of near-death and has to be revived by others. The hero has to pass through this experience in order to be reborn.

It is tempting to use the metaphor of a mountain ascent and descent to describe the life of any cyclist. For Charly Gaul we might say that the 1958 Tour de France was his summit, everything before it was ascent, everything after descent, but that would be reductive. Charly's life was more messy, more nuanced and more phased than that. His greatest triumph – as a man rather than just as a cyclist – was his union with Josée and the birth of his daughter.

No, rather than a banal cycling metaphor, let's look to the world of storytelling. Stories have shapes and these shapes are so ingrained into the way we recount tales that they have become archetypes. Storytellers, whether they are film directors or novelists or playwrights, consciously use these archetypes to build their narrative. The audience may not always be aware of the presence of these archetypes (hopefully the story itself is so diverting that no one is thinking about its construction), but instinctively they will understand them. They cannot help it – these narrative shapes have been present in human storytelling since language began.

One of the most recognisable, and satisfying, story archetypes is called voyage and return. *Alice in Wonderland*, *The Wizard of Oz* and *Robinson Crusoe* are some of the best-known examples of this type of story. In summary, a heroic figure, usually starting from a lowly or dissatisfied position, leaves their home and travels to a strange world. When they arrive in this new world they find it exhilarating, bewildering, uncomfortable. Gradually the experience becomes darker. They encounter resistance and danger, become frustrated or fearful. An enemy – the witch in *Wizard of Oz*, for example – turns the dream into a nightmare. The heroic figure has to pass a devilishly hard test in order to escape and return to their previous life, and when they do return, they are changed by the whole experience.

Voyage and return stories are satisfying because they reflect a fundamental human experience – that of going out into an unfamiliar world, experiencing new, unsettling things and then returning home. This might be a neolithic hunter going out on an expedition, or a student going to university. The journey doesn't even need to be a physical one. Like the shamans, it might be spiritual or it might be an emotional journey, like falling in love. When the heroic figure sets out they are often young, naïve and inexperienced, and they return changed. They start as a limited character and return whole.

The connection to Charly Gaul's story is clear. He was young and naïve when he set out into the world of professional cycling. He was certainly egocentric, and episodes throughout his career show that his feeling for other people was, at best, limited, but none of that is a criticism. Maturing, becoming less egocentric, becoming more sensitive to other people, is a universal process. Arguably professional athletes have a harder time of it because their world encourages them to prize ego. For a star cyclist like Charly Gaul, the machinery of his sport bolsters his ego. That is how he will perform. That is how he will slam his rivals in post-race interviews. Being nice gets you nowhere.

The enemy in Charly's story was not a person, like Louison Bobet, Georgette or Nicole, it was the loss of status that retirement brought. He was not ready for it, so his fight was not against some wicked other figure, but against himself, against his own history, and when he emerged from that fight he was ready to find other people who could make him happy, who could make him whole.

At home in Luxembourg

Stage 23

REJOINING THE PELOTON

With the support of Josée and Fabienne, Charly slowly reacquainted himself with the world of cycling that he had left behind nearly three decades earlier. In 1988 he was guest of honour at the publication party for Gaston Zangerlé's book *L'Ange de la Montagne et son Époque*. The city of Luxembourg had already secured the Grand Depart of the 1989 Tour de France and in 1988 Charly was approached by George Lanners, the chairman of the organising committee. Would Charly be interested in a role as a technical consultant? Lanners was persuasive, but it seems that Charly was already open to being persuaded, to being inveigled back into cycling. Perhaps he understood that things were very different now, that he could control media access to him and his family, and besides, the tone of the journalists was different. More respectful, more nostalgic. By 1988, too, Fabienne had fallen in love with cycling. Her parents had never hidden Charly's former occupation from her, but it was only in her early teenage years that he had really opened up to her. She had to ask him, though. He never kept books or magazine articles about himself, never watched cycling on the television and rarely volunteered information. With Fabienne growing up and books like Zangerlé's being published, Charly did not have much choice but to tell her of his achievements. Her teenage passion for the sport reignited Charly's love of cycling.

His job for the 1989 Tour was to work in the archives of the Ministry of Sport in Pulvermühle, alongside the archivist and writer Henri Bressler, acquiring and cataloguing documents and artefacts that were to be displayed in exhibitions to celebrate the Tour's Luxembourg stages. Bressler hoped to establish a Museum of Sport to permanently house the archive. From the start, Charly was a conscientious and popular employee. He and Bressler became friends as they sorted through the avalanche of memorabilia – most of it about Charly himself – that came to them from various collectors and old friends. Former team-mates and team staff got in touch to offer material. One day Jang Goldschmidt turned up at the Ministry with a huge suitcase of documents relating to his and Charly's time together.

Charly worked at the Ministry for eleven years. Like his time delivering Ford cars, it was a job that he didn't really need, yet it played a significant role in his journey back from solitude. Other writers have suggested that by working through his own archive, Charly was able to piece together his life, to understand the journey he had been on. This is a nicely poetic, if speculative, idea. Charly himself never publicly said anything to support it and, while he had been through dark times, Charly never lost sight of who he was. In his time as an archivist, he may have had a chance to reflect on his career, to remember specific people and races, but to suggest that he used the archive as a giant jigsaw puzzle of his own life is a little far-fetched.

More importantly, his time working for the 1989 Tour de France and beyond helped Charly reconnect with people whom he had lost touch with. Universally, he was greeted warmly. There were dinners and receptions held in his honour, speeches given, medals awarded. The cycling world, in particular everyone associated with the Tour de France, welcomed him back. The Tour loves to honour its heroes. It creates and maintains its mythology, and on a personal level there was genuine affection for this man who had so stunned everyone with his climbing in the 1950s. There was a sense in which the other old-timers were saying, 'You always were too sensitive! Cycling is a tough sport and you can't be popular forever, but there's no need to disappear – we are all friends!'

From 1989 he and Fabienne went to watch at least one stage of the Tour de France every year, and if the Tour visited Ventoux he would insist that he and Fabienne travelled to Provence. Speaking to a Belgian journalist, Fabienne later recalled, 'Every time a stage ended on the Ventoux, he wanted to go there. We kept getting passes to the VIP village, but he didn't care. He wanted to stand along the track. He had his favourite spot, a wall just below the top. To get to it we had to get up at night, otherwise he wouldn't be sure of his place. I have often seen the sunrise on the Ventoux with him.[114]

Charly bought his daughter a bike, then bought himself one so that he could ride with her, for company and safety. Now approaching sixty, he was riding more than he had for over twenty years. His weight, a product of his sweet tooth more than alcohol, fell away.

A new generation of cycling journalists travelled to Itzig, to make a pilgrimage to see this newly accessible legend. Charly welcomed them, Josée made them coffee and Fabienne entertained them, but there was still wariness. Several articles from the 1990s describe Charly's intensely watchful blue eyes, half-hidden behind the smoke from his cigar. His answers were not evasive, but they were hardly expansive either. He was not a raconteur like Big Gem.

In 1995 he was interviewed for *De Limburger* and spoke of the rumours that had circulated during the years he was away from public life:

'Gossip and backbiting,' says Charly Gaul now. 'From disappointed journalists, to whom I showed the door, because they only write lies. For the thrill. During my career I often fought with certain journalists. Because I got them out of the bathroom or chased them out of the restaurant. In the bath I wanted to wash and at the table I sat to eat. There was enough opportunity to interview me. But the men felt insulted . . . They were exclusively out for scandal. If they no longer need you, they attack you.'[115]

His love for the sport and the bicycle kept him going beyond 1963, the point at which his career really ended. By then he understood that he would never again climb as well as he previously had and, when members of the peloton began making fun of him, it hurt a great deal.

When asked about regrets, however, he would say that the only one of his career was the final stage of the 1960 Tour de France when he lost second place on the last day. He had no other regrets, which may seem surprising considering the number of tactical errors he made that lost him major races. Perhaps he had simply come to terms with the kind of rider he used to be and had decided not to be too hard on his twenty-five-year-old self. After all, what is the point in regret? Charly was not a nostalgic man; he enjoyed seeing old friends, but as the 90s wore on, he was more interested in watching and analysing contemporary racing than talking about his glory days. He certainly was not one of those former professionals who bemoan how soft and naïve the current generation of riders are.

In *How to Be Alone*, Sara Maitland tells the story of Anthony the Great (AD 251–356), one of the first Christian hermits and a 'founding father of monasticism'. At the age of thirty-four, Anthony went into the Egyptian desert and shut himself away in a ruined fort, building fortifications into the ruins to prevent the curious from disturbing him and perhaps to discourage himself from leaving. When he emerged twenty years later he was healthy, and – contrary to the expectations of those gathered to see him come out of the fort – very much sane.

This pattern is broadly reflective of Charly Gaul's life. His extreme isolation began at the age of thirty-five and, though he did not teach in the conventional manner, he did open himself up for interviews with journalists in a way that suggests he wanted to share his experiences. He also put himself at the service of the public, in his role at the Ministry of Sport. Afterwards, he retired again, to focus on enjoying family life and watching the sport he had fallen in love with all over again.

Stage 24

PARIS

In the summer of 1998 Charly decided that he wanted to mark the fortieth anniversary of his Tour victory by climbing Mont Ventoux, so with Fabienne and a Luxembourg friend, Carlo Bock, with whom he had dreamt up the idea, he set off for France. As they prepared themselves in Bédoin, it was warm and still with clear blue skies – a perfect Provençal day. Charly was nervous. He was sixty-five and, while he had been training for the climb, he knew more than anyone to respect the mountain. The trio agreed that if any of them were overcome by extreme fatigue, they would stop on the side of the road. From the start, Charly spun a small gear, reminiscent of his famous racing style. At times he grumbled about the steepness of the slope, but kept going.

As they climbed, a car came around a bend ahead of them, descending towards Bédoin. At first they did not notice that it had Luxembourg number plates. Then the car slowed and stopped, and its passengers climbed out. They stood on the side of the road, clapping. Come on Charly, they called down the road. Recognising their compatriot and hero, they had spontaneously decided to stop and cheer him up his beloved mountain. He gave them a brief wave and a smile. After so many years, here was a moment that encapsulated his whole life – the athlete overcoming the mountain, cheered on by his fans. For Charly it must have been a confirmation that his legacy was going to endure.

Charly, Fabienne and Carlo reached the summit, and while they rested there and enjoyed the view, Charly talked at length of his love for this place and for France. Then, goal achieved, they descended to their hotel and a glass of champagne on the terrace. To ascend Mont Ventoux with his daughter was a fulfilling end to a chapter of Gaul's life.

There was another cause for celebration in 1998. Marco Pantani accomplished the rare feat of winning the Giro d'Italia and the Tour de France. Beyond any other rider, Charly was a fan of Pantani. He saw something of himself in Pantani's attacking style, his courage in the mountains and perhaps in his erratic racing patterns too. Pantani could be dominant or strangely absent. The fans loved him and other riders feared him. Charly considered Pantani a natural heir. Forty years after the Angel of the Mountains won the Tour, *Il Pirata* took his own yellow jersey into Paris.

Charly also saw Pantani's fragility. Both men were introverts and had a few close friends, then a much bigger circle of people who wanted to be friends with them, but could not quite get in. Pantani's relationship with the media was more ambivalent than Charly's; the Italian loved the trappings of celebrity – the money, the women, the nightlife – and he understood that he was a brand. The bigger the brand, the bigger the celebrity lifestyle. Charly raced in different times. He enjoyed the financial gains of racing, but his idea of a good day off was to listen to records or do a bit of gardening. The two men became friends, talking whenever their paths crossed at the Tour or other races. Both men recognised something of himself in the other. In 1996 Pantani even had someone drive him from Italy to Luxembourg so he could pay Charly a visit at home.

Speaking to Luxembourg's principal newspaper, *Luxemburger Wort*, Henri Bressler said, 'Gaul looked at Pantani almost like a son. He really liked the Italian. They were alike. They were gifted climbers. Their kick in the mountains was identical. The lightness was impressive. The qualities in the climbs were innate to them. There they could make the difference. Gaul spoke Italian. The two had a high regard for each other. When Pantani died, Gaul was at the funeral and wept. I think that says enough.[116]

Pantani's problems began in 1999 when he was expelled from the Giro d'Italia for a haematocrit level of 52% – the UCI had set a maximum level of 50% for 'health reasons'. High haematocrit levels were closely associated with the use of erythropoietin (EPO). When he was disqualified, Pantani was comfortably leading the race with only one mountain stage remaining. Pantani fought to clear his name, but more allegations emerged. Unlike Gaul, Pantani faced a cycling media that – in the wake of the 1998 Festina affair – was prepared to expose doping.

Pantani denied everything, used the media to defend himself, made numerous half-baked comebacks, and slipped into paranoia and recreational drug abuse. His problems were played out in the media, but somehow they only seemed to intensify the fans' love for him. Charly defended his friend, telling the newspapers and the UCI to leave him alone; that reports of EPO abuse were exaggerated. His defence of Pantani, though clearly heartfelt, was dismissed as the opinion of an out-of-touch old man whose own career was retrospectively tainted with rumours of amphetamine use.

The Italian tifosi were considerably more forgiving of Pantani's poor performances than the Luxembourg fans were for Charly. Pantani paid the price for being one of the first cycling superstars to be exposed for doping. In the late nineties the authorities had neither the science nor the moral authority to take decisive action in such cases, so the revelations were fragmented and contested, leading to prolonged court cases and slanging matches in the media. The process led Pantani into dark places.

At his funeral a note that he had written in his passport was read out: 'For four years I've been in every court, I just lost my desire to be like all the other sportsmen, but cycling has paid and many youngsters have lost their faith in justice. All my colleagues have been humiliated, with TV cameras hidden in their hotel rooms to try and ruin families. How could you not hurt yourself after that?'

Surrounded by people who wanted him only for his money and fame, Pantani grew isolated from those who could have been close enough to help him. Charly was one of those people, as Matt Rendell notes in his book *The Death of Marco Pantani*: 'Marco had only ever listened to his grandfather . . . or grandfather figures . . . Charly Gaul might have got through to him.'[117]

Charly and Fabienne attended Pantani's funeral in Cesenatico. A crowd of 20,000 gathered outside the church in scenes reminiscent of Fausto Coppi's funeral in 1960. Inside, Charly sobbed loudly for his lost friend. He never quite got over Pantani's death, Fabienne said.[118] In the months that followed Charly's health began to deteriorate. He could only move about with the aid of a cane.

Pantani's downward spiral has been covered in numerous books and his death affected Charly deeply. He loved the Italian as a friend, admired him as a bike rider and identified with his personality. Did he identify, too, with Pantani's troubled later years? Did he see a parallel to his own life? In the late 60s Charly was spiralling. Divorce, alcohol, a failed business, a traumatic car crash – if unchecked, where would it have ended? Pantani was unable to save himself. Perhaps he could not see the glimmer of light through the chaos, as Charly could. Pantani's withdrawal from the world took him to a place from which he did not return; Charly's withdrawal into solitude led him to a happy future.

In October 2005 the city of Trento told Charly of their intention to lay a plaque at the foot of Monte Bondone, inscribed to him in honour of his 1956 ride up the mountain. Despite poor health Charly travelled to Italy for the unveiling ceremony, accompanied by Fabienne and Carlo Bock. There Charly met some of the people who had helped him get warm in the café that freezing day. Fabienne later said that autumn day in Italy was the last time she saw him truly happy.

Following a fall at his house in Itzig in November 2005, Charly suffered a broken kneecap and was admitted to hospital in Luxembourg. The surgery on his knee was successful, but shortly after he developed a pulmonary embolism. He died on 6 December, two days short of his seventy-third birthday. As he would have wished, his funeral was a small affair with close family and friends. Charly was buried in the cemetery in Itzig with a headstone that reads, 'Charly Gaul, L'Ange de la Montagne, Vainqueur du Tour de France 1958 et du Giro d'Italia 1956 et 1959.'

Obituaries in the cycling media picked out the obvious points from his life and career – the former butcher's apprentice who became the best climber in the history of the sport, who defeated the weather gods and the malevolence of Mont Ventoux, who enraged his enemies and suffered the consequences, who fell from grace and 'disappeared', emerging two decades later a changed man.

Those who knew him better, and thought more deeply about his life, put it more eloquently. Frank Wilhelm wrote, 'The rider we admired for his amazing exploits could also frighten us with his graceless days, his dropouts, his depression. It is this vulnerable, profoundly human side of the Angel of the Mountains which seems to me to be at the very basis of the myth he has engendered.'[119]

Surely he will continue to be remembered for those big moments in his career – the swirling snow of Monte Bondone, the volcanic drama on Ventoux, the biblical deluge of his ride through the Chartreuse Mountains – but let us also remember that there was another side to Charly Gaul. Here was a quiet man who loved riding his bike, but also struggled with the pressures of his sport and, above all, was a good friend, and a loving husband and father.

So the story of Charly Gaul's life is both a warning and a comfort. It is a warning because his talent was turned into a mythic narrative that came to symbolise something far beyond his own control or understanding. He simply wanted to win bike races, yet he became a national symbol of post-war regeneration, a cultural artefact. Perceived and portrayed as enigmatic by intellectual French cycling journalists, he was ascribed the same sphinx-like qualities as Greta Garbo. There was an assumption of hidden, perhaps disturbing, depths. Eventually, those who could not get close to him became bitter and dismissive. The way he carried himself, classic introvert behaviour, was described as arrogance. The gap between the truth of his life, particularly the unknowable interior life, and the myth widened. He was just a man, with flaws like any other.

Sport can be mistaken for an arena where human perfection is reached – physical and moral. Athletic heroes are given moral qualities far beyond what is reasonable. We know – if we care to admit it – that sport can only reflect the society it is a part of. Cheating, corruption, prejudice, anger, jealousy, fear – we can see them all in a single Tour de France if we care to look. And underneath these grand themes of good and evil, there are young men and women who are ill-prepared to play a public role, to become a myth.

Charly Gaul's story is a comfort, too, because he did not fall into the abyss. When myth and reality diverged, and he found himself stuck in the middle, he chose a new path for himself, that of solitude. It annoyed and confounded people. Over time it became attached to his myth, as if it was somehow inevitable that the Angel of the Mountains would become the Hermit of the Ardennes, but it was a conscious strategy and one that is rooted in its own history. For thousands of years men and women have used solitude to move forward with their lives, even if it appears outwardly to be a retreat. Charly Gaul knew what he needed to do. He was strong. He was a survivor.

Out for a training ride, 1961

EPILOGUE

The Luxembourg Institut National des Sports is a campus of buildings on a hill overlooking the ancient citadel. On a sunny September morning in 2022 I walked from my hotel in the banking district, down the cobbled street that the Grand Prix de la Forteresse climbed, crossed the Alzette river by a picturesque bridge, then began the long climb up to the Institut. A little early for my appointment at the Ministry of Sport archive, I lingered for a while to watch some track and field athletes training at the impressive athletics stadium. Outside a group of schoolchildren learning mountain biking skills whizzed past under the watchful eye of their teacher. It was a peaceful scene, reflecting the wider city – compared with London, Luxembourg City seemed very calm and well-mannered.

The archivists, Pit and Nadine, seemed slightly stunned that I had travelled from London specifically to come to their little office. I was very grateful that they had already pulled together the archive's material on Charly Gaul and, fortified by coffee, I sat down to work through every newspaper clipping, official document, photocopied magazine article and more. It took two days. Many of the documents had a handwritten reference on them, the publication title and a date. The photographs were mounted on cardboard with the date they were taken and the event written neatly at the top. Often these titles were carefully underlined in a different colour. I wondered whether Charly himself had written these references. As most of them were dated before 2000, when he retired from the archive, it seemed likely. The handwriting was as neat as his signature.

I do not believe that Charly needed the archive work to piece together the puzzle of his own life. From what I have come to know of him and from the various interviews he gave during that period, by the 1990s he was at peace with himself and, having a thoughtful and reflective personality, was fully aware of his own history. If there was a time when his life was fragmented and confused, it was probably the late 1960s and early 1970s. All the same, to spend all day in an office, sorting through documents about your own career, is quite a strange job, especially considering his ambivalent, at best, attitude to journalists.

It is important to remember that Charly undertook this work when he was in the gradual process of reconnecting with cycling. His home life was happy, and from 1989 he had been welcomed back into the fold by former colleagues and acquaintances. His archive work was part of that process. He was a popular figure around the building, gentle and cheerful, and that seems to tell us he was happy in his work. It was not a painful reconciliation process; it was a kind of sorting of his affairs before his second retirement.

As a literary form, biography has its limits. It gives us facts, quotes, anecdotes, the opinions of others and much more, yet the true nature of a person can elude us. His or her interior life – unless we are lucky enough to have diaries – has vanished. I never met Charly Gaul and I suspect that, even if we had been contemporaries, my nationality and woeful language skills would have precluded any chance of getting to know him well. Gaul passed away before I first heard of his story. The people that I met through the research process of this book were friendly and helpful, yet I also know that, partly because of doping, cycling holds its secrets close. Every rider has his trusted inner circle, usually family and a few close friends and colleagues. Throw in the professional peloton's infamous *omertà*, and it can take a journalist many years to get anywhere near the meaningful truth. Charly Gaul had a handful of trusted journalists who had enviable access to him during his career. Every other journalist had to piece together the picture, as I have attempted to do more than half a century later. Perhaps Gaul remains elusive, even after this book. If so, I am okay with that. I hope only that he seems a little more rounded, a little less cartoonish.

Occasionally, as I wrote this book, I imagined that I felt Charly's presence. Not as a ghost, or some kind of hallucination, more in the sense of wondering what he would think if he knew of me sitting here in London, in 2023, writing about his life? Perhaps he'd be amused, but more likely he would be dismissive. Just another hack perpetuating a myth, which is also fine with me. Some are meant to write, some are meant to pedal.

PALMARES

Major career results as a professional

1953 (riding for Terrot-Hutchinson)
1st overall, Flèche du Sud – 1st, Stage 1a (team time trial)
2nd overall, Critérium du Dauphiné
1st, Mountains Classification
3rd overall, Tour de Luxembourg
3rd, Grand Prix Robert Grzonka
6th, Road Race, UCI World Championships
7th overall, Circuit des Six Provinces
8th, Polymultipliée

1954 (Terrot-Hutchinson)
1st overall, Circuit des Six Provinces – 1st, Stage 3
1st, Luxembourg National Cyclo-cross Championship
2nd overall, Tour de Luxembourg – 1st, Stage 4
3rd, Road Race, UCI World Championships
4th overall, Critérium du Dauphiné
1st, Mountains Classification – 1st, Stage 6
5th, Polymultipliée
9th, Züri–Metzgete

1955 (Magnat-Debon)

1st overall, Tour du Sud-Est – 1st, Stage 7

3rd overall, Tour de France

1st, Mountains Classification – 1st, Stages 8 and 17

3rd overall, Tour de Luxembourg

5th, Gran Premio di Lugano

6th overall, Tour de Romandie

6th, Polymultipliée

1956 (Faema-Guerra)

1st overall, Giro d'Italia

1st, Mountains Classification – 1st, Stages 7, 13 and 18

1st overall, Tour de Luxembourg – 1st, Stage 2

1st, Luxembourg National Road Race Championship

1st, Mountains Classification, Tour de France – 1st,
    Stages 4a and 18

3rd overall, Roma – Napoli – Roma

1st, Mountains Classification

3rd, Mont Faron Road Race

3rd, Mont Faron Hill Climb

4th, Gran Premio di Lugano

6th, Grand Prix Genève

7th, Giro Dell'Emilia

1957 (Faema-Guerra)

1st, Luxembourg National Road Race Championship

1st, Stage 2b, Tour de Luxembourg

4th overall, Giro d'Italia – 1st, Stages 2 and 19

5th, Mont Faron Coast Race

4th, Gran Premio di Lugano

1958 (Faema-Guerra)

1st overall, Tour de France – 1st, Stages 8, 18, 21 and 23

1st, Grand Prix de la Forteresse

1st, Mont Faron Hill Climb

3rd overall, Giro d'Italia – 1st, Stage 14

3rd overall, Challenge Desgrange – Colombo

5th overall, Grand Prix Bali – 1st, Stage 3

8th overall, Tour de Luxembourg

9th, Critérium des As

10th, La Flèche Wallonne

1959 (EMI)

1st overall, Giro d'Italia

1st, Mountains Classification – 1st, Stages 3, 7 and 21

1st overall, Tour de Luxembourg

1st, Luxembourg National Road Race Championship

1st, Stage 17, Tour de France

1st, Stage 7, Roma – Napoli – Roma

1960 (EMI)

1st, Luxembourg National Road Race Championship

3rd overall, Giro d'Italia – 1st, Stage 22

10th overall, Tour de Luxembourg

1961 (Gazzola-Fiorelli)

1st overall, Tour de Luxembourg

1st, Mountains Classification – 1st, Stage 3

1st, Luxembourg National Road Race Championship

3rd overall, Tour de France – 1st, Stage 9

4th overall, Giro d'Italia – 1st, Stage 20

4th, Tour de Romandie

7th overall, Challenge Desgrange – Colombo

9th, Coppa Sabatini
10th, Circuit des Four Cantons

1962 (Gazzola-Fiorelli)

1st, Luxembourg National Road Race Championships
1st, Luxembourg National Cyclo-cross Championships
9th overall, Tour de France
1963 (Gazzola-Fiorelli and Peugeot-BP-Englebert)
8th Züri–Metzgete

ACKNOWLEDGEMENTS

Writing this book would have been impossible without the help of a number of people. Thank you to Fabienne Gaul for sharing her time and memories. Frank Wilhelm, academic and Gaul super-fan, gave me invaluable insights and prompted my thinking about mythology. Robert Philippart gave me an exemplary lesson in Luxembourgish history. Pit Hess and Nadine Geisler at the Luxembourg Ministry of Sport Heritage department were generous with their time, energy and coffee. Dries de Zaeytijd helped me discover many treasures within the archive of Koers Museum of Cycle Racing in Roeselare, Belgium. Thank you also to Henri Bressler, Edmond Fries, David Lavallee, Gareth Cartman, Charlotte Wilson, Matt Rendell and Andy McGrath, Dale Archer and all those that have permitted me to quote from their publications. Lastly, thank you to my agent, James Spackman, my editors, Richard Milner and Tania Wilde, and all the team at Quercus who made this book a reality.

A NOTE ON SOURCES

Primary sources about Gaul's life are scant, at least compared with other famous cyclists. Gaul himself kept few archives from his career. Therefore, my sources for this book have been mainly secondary – stories and facts handed down through the years by way of cycling books, magazines and, more recently, websites. Most of these are included in the bibliography. Thank you to all those writers and editors who have kept alive the stories of twentieth century cycling. Our sport can be prone to misty-eyed nostalgia, but its mythology gives weight to the exploits of today's generation of riders. A sense of history is reassuring.

There are a lot of books about the history of cycling. Scan the index of any of these books focused on the middle of the twentieth century, or on mountains and climbers, and you'll find Charly Gaul's name listed against several page entries. Flick to these entries, however, and you will find that the text about Gaul is brief. His legend has been reduced to 'climber' and 'strange' and 'recluse'. The truth about him is elusive, slippery. An athlete is defined by his accomplishments and then by any quirks that attach themselves to his story. The definition ends there. But every athlete is also a man or a woman with a more complex and rambling life. In some cases, the sporting accomplishments that come to define that person only cover a handful of years.

Such was Charly Gaul's fate. Arguably, his tragi-heroic ride to Monte Bondone – one day – defined his place in cycling history.

As I hope this book has shown, cycling journalism has historically been an ephemeral affair. Newspaper stories were often written quickly and with incomplete information, riders were misquoted and misconstrued. What was said in the heat of the minutes after a race finish was often later regretted, but by then impossible to withdraw. In the middle of the twentieth century, cycling's epic qualities attracted a certain type of writer – men who wanted to see through the sport to something deeper, something more profound than pedalling a bicycle. Perhaps they wrote their pieces, a glass of absinthe at their elbow, with an ironic smile, not expecting them to last much longer than the next day's *L'Équipe*. But they endured. And now the internet means their words – and all their inaccuracies – can be recycled endlessly.

Which all adds up to a distinctly shaky foundation on which to base the story of a man's life. Charly Gaul was a private man. He did not write anything down. During his career he confided only in his closest friends, who have also now passed away.

The bibliography on the next page is the blend of history and analysis that I have used to research this book. I have also consulted websites, archive materials, periodicals and documentaries too numerous to list here. During the writing of this book, I hope I have been able to sniff out any suspect storytelling, any elegant embroidery, but – as more than one cycling writer has noted – you really cannot believe anything written about the history of our beautiful sport.

BIBLIOGRAPHY

Allchin, Richard and Bell, Adrian, *Golden Stages of the Tour de France*, Sport and Publicity, 2013

Armstrong, Karen, *A Short History of Myth*, Canongate, 2005

Barthes, Roland, *Mythologies*, Hill and Wang, 2012

Beevor, Anthony, *Ardennes 1944*, Viking, 2015

Best, Isabel, *Raincoats are for Tourists, the Racing Secrets of Raphaël Géminiani*, Rapha Racing, 2020

Blondin, Antoine, *Tour de France: Mythos & Legende*, Egoth, 2018

Blondin, Antoine, *Tours de France: Chroniques de "L'Équipe"*, La Table Ronde, 2001

Bobet, Jean, *Tomorrow We Ride*, Mousehold Press, 2004

Booker, Christopher, *The Seven Basic Plots*, Continuum, 2004

Bressler, Henri, *Charly Gaul*, Editions Schortgen, 2021

Bressler, Henri and Thill, Fernand, *Histoire du Cyclisme Luxembourgeois*, Editions Schortgen, 2011

Busch, Akiko, *How to Disappear: Notes on Invisibility in a Time of Transparency*, Penguin, 2019

Cain, Susan, *Quiet*, Penguin, 2013

Cartman, Gareth, *Koblet & Kübler*, self-published, 2022

Chany, Pierre, *La Fabuleuse Histoire du Tour de France*, Editions de la Martinière, 1997

Cossins, Peter, *Climbers*, Octopus Books, 2022

Dauncey, Hugh and Hare, Geoff, *The Tour de France 1903–2003*, Frank Cass, 2003

Desforges, Jacques, *Grimpeur Ailé*, Editions Publibook, 2003

Fallon, Lucy and Bell, Adrian, *Viva la Vuelta!*, Mousehold Press, 2013

Fife, Graeme, *Brian Robinson – Pioneer*, Mousehold Press, 2010

Fife, Graeme, *Tour de France*, Mainstream Publishing, 1999

Foot, John, *Pedalare! Pedalare!*, Bloomsbury, 2011

Fotheringham, William, *Fallen Angel – the Passion of Fausto Coppi*, Yellow Jersey Press, 2009

Friebe, Daniel, *Eddy Merckx*, Ebury Press, 2012

Géminiani, Raphaël and Claude Dubois, *Mes 50 Tours de France*, Editions du Rocher, 2003

Guillame, François, *Du Tour de Frantz au Tour de Gaul*, Editions APESS, 2006

Haag, Emile, *The Rise of Luxembourg*, Ernster, 2021

Hill, Richard, *The Art of Being Belgian*, Europublic, 2005

Howard, Paul, *Sex, Lies and Handlebar Tape*, Mainstream, 2008

Koller, Alice, *The Stations of Solitude*, Bantam, 1990

Kroon, John, Netherlands wins the Tour! in *En God Schiep de Sprinter*, De Muur 2018

Laborde, Christian, *L'ange qui aimait la pluie*, Editions Michel Albin, 1994

Lanfranchi Pierre, Holt, Richard and Mangan, J.A. (eds.), *European Heroes: Myth, Identity, Sport*, Frank Cass, 1996

Maitland, Sara, *How to Be Alone*, Pan Macmillan, 2014

Mersch, François, *Bergauf, Bergab mit Charly Gaul*, Imprimerie Bourg, 1975

Moore, Richard, *In Search of Robert Millar*, Harper Sport, 2008

Moran, Joe, *Shrinking Violets*, Profile Books, 2016

Nicholson, Geoffrey, *The Great Bike Race*, Velodrome Publishing, 2016

Ollivier, Jean-Paul, *La Légende de Louison Bobet*, Flammarion, 1984

Skelton, Tim, *Luxembourg*, Bradt, 2014

Sykes, Herbie, *Dear Hugo*, Rapha Racing, 2022

Thill-Somin-Nicholson, Marguerite, *Surviving the Nazi Occupation of Luxembourg*, Xlibris, 2008

Truyers, Noel, *Kings of Cycling*, Coda, 1993

Vassaux, Willy Harold, *Le Luxembourg au Tour de France*, 2002

Weiss, Allen S., *The Wind and the Source – In the shadow of Mont Ventoux*, State University of New York Press, 2005

Woodland, Les, Cycling's 50 Triumphs and Tragedies, McGann Publishing, 2015

Zangerlé, Gaston, Charly Gaul, der Engel der Berge, Schortgen Editions, 1998

Zangerlé, Gaston, La Saga Charly Gaul, Éditions Saint Paul, 2006

REFERENCES

Part One

1   Gaston Zangerlé, *Le Saga Charly Gaul*.

2   Emile Haag, *The Rise of Luxembourg*.

3   Marguerite Thill-Somin-Nicholson, *Surviving the Nazi Occupation of Luxembourg*.

4   Spangdahlem Air Base website: www.spangdahlem.af.mil/News/ Features/Display/Article/297042/national-museum-of-military-history-in-diekirch-brings-history-alive/

5   *Ibid.*

6   François Mersch, *Bergauf, Bergab mit Charly Gaul*.

7   Cycling Legends website: www.cyclinglegends.co.uk/index.php/features/big-reads/92-charly-gaul

8   Cycling Revealed website: www.cyclingrevealed.com/May11/May_feature11_Grossglck.html

9   Mersch, *Bergauf, Bergab mit Charly Gaul*.

10 Richard Hill, *The Art of Being Belgian*.

11 Emile Haag, *The Rise of Luxembourg*.

12 Author's conversation with Frank Wilhem, 29 September 2022.

13 *Sporting Cyclist*, February 1959.

14 *Ibid.*

15 Frank Wilhelm, *Les Gants de Charly Gaul*, 2011.

16 Jacques Desforges, *Grimpeur Ailé*.

17   Pierre About, *L'Equipe*, May 1954.

18   Pierre Chany, *L'Equipe*, February 1956.

19   Frank Wilhelm, *Les Gants de Charly Gaul*, 2011.

20   Roland Barthes, *Mythologies*.

21   Jean-Paul Ollivier, *La Legende de Louison Bobet*.

22   Pierre Lanfranchi, Richard Holt and JA Mangan, *European Heroes: Myth, Identity, Sport*.

23   Roland Barthes, *Mythologies*.

24   Mersch, *Bergauf, Bergab mit Charly Gaul*.

25   Bobet, Jean, *Tomorrow We Ride*.

26   Paul Maunder, 'Mont Ventoux: Fear and the Mountain', *Rouleur Journal*, July 2021.

27   Isabel Best, *Raincoats are for Tourists: The Racing Secrets of Raphaël Géminiani*.

28   Jean Bobet, *Tomorrow We Ride*.

29   Isabel Best, *Raincoats are for Tourists: The Racing Secrets of Raphaël Géminiani*.

30   Roland Barthes, *Mythologies*.

31   Gaston Zangerlé, *Charly Gaul, der Engel der Berge*.

32   Les Woodland, *Cycling's 50 Triumphs and Tragedies*.

33   Mersch, *Bergauf, Bergab mit Charly Gaul*.

34   Soigneur website: https://soigneur.nl/race/part-3-gaul-monte-bondone/

35   Mersch, *Bergauf, Bergab mit Charly Gaul*.

36   John Foot, *Pedalare! Pedalare!*

Part Two

37   Gaston Zangerlé, *Charly Gaul, der Engel der Berge*.

38   Jacques Desforges, *Grimpeur Ailé*.

39   *Ibid*.

40   *Ibid*.

41   François Mersch, *Bergauf, Bergab mit Charly Gaul*.

42   Roger Frankeur, *L'Equipe* 1959.

43 Frank Wilhelm speech, given in December 2005 to commemorate Gaul's life.

44 Jean Bobet, *Tomorrow We Ride*.

45 François Guillame, *Du Tour de Frantz au Tour de Gaul*. Translation author's own.

46 *Ibid.*

47 Christopher Thompson, *The Tour in the Inter-War years – Political Ideology, Athletic Excess and Industrial Modernity*, in Hugh Dauncey and Geoff Hare (eds.), *The Tour de France 1903–2003*.

48 Jean Bobet, *Tomorrow We Ride*.

49 François Mersch, *Bergauf, Bergab mit Charly Gaul*.

50 Jean Bobet, *Tomorrow We Ride*.

51 *Ibid.*

52 *Ibid.*

53 Les Woodland, *Cycling's 50 Triumphs and Tragedies*.

54 François Mersch, *Bergauf, Bergab mit Charly Gaul*.

55 Antoine Blondin, *Tours de France: Chroniques de 'L'Équipe*.

56 François Mersch, *Bergauf, Bergab mit Charly Gaul*.

57 *Sporting Cyclist*, February 1959.

58 Roland Barthes, *Mythologies*.

59 *Sporting Cyclist*, February 1959.

60 Frank Wilhelm speech, 2005.

61 Mersch, *Bergauf, Bergab mit Charly Gaul*.

62 *Ibid.*

63 *Cycle Sport*, August 1999.

64 Desforges, Jacques *Grimpeur Ailes*.

65 Zangerlé, *Charly Gaul, der Engel der Berge*.

66 Isabel Best, *Raincoats are for Tourists: The Racing Secrets of Raphaël Géminiani*.

67 Thom Hartmann, *ADHD: A Hunter in a Farmer's World*, Healing Arts Press, 2019.

68 Author conversation with Dale Archer, April 2023.

69 Totally ADD website: www.totallyadd.com/adhd-video/greg-lemond-cycling-and-exercising/

70   Dale Archer, 'How ADHD Puts Athletes in the Zone', *Forbes*, 16 July 2014: www.forbes.com/sites/dalearcher/2014/07/16/how-adhd-puts-athletes-in-the-zone/

71   Harvard Health Publishing website: www.health.harvard.edu/blog/is-it-adhd-or-autism-201510278462#

72   Mersch, *Bergauf, Bergab mit Charly Gaul*.

73   *Ibid.*

74   *Ibid.*

75   The account in this section is all taken from François Mersch, *Bergauf, Bergab mit Charly Gaul*.

76   Paul Howard, *Sex, Lies and Handlebar Tape*.

77   Richard Allchin and Adrian Bell, *Golden Stages of the Tour de France*.

78   *Ibid.*

79   *L'Equipe*, July 1959.

80   Paul Howard, *Sex, Lies and Handlebar Tape*.

81   Mersch, *Bergauf, Bergab mit Charly Gaul*.

82   Zangerlé, *Le Saga Charly Gaul*.

83   Mersch, *Bergauf, Bergab mit Charly Gaul*.

84   *Sporting Cyclist*, August 1959.

85   Desforges, Jacques *Grimpeur Ailes*.

86   *Ibid.*

87   *Sporting Cyclist*, August 1959.

88   Mersch, *Bergauf, Bergab mit Charly Gaul*.

89   *Ibid.*

90   *Ibid.*

91   *Ibid.*

92   Jean Bobet, *Tomorrow We Ride*.

Part Three

93   *Sporting Cyclist*, February 1959.

94   Jean Bobet, *Tomorrow We Ride*.

95   *Sporting Cyclist*, September 1961.

96   *L'Equipe*, July 1961.

97   Paul Howard, *Sex, Lies and Handlebar Tape*.

98   *Ici Paris*, 1961.

99   Jean Bobet, *Tomorrow We Ride*.

100 Philippe Brunel, *L'Equipe*, July 2001.

101 *Ibid.*

102 *Sporting Cyclist*, February 1959.

103 Gaston Zangerlé, *Le Saga Charly Gaul*.

104 Jean Bobet, *Tomorrow We Ride*.

105 Chany, Pierre, *La Fabuleuse Histoire du Tour de France*, Nathan, 1988.

106 Gareth Cartman, *Koblet & Kübler*.

107 Brigit Katz, 'The profound loneliness of Greta Garbo', Smithsonian Magazine website: www.smithsonianmag.com/smart-news/profound-loneliness-greta-garbo-180967417

108 Philippe Brunel, *L'Equipe*, July 2000.

109 Mersch, *Bergauf, Bergab mit Charly Gaul*.

110 Article in *De Limburger*, 1995, from Luxembourg Ministry of Sport archive.

111 Alice Koller, *Stations of Solitude*.

112 Joe Moran, *Shrinking Violets*, Profile Books, 2016.

113 Philippe Brunel, *L'Equipe*, July 2000.

114 Jeroen Denaeghel, Charly Gaul, the climber turned hermit: www.jeroendenaeghel.be/charly-gaul-de-klimmer-die-kluizenaar-werd

115 Article in *De Limburger*, 1995, from Luxembourg Ministry of Sport archive.

116 Interview with Henri Bressler by Joe Geimer, *Luxemburger Wort*, May 2021.

117 Matt Rendell, *The Death of Marco Pantani*, Weidenfeld & Nicholson, 2015.

118 Henri Bressler, *Charly Gaul*.

119 Frank Wilhelm speech, December 2005.

INDEX